LIGHTING IN AMERICA

Cover illustration: Lighting devices of the late seventeenth through the early nineteenth century. Photograph by George Fistrovich.

LIGHTING IN AMERICA

From Colonial Rushlights to Victorian Chandeliers

A NEW AND EXPANDED EDITION

Edited by Lawrence S. Cooke

THE MAIN STREET PRESS • PITTSTOWN, NEW JERSEY

Articles included in this volume are printed exactly as they appeared in the following issues of *The Magazine* ANTIQUES.

Part I. A Note About Rushlights, August, 1944; Early American Lamps, I, Open Lamps, December, 1927; The Lamps of Colonial America, October, 1937; Notes on Early Ohio Lighting Devices, August, 1934; American Pottery Lamps, August, 1953; Early Pottery Lighting Devices of Pennsylvania, May, 1940; On the Trail of the Betsy Lamp, February, 1924; Further Light on Betty Lamps, April, 1929; Some Old Lamps, December, 1926; The Light of Other Days, March, 1933.

Part II. The Whale Oil Burner: Its Invention and Development, April, 1935; Early American Lamps, II, Closed Lamps, January, 1928; American Glass Lamps, April, 1936; Glass Lighting Devices, December, 1970; Miniature Glass Lamps, September, 1937; A Regional Collection of Glass Lamps, May, 1941; Three Maine Pewterers, July, 1932; A Lamp Dealer Illustrates His Wares, June, 1939; The Etiquette of Nineteenth-Century Lamps, September, 1936.

Part III. Brass Candlesticks, I, September, 1950; Brass Candlesticks, II, November, 1950; Brass Household Candlesticks of the Gothic Period, December 1967; Dating English Brass Candlesticks, December, 1969; A Chronology of English Candlesticks, March, 1930; Benjamin Gerrish, Brazier, March, 1964; American Tin Candle Sconces, August, 1936; Eighteenth-Century Lighting Devices: Wall Fittings and Candlesticks, October, 1932; English Brass Chandeliers in American Churches, August, 1966; Chandeliers in Federal New England, March, 1972.

Part IV. Paul Revere's Lantern, December, 1930; An Historic Lamp, April, 1928; Patented Lamps of the Last Century, February, 1934; Lard Oil Lamps, November, 1938; The Canting Lamp, June, 1935; Early Firemaking Devices, March, 1929; Sundry Candle Molds, June, 1937; Old-Time Iron Snuffers, November, 1929; New Thoughts on Eighteenth-Century Lighting, January, 1955; Food Warmers and Their Lamps, August, 1964; Old Sturbridge Village, Lighting Devices, September, 1955; Henry Ford Museum, Lighting, February, 1958; Lighting Devices and Practices, February, 1983; The Lamps and Candlesticks of the Meriden Britannia Company, February, 1977; Cornelius and Company of Philadelphia, December 1983.

Revised Edition 1984

Published by The Main Street Press, Inc., William Case House, Pittstown, New Jersey 08867

Distributed by Kampmann & Company, Inc., 9 East 40th Street, New York, New York 10016

Published simultaneously in Canada by Methuen Publications, 2330 Midland Avenue, Agincourt, Ontario M1S 1P7

Printed in the United States of America

Library of Congress Cataloging in Publication Data

Main entry under title:

Lighting in America
   Articles for Antiques.
   Includes index.
   1. Lamps—United States—History. 2. Lighting,
Architectural and decorative—United States—History.
3. Lighting—United States—History. I. Cooke,
Lawrence S. II. Antiques (Orange, Conn.)
NK6196.L53 1984   749'.63'0973   84-897
ISBN 0-915590-40-9 (pbk.)

Contents

Introduction

Within two short decades after the United States achieved its independence, lamps began to burn more brightly. New England whalers out of Nantucket and New Bedford brought back whale oil to feed the newly invented lamps of Argand and Miles. With the opening of the Northwest Territory, refined lard oil from Ohio soon became available to light the solar lamps of the East Coast. The rich natural resources of turpentine in the South and petroleum in Pennsylvania would fuel the camphene and kerosene lamps long before the young country celebrated its Centennial in 1876.

The history of lighting, primarily a record of scientific and technological development, studied as a reflection of the cultural advancement of the period, has long been of interest to the historian, the scholar, and the antiquarian. Many articles by writers in this field have appeared in the pages of *The Magazine* ANTIQUES during the past half century. These, as well as notes pertaining to lamps and lighting devices, comprise over seven hundred entries. From this imposing "library" of early lighting history, forty-one major articles by well known collectors, writers, and scholars such as Charles L. Woodside, Arthur H. Hayward, Lura Woodside Watkins, Rhea Mansfield Knittle, Leroy Thwing, C. Malcolm Watkins, John Kirk Richardson, Stephen Van Rensselaer, to name but a few, have been carefully chosen for *Lighting In America*.

Not surprisingly, some of these pioneering writers relied to a great extent on guesswork, and this accounts for occasional errors in their articles. The degree of conjecture involved in ascribing dates, provenance and history to most devices made prior to 1800 is evidenced by such phrases as "game of guesswork," "lack of definite information," "difficult to ascertain with exactitude," "do his own guessing." Prior to the nineteenth century, wills, inventories, and a few housekeeping books furnished most of the clues to supplement the guesswork. The errors of guesswork are further compounded by the fact that— perhaps more than in any other field of collecting— lighting is vulnerable to the overzealous enthusiasm of the collector. This weakness is sometimes exploited by anxious-to-please dealers, often giving rise to misinformation. Non-lighting items are described as lamps, and early twentieth-century devices are ascribed to the Middle Ages. On an "educational" television program, a miner's cap lamp, illustrated in an early twentieth-century Sears, Roebuck catalog, was described as a priceless lamp of extreme antiquity!

A classical example of misinformation is the description of a multi-spouted candy runner as a "wax pourer-candlemold filler" by Carl W. Drepperd in his *A Dictionary of American Antiques,* 1952. One year later he tried to correct his error in his *Handbook of Tomorrow's Antiques.* Since then, the error has lived on in print, in Mary Earle Gould's *Antique Tin and Toleware,* 1958, and in an issue of *The Rushlight Bulletin* (corrected in the next issue), and has even appeared in a candlemaking exhibit of a leading museum, as shown in an illustration on p. 182.

Another persistent canard is the appellation of "witch lamp" for the documented cast iron baker's oven lamp. One marked example, properly identified in the lighting collection of Old Sturbridge Village, has been found illustrated in an early catalog of the Edward Katzinger Company of Chicago, forerunner of Ekco Products Company.

One mystery, as yet unsolved, is the identity of the so-called "pig lamp." It seems to have been used as a shop lamp, but whether for light or heat we cannot be sure. In his article "Patented Lamps of the Last Century" (pp. 126–128), Arthur H. Hayward incorrectly calls this a guest-room lamp, and Leroy Thwing in his book *Flickering Flames* disputes this description.

One legend that may be true, but unproved, is the attribution of the invention of the twin-tube whale oil burner to Benjamin Franklin. There is evidence that he did devise a float lamp (letter from Benjamin Franklin to John Pringle, Philadelphia, December 1, 1762). Franklin certainly was a prolific inventor and scientist, but until we have some definite *proof* we must reserve judgment about the origin of this burner.

We can only "guess" as to who first associated the pierced tin lantern with Paul Revere. It is not, necessarily, an incorrect identification. One mark of the seasoned lighting collector is the patronizing correction of the neophyte, or the auctioneer, who calls a pierced tin lantern a "Paul Revere lantern." Those who believe they know better point out that "Paul could not have seen the feeble light from the distant church belfry, and besides, one of the glass-sided originals is in the Concord Antiquarian Society". Both lanterns are illustrated in the article "Paul Revere's Lantern" (p. 123). But, perhaps the neophyte collector is right. He does not call it the "Christ Church lantern." In Revere's period a night rider might well have carried a tin lantern as we carry a flashlight today, not to see the way but to have instant light when needed. In fact at least two paintings of Paul Revere's ride show such a lantern attached to his saddle-horn. This does not prove that he carried a lantern, but if he did, it would likely have been a pierced tin type. Again —as with "Franklin's" twin tube burner, and many of the other guesses—maybe it was and maybe it wasn't.

Lighting progress in the nineteenth century is much easier to document, a fact reflected in Malcolm Watkins' article "A Lamp Dealer Illustrates His Wares," Major L. B. Wyant's "The Etiquette of Nineteenth Century Lamps," and "Three Maine Pewterers" by Charles L. Woodside and Lura Woodside Watkins. Glasshouse catalogs and invoices, periodical advertisements, and especially patent records furnish a wealth of information accurately recording the development of American lighting. The United States Patent Office Annual Reports, 1848–1871, and the weekly Patent Office Gazette, 1872 —, are excellent original sources for research of lighting progress during the highly innovative years of the Industrial Revolution. The problems of burning cheap and plentiful lard and lard oil were ingeniously solved by hundreds of hopeful inventors while others were concocting patented, but hazardous burning fluids, usually from spirits of turpentine (camphene) and alcohol. The use of these explosive mixtures provided a market for still more inventions of safety lamps, burners, and containers. Kerosene, a low cost, safe and clean fuel, not only rendered obsolete the existing light sources but offered a field day for ingenious Yankee inventors who produced an amazing array of gadgetry for filling, lighting, extinguishing, and properly using this new fuel. Given a patent date, it is not difficult to determine the patent number and patentee, and with this information a copy of the original patent can be secured from the Commissioner of Patents, Washington, D. C. Also of value to the researcher are nineteenth-century issues of the *Scientific American* which carry not only weekly listings of the United States patents as issued but also contain many articles on lighting development, technology, and the proper "management" of lamps and candles, as well as occasional advertisements for lamps and fuels.

Among the books on lighting that the collector will find most useful is *Early Lighting, A Pictorial Guide,* written and published by the Rushlight Club in 1972. Over four hundred devices, clearly illustrated and described, are arranged and numbered for easy identification and organization of a collection. *The Heritage Of Light* by Loris S. Russell, University of Toronto Press, 1968, although stressing Canadian backgrounds, reflects a high quality of scholarship and is of value to American collectors. It is outstanding in its treatment of the kerosene era, a period which occupies approximately sixty percent of the contents. *Flickering Flames,* written for the Rushlight Club by Leroy L. Thwing, 1958, contains much useful information not found elsewhere, but its lack of an index and use of small group illustrations make it difficult to use for ready reference. *Smithsonian Bulletin No. 141,* "Collection of Heating and Lighting Utensils in the United States National Museum" by Walter Hough, 1928, long out of print and scarce, is noteworthy for accuracy in an early pioneering work.

The only periodical devoted solely to early lighting, *The Rushlight,* a quarterly bulletin of the Rushlight Club, has been published continuously for over forty years. A detailed index facilitates its use in research.

Although *Lighting In America* is of primary interest to the lighting enthusiast, it is also of importance to other antiquarians since lighting devices often form a prominent part of other collections such as ceramics, glass, iron, brass, etc., as well as being an appropriate part of the furnishings of any period interior. In fact lamps are the only antiques that logically can be electrified for modern illumination. The making of a lamp, however, from an early candlemold is just as ridiculous as electrifying a coffee grinder or a flatiron.

Some lighting collectors bring life to their collections by burning lamps. Candlewood for splint holders is available from mail order sources in the South and some country stores elsewhere. Prepared rushes for rush holders are often for sale by the Rushlight Club or are easily made from detailed instructions in the opening article, "A Note About Rushlights" by Thwing. The secret of making successful rushlights is to be found in the use of meadow rushes, *juncus effusus,* keeping them moist until peeled, and then in drying them thoroughly before dipping.

Modern salad oil burns well in betty lamps and whale oil lamps as does vegetable shortening in grease and lard lamps. For best results the fuel must be at or above room temperature. Simple strips of cotton flannel make good wicks for betty lamps and lard lamps. Plumbers' wicking, upholsterers' welting, or old fashioned string mop heads, if not chemically treated, all make suitable wicks for whale oil or fluid burners.

One of the greatest satisfactions of "show and tell" is the demonstration and production of a flame from a tinderbox, as described by Lura Woodside Watkins in her article "Early Firemaking Devices", Part I, (pp. 133–135). The tinder is merely a charred cotton or linen rag, and the spunks are easily made by dipping the tips of slivers of wood in melted sulphur. The secret of success lies in the quality of the flint and the steel. In Part II of the same article William F. Noe graphically describes the Dobereiner lighter, by far the most ingenious and sophisticated firemaking device of the early nineteenth century.

As will be obvious from reading *Lighting in America,* there are almost as many kinds of lighting collections as there are collectors. Some specialize in limited categories such as rush holders, patent lamps, firemaking devices, or even kerosene burners or electric light bulbs. Others cover a broad spectrum from Roman and Grecian classical lamps right up to the highly successful Hitchcock mechanical kerosene lamp of the late nineteenth century. A lighting collection can fit your taste or your pocketbook.

The following anthology, containing the best lighting articles of fifty years in *The Magazine* ANTIQUES, should not only introduce the reader to this fascinating subject but provide inspiration in the pursuit of his hobby.

For further information on lighting the reader may consult other articles from *The Magazine* ANTIQUES which have not been included in this volume. Among these are:

"Iron in Early American Lighting," Arthur H. Hayward (May, 1923); "National Types of Old Pewter," Howard Herschel Cotterell (March, 1924); "The Boston and Sandwich Glass Company," Priscilla C. Crane (April, 1925); "The Village Tinsmith," Mabel M. Swan (March, 1928); "Candlesticks and Snuffers," Edward Wenham (December, 1930); "Some Early English Lighting Devices," R. W. Symonds (June, 1932); "Early English Hanging Light Fixtures," R. W. Symonds (August, 1932); 'The Cost of Lamp Glassware," Harrold E. Gillingham (July, 1935); "The Trail of the Miner's Candlestick," Ruby T. Scott (March, 1937); "Lighting Devices, From Stratford Lee Morton Collection," n.a. (April, 1938); "Old Brass Candlesticks," F. Gordon Roe (June, 1938); "Electioneering Without Electricity," Edward A. Rushford, M.D. (November, 1938); "Old English Candlesnuffers," G. Bernard Hughes (November, 1946); "New England Glass Company Invoices, Part III, Helen McKearin (December, 1947); "Electric Light in Antique Settings," Malcolm Watkins (December, 1947); "Light, An Eighteenth-Century Interest," Jean Gorely (October, 1949); "Williamsburg, Lighting," n.a. (March, 1953); "Deerfield, Lighting," n.a. (September, 1956); "English Brass Candlesticks," Robert Sherlock (September, 1959); "Quillwork: American Paper Filigree," Edith Gaines (December, 1960); "Lighting Devices from a New Hampshire Collection," Howard W. Stone (July, 1964).

I   Primitive Lamps

The articles chosen for this section cover the various primitive lighting devices and sources in common use in the colonial period in North America, but which, as in the case of the betty lamp, found occasional use well past the middle of the nineteenth century. The solid fuel light sources of the period such as splints and rushes are included here, but candles are covered in a separate section.

Simplest of all is a splint of pitch pine, known in New England as candlewood and in the South as fatwood or lightwood. It is nature's own candle. The cellulose "wick" impregnated with the fuel—pitch—required only splitting to become a splint, and a simple iron holder enabled it to be burned in a horizontal position. Greasy black smoke and dripping pitch largely limited it to use in the great kitchen fireplace where many houehold chores were carried on. Pine knots, burned outdoors in iron cressets, were used for night fishing and on wharves where smoke and dripping were no problem.

Another primitive solid fuel light source is the rushlight. As described by Leroy Thwing (pp. 13-15), it is simply a peeled, dried length of meadow rush, *juncus effusus* (not cattail), dipped in tallow and burned in a rush holder at a forty-five degree angle. First hand descriptions of rush preparation are recorded in Gilbert White's *Natural History of Selborne,* 1775, William Cobbett's *Cottage Economy,* 1821, and in Gertrude Jekyll's *Old English Household Life,* 1925. Unlike candlewood splints, the rushlight burned with a clear steady light, free from odor and smoke, and did not drip. It did require a little more preparation, but its cost was minimal. Rushes were sometimes dipped many times to form a rush candle which was burned in a vertical position. Since rush candles did not require snuffing, they were used in nursery lamps and in ships' lanterns where they did not need constant attention. This feature may explain their commanding a premium price from a Boston chandler, as noted by Thwing.

When and where the "lamp" was discovered or invented will never be known, but we do know that a simple saucer or pan filled with animal or vegetable fat, and some form of porous wick, remained virtually unchanged for several millenia. The crusie with its wick trough was a slight improvement over the simple saucer or pan lamp but presented the drawback of dripping excess fuel. The double crusie, sometimes called a "Phoebe," offered a makeshift solution to the dripping problem and permitted the canting of the reservoir to better feed the wick.

The use of an integral wick support, typical of the betty lamp, represented a true invention; the drip running back into the reservoir made it a "better lamp." As defined by Charles L. Woodside in "Early American Lamps" (pp. 16-18), they usually were of an "open" type, although some of the later betty lamps were covered but not spill proof. The lamps of this period burned any grease or oil available and were apt to be smelly, messy, and demanding of constant attention. The resulting illumination was pitiful compared to nineteenth-century lamps, yet their use persisted in some rural areas well into that century. Peter Derr was still making betty lamps in Berks County, Pennsylvania, as late as 1860. Fortunately, Derr signed and dated his products, making their identification possible. The low betty lamp, if not suspended from a chair back or wall, required a stand or "tidy" to raise it to a useful position. A tin betty and tidy made for each other is known as an "Ipswich betty," and if permanently joined is called a "Portsmouth betty."

Lamps of the colonial period commonly were limited to table types and an occasional chandelier. Except for examples of peg lamps used in candleholders and a few ships' gimbal lamps, wall versions are scarce, and floor models are almost nonexistent. On the other hand, it is interesting to note that rushlight holders, as well as candleholders, were made as table stands in floor and pendant models. There was, also, an offset type for wall mounting. In comparing the splint, rushlight, and candle to the various types of lamps, it helps to understand how they work. In the first three the flame seeks the fuel, whereas in lamps the fuel must be brought to the flame. This delivery is accomplished with the help of heat, gravity, and capillary attraction in the primitive lamps and sometimes by clockwork. mechanical means, or atmospheric pressure in the later more advanced lamps.

In a section that necessarily depends much on conjecture, Malcolm Watkins' "Lamps of Colonial America" (pp. 19-23), is outstanding for its scope and accuracy, and is especially recommended reading.

A NOTE ABOUT RUSHLIGHTS

By LEROY THWING

RUSHLIGHT HOLDERS are found often enough today to imply that rushlights were in common use in early America. Yet careful investigation in New England forces the conclusion that in that part of the country, at least, rushlights were used little if at all in colonial days. While inventories of estates kept in the Massachusetts Probate Court records list manifold household furnishings and utensils, including all kinds of lamps, candlesticks, and lanterns, with one exception no mention has been found of rushlight holders, or even of any device with a strange name that might be assumed to have been a rush holder.

The single exception thus far found is a late eighteenth-centry Boston chandler's bill, which lists Rush Candles at 11 d., and [common] candles at 9 d. The chandler is listed in the 1789 Boston directory: "Lovering, Jos. and Sons, manufacturers of Spermaceti and Tallow Candles, hard and soft soap, Poland Starch and Hair Powder, No. 49 State St." The fact that his rush candles cost more than those with cotton wicks does not point to their extensive production at that time and place.

The origin of the many surviving rushlight holders is obscure. A few seem to have a record of ownership in the same family for several generations — a sort of evidence which should not be taken too seriously, yet should not be considered valueless. It would indeed be strange if a few rush holders were not brought from England, or made here, but it is safe to conclude that they were never used here to the extent that they were in England, and that rushlights were never as common in early Massachusetts homes as rushlight holders are on dealers' shelves and in private collections today.

Two thousand years ago Pliny mentioned that certain rushes were used as wicks for both lamps and candles. The original English name for lights made of rushes seems to have been

FIG. 1 (*above and right*) — RUSHLIGHT MAKING. Reproduced from *Old West Surrey* (1904) by Gertrude Jekyll.

FIG. 2 (*below*) — EARLY MENTION OF RUSHLIGHTS. Bill of Joseph Lovering & Sons, dated *Jany. the 27 1786*, which itemizes *Candles* at 9d. and *Rush Candles* at 11d. *From the Davis papers, Massachusetts Historical Society.*

rush-candle; its earliest noted use was in 1591. Many English writers of later centuries used the word *rushlight*, usually in the depreciatory sense of being a poor thing at best, as in these lines written by a minor poet in 1774:

A rushlight in a spacious room,
Burns just enough to form a gloom.
    (*Lloyd*)

Rushlights are described in the *London Gazette* in 1710 as "small rushes once dipped or drawn through Grease or kitchen stuff." A more detailed and often quoted description is found in Gilbert White's *Natural History of Selborne* (1775). White says that the soft rush *Juncus effusus* is the best for rushlights. As soon as the rushes are cut, they must be put in water and kept there until they are peeled, which is done by removing all of

13

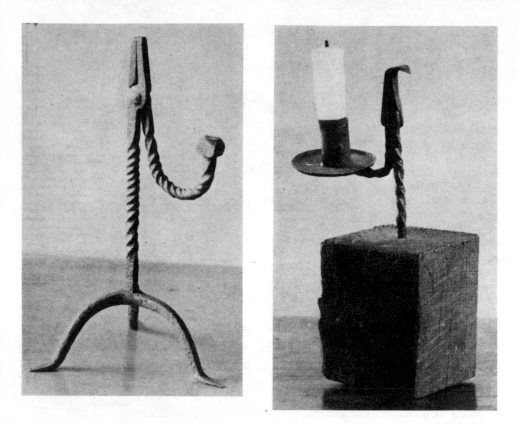

(Fig. 1); a rushlight as shown in a holder is evidently quite flexible. On the other hand, rushlights made for the Victoria & Albert Museum by a well-known film of English chandlers, of which I have had a number, had evidently been dipped several times, just as candles are dipped, for they were larger than a lead pencil.

Walter Hough, in his invaluable *U. S. National Museum Bulletin 141,* does not use the word rushlight but refers (p. 17) to the light used in a clip holder as a "fatted rush" and seems to distinguish it from the rush candle which was dipped more than once: "Rush candles in the British Isles preceded the candle with the textile fiber wick, and followed the fatted rush . . . were dipped in hot fat and put away to season. Later they were 'dipped' by the usual domestic process . . ." The once-dipped and the multiply-dipped rush are illustrated in Plate I of this *Bulletin,* and described respectively as "Rush soaked in grease" and "Tallow dip with rush wick." The two are quite different in appearance, and for our

the "rind" except a single narrow strip left to support the pith. Then they are dipped in "scummings"; the addition of a little beeswax to the fat is advised if a less greasy product is desired. White says that a rush 2 feet 4½ inches long, "being minuted," burned nearly an hour.

William Cobbett (*1762-1853*), who sometimes wrote under the descriptive pen name of Peter Porcupine, says in his *Cottage Economy,* "The rushes thus prepared [i.e., peeled], the grease is melted and put into something as long as the rushes are. The rushes are put into the grease, soaked in it sufficiently, then taken out and laid in a bit of bark taken from a young tree." He adds: "I was bred and brought up by rushlight. And I find that I do not see less clearly than other people. Candles were not much used in labourer's dwellings when I was a boy. My grandmother who lived to be nearly ninety, never, I believe, burnt a candle in her house in her life."

Rushlights have been made in England within the past fifty years. I have discussed them with a gentleman who has seen them hanging in bunches in a shop in the "marsh country" and described them as something smaller than a lead pencil. This is corroborated by illustrations in Gertrude Jekyll's *Old West Surrey* (1904). That writer, quoting a countrywoman ninety years of age who demonstrated the process for her, says that the rushes were drawn through the fat but once, and her pictures of them, before and after, show little difference in appearance.

purposes we may conveniently use the terms with specific meanings. However, I know of no such distinction in eighteenth-century England, where the names for "fatted rushes" doubtless varied with time and place. In my own limited experiments, I find that a rush soaked once in fat burns as brightly as one dipped five or six times, but not so long. If rushes are as easy to peel as Gilbert White says they were, I see no inducement for dipping them more than once.

I have found no direct evidence that candles of common size with rush wicks were ever made. Many rushlight holders have a separate socket which might have been designed to hold such a light, but it could equally well have held a candle with a cotton wick. Rush candles of this size would have burned very satisfactorily. An experimental candle about an inch in diameter with an English rush wick burns as well as any candle, and probably better than an early eighteenth-century candle. The rush curves nicely out of the flame, and the end is consumed, which makes for uniform height of the flame. We do not need to use snuffers frequently as our ancestors did, because candle wicks are now braided with one tight strand which curls the wick just as the rush wick curls naturally.

Rushes suitable for rushlights must have an absorbent pith. Under a ten-power magnifying glass, the pith of a soft rush looks like a mass of absorbent cotton. The Norwegian name "cotton grass" is descriptive. Where such rushes are plentiful, the use of rushlights is probable. Gilbert White implies that they were common in England in 1775. "I shall make no apology for troubling you with the detail of a simple piece of domestic economy...the use of rushes instead of candles, which I am aware prevails in many district..." Probably suitable

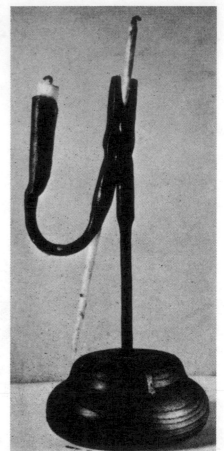

FIG. 6 — A REPRODUCTION RUSHLIGHT AND CANDLE HOLDER. Too heavy to be typical, but showing both rushlight and rush-wicked candle in place. Height, approximately 11 inches. *From the New York Museum of Science and Industry.*

rushes were lacking in certain parts of the country, and they seem to be equally lacking in New England. We have soft rushes here, but while English and Irish rushes are over a quarter of an inch in diameter, the largest New England soft rushes I have seen are less than an eighth. A rushlight twelve inches long made from a Maine rush will burn about ten minutes — less than half as long as those mentioned by White.

The New England colonists who apparently made such scant use of rushlights may have come from parts of England where rushlights were unknown, or they may have been discouraged by the small size of our soft rushes.

It has been suggested that a number of the small New England rushes could be made into a bundle and then dipped, thus making the rush wick the same size as the larger English rushes. This is, of course, a possibility, but there is no evidence that it was done.

We can, however, hold an open mind on the subject of rushlights in America, bearing in mind that while new evidence may prove that they were used here, nothing can ever prove that they were not.

FIG. 7 (*below*) — RUSHLIGHT HOLDER. Of spring type, this example does not require the counterpoise on end of the short arm, which is provided in other examples shown by a knob or by the candle socket. Height, approximately 10 inches. *From the collection of Gerald Fox.*

FIG. 8 — GERMAN SPLINT OR RUSH HOLDER. Of spring type. The iron antedates the wooden standard, which has a spring clip to fasten it to table edge. Height, approximately 16 inches. *From the collection of Julius Daniels.*

Early American Lamps

By CHARLES L. WOODSIDE

Illustrations from the author's collection

Part I: Open Lamps

ASIDE from those utensils essential to proper conduct of the household in Colonial days, the lamp and the candle held the place of greatest importance. To be sure, the great fireplace gave forth its glowing radiance, illuminating the room sufficiently to enable one to carry on some of the work or pleasure incidental to long winter evenings; but, after all, it could not, for many purposes, supply the place of the lamp or candle.

GREASE LAMPS

The first lamps used by the colonists were brought over from the home countries. They were of the "open" type, designed for burning oil or grease,

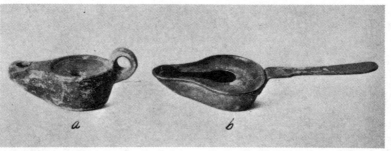

Fig. 1 — THE TRADITIONAL LAMP
a. Terracotta Roman lamp, A. D. 79.
b. Tin Betty lamp, American, 1790.

and were exactly similar in principle to those which had been in use, in every part of the world, from time immemorial.* They consisted essentially of a bowl, or receptacle, for the oil or grease, a spout or slot at one end in which to lay the wick, and a handle at the other end by which to carry the apparatus.

Strange as it may appear, this ancient lamp remained exactly the same during the many centuries of the existence and use of this type — the only type known — centuries during which the world steadily advanced in learning, science, and the fine arts, when the need of a better light must have been keen. Change and variation in

*The origin of the lamp is unknown. Its beginnings are shrouded in the mists of antiquity. We do not know who first made and used them, but we know that lamps were in use six thousand years ago, for the excavations of the ancient cities of Babylonia and other countries of the East have yielded numberless specimens, indicating that they were in comparatively common use there at that time.

At first these lamps were made of clay, and were probably dried in the sun. Then, in the passing of centuries, they were made of iron, copper, bronze, alabaster, and other materials. In Rome and Greece, where the fine arts had reached a high degree of attainment, lamps were made in great beauty of form and variety of detail, and were used for decorative as well as for useful purposes. The spread of the Roman Empire carried these lamps with it to the remotest corners of Europe and they became known as "Roman" lamps; and eventually some of them came to America with the Pilgrims.

form and material and in detail occurred, to be sure, and in the substances that were burned in the lamps; but the very same "open" type prevailed, with the receptacle for the oil or grease and the slot for the wick. The principle remained unchanged until this type was superseded by the "closed" lamp late in the eighteenth or early in the nineteenth century.

A comparison of the lamps shown in Figure 1 will make this clear. The one on the left is a "Roman" lamp, made of terracotta, and found about one hundred years ago in the excavations of the ruins of Pompeii by an American tourist, who brought it home. In his family it has since remained, until recently added to my collection through the courtesy of his great granddaughter. As Pompeii was destroyed by the eruption of Vesuvius in the year 79 A. D., we may assume that this lamp is more than eighteen hundred years old. The lamp at the right is a Colonial Betty, made probably about 1790. The similarity between these two lamps is really astonishing, the more so when we consider that they were made four thousand miles apart in distance and seventeen hundred years apart in time.

FIRST COLONIAL LAMPS IMPORTED

When the Pilgrims came, they brought some of these lamps with them from Holland and England, where such articles were in more or less common use. The simplest form was that of a saucer with one or two lips at the edge to hold the wick. There was likewise a form more nearly like that of the old Roman lamp, with a long nose or slot for the wick; whence the name of "slot" lamp. That shown in Figure *3a* is of wrought iron, six inches long, and has a handle for carrying, and a hook by which it may be hung up.

In these lamps were burned any grease, scraps of fat, fish oil or whale oil, according to what might be at hand for the purpose. The wicks were usually pieces of twisted cotton rag. When lighted,

Fig 2 — OLD EUROPEAN LAMPS (*for grease or oil*)
a. Brass lamp with drip spout, one wick. Dutch, 1750.
b. Pewter Betty lamp, two wicks. French, 1800.
c. Brass lamp, one wick. Venetian, 1850.
Heights, 10½", 5¼", and 12½".

they smoked considerably, and usually smelled badly, especially if fish oil was used. Moreover, these lamps had a rather untidy habit of dripping oil or grease on any object beneath them, whether table, floor, or the food in preparation for the family meal; for the wick often drew up the oil faster than it could be burned, and spilled the surplus without regard for consequences.

PHOEBE LAMPS

Because of this untidy habit, some one conceived the idea of placing one slot lamp within another of larger size, so that the lower and larger one might catch the drippings from the upper one in which the light burned. This arrangement was much cleaner than that which the single lamp afforded, and the drippings were thus saved to be burned later, a matter of considerable importance in early days when fats and oils were not plentiful. These combined lamps were called *Phoebe* lamps; but why I am unable to tell.*

THE BETTER BETTY LAMP

There was, however, a decided objection to this arrangement: it required two lamps in the place of one, and lamps were scarce and costly. Whereupon some genius conceived the idea of a wick holder, placed in the slot, with the lower end fastened to the bottom of the lamp. The advantage of this plan was immediately evident: The lamp at once became neat and clean, for the drippings from the wick ran back into the oil bowl of the lamp and were eventually consumed. Furthermore, the heat from the wick was transmitted through the wick holder to the grease in the bowl, thus keeping it in a fluid or semi-fluid state. And then, after a while, some other genius added a cover to the oil bowl, which still further improved the lamp by confining the heat within, and thus increased its neatness, cleanliness, and better burning qualities.

These lamps, with the separate wick holder in the slot, were called *Betty* lamps; but whether the Betty and the Phoebe were first so called by our ancestors here or abroad I am unable to say. Neither does any one appear to know just why they were so called. My grandmother, Mrs. Henry Marquand, used to say that the name of the Betty came from the word *better*, because such lamps were considered far better than the slot lamps or Phoebe lamps. They were better (and eventually Betty) lamps.†

All of these lamps are shown in Figure 3. The one marked *a* is a slot lamp; *b* is a Phoebe; *c* is a Betty without a cover and

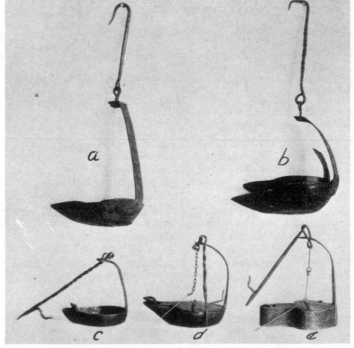

Fig. 3 — WROUGHT IRON LAMPS
 a. Slot lamp, 6″, capacity 2 fluid oz.
 b. Phoebe lamp, 6″, capacity 1¾ fluid oz.
 c. Betty lamp, 3¼″, with wick holder but without cover, capacity ¾ oz. An unusually small specimen.
 d. Betty lamp, 4¼″, with wick holder, hinged cover, hook and wick pick, capacity 1 oz.
 e. Another, 4″, capacity 2 oz.

showing the wick holder, and *d* is a full-fledged Betty with wick holder, cover, handle, hook for hanging, and wick pick for adjusting the wick.

PINE KNOTS AND RUSHLIGHTS

The Betty lamp was very popular in the Colonies. It was the standard type of lamp from the earliest days down to the advent of the whale oil or closed type of lamp in 1820. The Bettys did not come into general use at first, for only the well-to-do could afford to have them. The early colonists in general depended for their lights mainly upon the pitch-pine knot — the pitchy pine wood cut into thin strips about eight inches long called *candle-wood* — the rushlight made from dried rushes soaked in grease, the crude slot lamp, and the precious candle.

As there were but few skilled artisans in the Colonies — and these were employed in the more important work of house building — the early lamps were imported. But after a time, as the country became more settled and prosperous and the necessities of life had been provided so that living had become more comfortable and convenient, one of the first matters to be considered and most desired was the means for providing better lighting in the home.

The increasing need for ordinary household utensils had brought into activity that very important person, the village blacksmith, and soon his shop could be found in every town. Most of the domestic Betty lamps, I imagine, were made in these shops. Except in a general sense, there was no set pattern to be followed, and each workman fashioned them according to his own fancy. There was not much attempt at ornamentation, but all bear evidence of the careful and painstaking toil with which the work was done.

EARLY LAMP FUEL

The Betty lamp gave a comparatively good light for its time. Experiments with fish oil, grease and whale oil show that the light produced varied with the material burned and with the size and material of the wick. Fish oil gave the poorest light, and was inclined to be somewhat smoky and odorous. Grease and fats were better, especially if they were in a somewhat fluid condition. With whale oil, which, after 1760, was quite generally burned in these lamps, especially in the coast towns, the light produced was more satisfactory and was about equal to that given by two ordinary candles of our own day.

LAMP SUPPORTS

All of these lamps were intended to be set on the table, or to be hung on a hook on the wall, or on the back of a chair, or wherever convenience might require their placement. But this arrangement was not always satisfactory, especially for use at the table, where the lamp's low position prevented the spread

---

*It has been suggested by Mrs. Mary Debevoise Cole that this name was derived from the light-giving Phoebe, also known as Artemis, or Diana, who was goddess of the moon. Her brother Phoebus Apollo was god of the sun. *Ed.*

†On this point see ANTIQUES, Vol. XII, page 211. The explanation offered there seems reasonable.

of its light. Stands of various kinds came into use, of wood, or iron; and one of these, of turned maple, is shown in Figure 4 with a cast iron Betty lamp on its top.

Then followed lamps on pedestals like the Pennsylvania pottery lamp. A very rare specimen is shown in Figure 5a, at the left. In the same illustration are to be found a swinging iron lamp (b) with upright wick holder in the centre of the oil bowl; and the cast iron lamp (c), also a rare specimen, at the right. There were, besides, stands having an upright rod to which was attached a Betty lamp that could be moved up and down, as desired — a great convenience.

TIN LAMPS

About 1750 tin plates began to be imported from abroad. Almost no tin at all was known to exist in the colonies, and consequently no tin plate was made here. During the Revolutionary War all importations of this material ceased. Bishop states that "tin could not be had in 1776 sufficient to make canteens and kettles for the army." By 1785 importations were resumed, only to be again interrupted by the War of 1812; but, soon after the close of this conflict, importations of tin began again, and this desirable material was then to be had in plenty to meet the demand of the great tin era which followed.

IPSWICH LAMPS

Tin plate was easily workable and the household and other utensils made from it were neat in appearance and comparatively free from rust. Betty lamps, too, were made from tin, and, apparently, were very popular.

Fig. 5 — RARE GREASE LAMPS

a. Pennsylvania pottery grease lamp, of greenish brown color, for one wick. Height, 6″, capacity 2 oz.

b. Wrought iron swinging grease lamp, with upright wick holder in centre of bowl. Height, 7½″, capacity 1 oz.

c. Cast iron grease lamp, for two wicks. Height, 5″, capacity 2½ oz.

Not many remain to this day, however, for the material was not very durable, and I imagine most of the tin lamps were discarded, from time to time, after a few years' wear. It has been said that a tinsmith, or perhaps I should say a "tinner," as such workmen were called in early days, who lived in Ipswich, Massachusetts, appreciating the advantage of a light elevated on a stand, made a combination affair of tin plate consisting of a saucer-like base, an upright with a small shallow receptacle on its top, and a Betty lamp. The lamp rests in the receptacle when in ordinary use, but could be carried about or hung up in the usual manner independent of the stand.

This contrivance as a whole was known as an *Ipswich Betty*, from the place of its origin. I have never been able to verify this story; but, in any event, many lamps of this type, called by this name, were made and used, though they are comparatively rare today. Figure 6 shows one of these lamps. It was probably made about 1800, and was found in an old barn in a New Hampshire town. It measures twelve and one half inches in height, and is a fine specimen of this rare type, in perfect condition.

It would be virtually impossible to ascribe any chronological order to these so-called *open* lamps. The different forms were made indiscriminately during periods which often overlapped. About all that can be said is that this open type of lamp, in one form or another, continued in more or less general use until long after the advent of the so-called *closed* or *whale oil* type of lamp in 1820 or thereabouts.

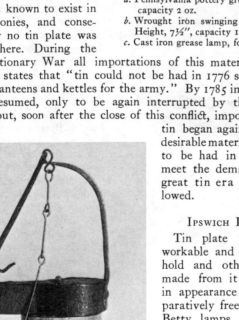

Fig. 4 — LAMP STAND
Turned maple, 6″ high, with cast iron Betty lamp on top. Length 4″, capacity 1¾ oz.

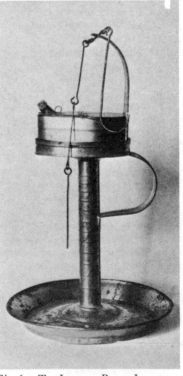

Fig. 6 — TIN IPSWICH BETTY LAMP AND TIN LAMP STAND
Height of stand, 8″. Extreme height, 12½″.

The Lamps of Colonial America

By Malcolm Watkins

Note. The exhibit of lighting devices held by the Rushlight Club in Boston during October 1935 afforded opportunity for first-hand study and for comprehensive photography, without whose aid these notes could hardly have been prepared or adequately illustrated. — *M. W.*

THE "study" of early lighting in America is really a game of guesswork. It is always entertaining: but he is presumptuous who would suppose that he can draw anything like certain conclusions concerning the early lamps used by the American settlers before the Revolution. There is nothing, either verbal or graphic, to tell us what were the "lamps" mentioned in old records, or which among the early lamps now surviving were actually used by our colonial forebears.

However, we may be permitted a few hypotheses — guesses — from which we may build a foundation a little less flimsy, I believe, than that which now exists. It will be essentially a patched affair, consisting of evidential scraps gleaned from old records, bits of information about lamps used in those parts of Europe whence the colonists came, and a good many vaporous conjectural props.

Yet to start with, we find some hearteningly solid material. This is that lamps were assuredly used by the earliest of the Pilgrim settlers. In 1621 Edward Winslow wrote to prospective colonists still in England, advising them to bring "cotton yarn for your lamps."[1] This disposes of the theory that lamps could not have been used by the very first comers because of the scarcity of tallow before the advent of cattle, sheep, and hogs. As a matter of fact, fish oil was bountifully available in the coastal settlements. Indeed, Governor Winthrop, in his journal, speaks of the capture of whales and mentions a sloop which sank with three hogsheads of train oil on her deck.

At a later period, tallow also was used. And here we find ourselves at our first conjectural step. In an inventory of the mortal possessions of one William Woodcock, a shopkeeper of Salem who died in 1660,[2] we find listed, among other items, "1 slutt," worth twelvepence, as well as "1 lamp, and iron bearer, 12d." As lamp collectors know, the term *slut lamp*, as a synonym for grease lamp, is often heard today. It is no mere catch term, for *slut* (in this connection) is given full authority in Murray's *A New English Dictionary*, where it is defined as "a piece of rag dipped in lard or fat and used as a light." Accompanying quotations indicate that *sluts* of this description were stuffed into bottle mouths and other receptacles. The transfer of the designation *slut* from a tallow-burning rag wick to a crude form of lamp employing such a wick may be assumed as obvious. Certainly a rag wick would not have been worth twelvepence. A

almost assuredly burned fish oil. The slut lamp continued in use until a very late period, particularly in the Middle West, where pioneer conditions persisted until well into the nineteenth century and where crude lighting devices would have been less out of place than in the more formal interiors of the East.[3]

But the *lamp*, as distinguished from the *slut*, presents a more difficult problem. Never, when a lamp is mentioned in an old inventory, do we find it described. Occasionally we learn that the item is of tin, or pewter, or iron, but never does any inventory thus far examined give explicit details of the form. Assumptions from now on will have to be made for the most part on the basis of types known to have been used in European nations from which American colonists came.

In Great Britain, two types of primitive lamp were used in the seventeenth century. The first of these was generally known as the *crusie*. This was a lamp with two identically-shaped dishes — usually ovoid — one fitting inside the other, the lower attached to the upward-curving hanger which supported it. Each of the dishes had a groove or channel (as many as four when the lamp was other than ovoid). The upper dish was the oil reservoir and the channel was designed to hold the wick. The similarly shaped lower receptacle was intended only to catch any excess oil that might drip from the wick. Occasionally crusies are found unequipped with a secondary dish. They are to be distinguished from an ordinary double crusie that has lost its reservoir by the absence of any hook or ratchet on the hanger by which a reservoir could be attached to the rest of the lamp.

These crusies seem to be among the most ancient of lamps. They appear to have been used in the remoter parts of Great Britain, particularly near the coast. They predominate in Scotland, and examples have been identified from Cornwall, where they were called *chills*, and the Channel Islands, where they were

"slutt," it is safe to say, was a grease lamp, and grease lamps were doubtless distinct from ordinary lamps, which (along the seaboard, at least)

designated *cressets*.[4] Crusies are still used in Iceland in the north, and Spain in the south. Mrs. Moore[5] shows one that she says was found in Damascus. I know of no French double crusies, though Hough[6] illustrates a single one. Of course, the familiar French bronze wick-channel lamp, with the canopylike cage over the reservoir and the little detachable drip pan beneath, is obviously a refinement of the crusie. Hough

Fig. 1 — Slut Lamps
a. Said to have been made at the Marble Furnace, Adams County, Ohio, *c.* 1830. *From the collection of William A. Dick, Jr.*
b. Late type of cast-iron grease lamp. Cover missing. *From the collection of Mrs. William C. H. Brand*
c. Found in a New Hampshire barn. Its unique shape places it in a class by itself. It is probably older than the others. *From the Charles L. Woodside collection*

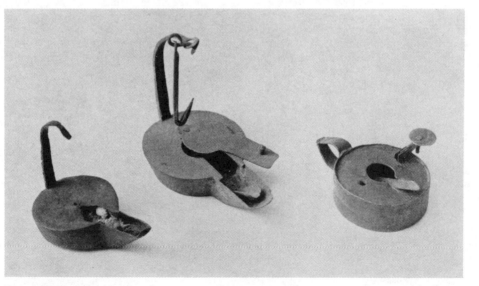

Fig. 2 — Wick-Channel Lamp, or Single Crusie
From the Charles L. Woodside collection

Fig. 3 — Two Double Crusies (Called "Phœbe Lamps" in New England)
a. An iron crusie found in a recently opened sixteenth-century Scottish coal mine. *From the collection of Mr. and Mrs. Stephen Jacobs*
b. A copper crusie made in Iceland during the summer of 1935. Such lamps are still sold for actual use in regions not reached by electricity. *From the collection of Mr. and Mrs. William M. Kuhn*

Fig. 4 — Iron Four-Wick Crusie Lamps like this are found both in Spain and in the British Isles.
From the Wells Historical Museum

attributes this lamp to northern France, which places it, like all the other crusies we have found, not far from the coast.

Without more adequate knowledge it is useless to hazard any guesses regarding the original source of the general type, but it seems fair to assume that the crusie was transmitted by seafaring people from the eastern Mediterranean almost to the Arctic Circle. This leaves out of account wick-channel lamps found as far east as Java, which have every appearance of being descended from the crusie.

The etymology of *crusie* tells us little of the lamp's source. It is bound up with various French idiomatic forms, among them *crasset* and *cræssus*, as well as old French forms suggested by Murray, which include *creuseul, croisel,* and *cruseau.* There is a hint of the same root in the Basque name for the crusie, *kurtsulu.* The Basque fishing people, it should be noted, used this lamp exclusively before the advent of kerosene and electricity. It burned fish oil.

That the crusie should have been carried across the Atlantic by English settlers (and perhaps, as well, by Spanish conquerors) appears almost certain. This surmise is substantiated by

is frequently encountered. But it is usually called a *phœbe,* a name apparently never used in Europe. The designation is probably an American colloquialism. All in all, it should not be surprising to find the crusie in any of the colonies, even if there were no collectors or antique dealers to redistribute them today.

The second type of lamp used in seventeenth-century England, and hence almost assuredly in America, was the *betty.* The term *betty lamp* seems to have been applied indiscriminately to all lamps related to the crusie. For convenience's sake, however, we shall use it to designate a particular form. This form is more advanced than the crusie and apparently derives both from the crusie and from the classic Roman lamp. Its essential distinguishing characteristic is a *slanting support* for the wick within the reservoir. Thus the wick no longer lies directly in the nose of the lamp, but is suspended above the latter so that excess oil will run back into the reservoir. This obviates the need for a drip pan. The lamp usually has a curving hanger like that of the crusie. It is almost always flat on the bottom with either flaring or vertical

the fact that in America today the open lamp with a deep pan

Fig. 5 — Betty Lamps
a. Used by pioneer family that settled in Quincy, Illinois, early in the nineteenth century. *From the collection of Glen E. Toalson*
b. Typical betty lamp; distinguished by a wick support, and in this instance by a cover. *From the collection of F. E. Gage*
c. A betty of unusual shape. Germanic origin. Said to have been made near Hebron, Ohio, in the Black Swamp region of Licking County. The cover is a hinged lid. This form is of German derivation. *From the Charles L. Woodside collection*

sides. It may or may not be covered, a circumstance depending somewhat on national source. It may be formed of tin, brass, or pewter, though most frequently it will be of iron.

The betty lamp is found in Italy, France, Germany, the Low Countries, Great Britain, and to some extent in virtually all of eastern Europe. It predominates, however, in Italy, Germany, France, and Belgium. In Italy it has been used until recently, apparently with little alteration. Italian and French bettys usually have no covers, being merely open pans with the necessary wick and hanger accessories. Those from the north of Europe — Germany, the Low Countries, and England — are commonly enclosed at the top and often have vertical sides.

When the wick-support lamp first came into use is as uncertain as the origin of most of our primitive lamps. One is tempted to believe, at any rate, that the type is earlier than the records show. D'Allemagne, in *L'Histoire du Luminaire*, believes that bettys were first introduced into France as late as the fifteenth century. The earliest dated example of a wick-support lamp that I have seen is a soapstone specimen marked *1584*.

The origin of the name *betty* has long been a matter of conjecture. To date, the most thorough elucidation of the subject occurs in an article *Further Light on the Betty Lamp*, by Charles L. Woodside, in ANTIQUES for April 1929. Mr. Woodside reveals that according to Murray, *betty* is probably derived from *beet* or *bete*, an old form meaning *to kindle*, and also *to make better*. He recalls his grandmother's remark that her betty lamp was really a "better lamp" (than the more primitive crusie), and infers that the second meaning of *beet* or *bete* should be associated with *betty*. Murray's study of the word, however, seems to point rather to the first meaning. The following citations from that authority will, perhaps, clear up a not too important but much-discussed point:

BEET, BETE (bīt). V. Obs., exc. dial.
Forms: 1 bóetan, bétan, 2–5 beten, 3–5 bete, 5–6 beete, 6 Scottish beit, 8 beet; (3 betten, 5 beton, bet, beethe, beytt.). Past tense, bet: 1 bette, 2–5 bette, 4 bett, bet (bete, beit). Past participle, bet; 1 beted, 1–5 bet, 3–5 ibet, bett (4 bete, bette)

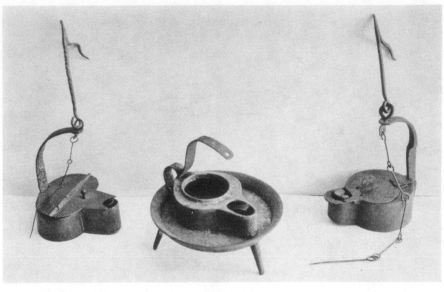

Fig. 6 — LATER PENNSYLVANIA-TYPE BETTY LAMPS
   a. Brass. Dated *185[?]* within shaft. *From the collection of Stephen Van Rensselaer*
   b. Lamp and integral three-legged saucer. Cast-iron lid is not shown. *From the collection of Stephen Van Rensselaer*
   c. Betty lamp marked *J. S.* and dated *1852*. *From the Charles L. Woodside collection*

Fig. 7 — TIN BETTY LAMPS
   Probably from Pennsylvania. First half of the nineteenth century. *From the collection of Mr. and Mrs. Earle E. Andrews*

II. To beet a fire
The dev. of this (the chief extant) sense, the antiquity of which is shown, not merely by the O S fýr bétan, but by its existence in the other Teutonic languages (cf. Dutch vuur boeten, Low German für böten, etc.), is somewhat obscure, from the fact that in the earliest instances it appears to mean, not to *mend* a fire, but as in modern Dutch, to *make, kindle, put on* a fire. Perhaps this is to be explained by the primitive conditions (which prevailed more or less till the days of phosphorous matches) according to which fire was not generated anew each time it was required, but was usually propagated by a "glede" from an existing fire, often carried and kept alive for days (cf. *Genesis* xxii 6), which was surrounded with combustibles and beeted into a blaze, when a fire was required.

* * *

4. To make, kindle, put on (a fire)
   c. 885 K. Aelfred Oros. vi. xxxii. Da het he betan baerinne.
   c. 1325 Seuen Sag. (W.) 2122 The clerkes . . . bet a fir strong and sterk.
   c. 1386 Chaucer Knts. T. 1434 Tuo fyres on the auter gan sche Beete.
   1430 Chev. Assigne 157 The goldesmyth gooth & beetheth hym a fyre.
   c. 1500 Sir Aldingar 53 in Furniv. Percy Folio 1. 168 And fayre fyre there shalbe bett.
   1513 Douglas Aeneis VII Prol. 127 Bad beit the fyire, and the candill alycht
   1875 Lancas. Gloss. (E. D. S.) s.v. *Beet*, tha mun get up an' beet t' fire to-morn.

5. To mend, make up, keep up, add fuel to, feed (a fire) Still in Sc. 1857 Lancas. Gloss. Then aw bettud fire, un rattl't fire-potter orgen't back o' the grate. . . .

BEETING. The action of making good, mending, repairing; making (a fire), kindling.
   1517 Churchw. Acc. Heybridge, Essex (Nichols 1797) 168 Half of betynge lyght ageynst the feste of the Natyvyte of oure Blessed Lady.

BETTING. Obs. variant of Beeting. Material for a fire, fuel.
   1521 Item payd for viij li. of pyche for the bettyngs to the Cressets, viij d.

It is clear, I think, that from one of these forms and meanings came the word *betty* as applied to a certain class of lamps. The reader may choose for himself. I am inclined to think that virtually all must be taken into account, with the exception of that which simply means to make good. Though there is not much evidence to support such a view, it is nevertheless probable that the Dutch and Germans who came to this country may have independently derived *betty* from their own *boeten* and *böten*. Our supposition concerning the derivation of *betty* from old English, meanwhile, is supported by Cotterell's extract from the records of the Worshipful Company of Pewterers of London for 1693/4.[7] This reads: "Among goods seized by the clerk on 26th Sept. from Wm. Barton were one Betty Pot marked T. C. and two wine quarts deep-lipped of Anthony Redhead's make and stamped on the lid with the sign of the swan." This "betty pot" was probably a vessel designed to hold lamp fuel. If we are willing to believe that *betty* came to mean lamp fuel, we can easily assume that at some date it was transferred to the lamp itself. This probably occurred in America, and at a fairly late date, for old records never mention *betty* lamps.

Whatever the origin of *betty*, we have the lamp bearing that name, today the most widely represented of all American primitive types. The surviving majority of them come from western Pennsylvania and Ohio, where the German settlers produced betty lamps abundantly in iron, copper, and tin. It is surprising how late these lamps were made. Some of them bear dates subsequent to 1850. For particular local use special adaptations of the betty lamp were devised of local materials, so that we find not only many variant derivative forms in tin, but also many in heavy cast iron suitable for use in

Fig. 8 — Lamps Made Either in Germany or Pennsylvania
a. Crude type of swinging-saucer lamp. *From the collection of Mr. and Mrs. Lewis N. Wiggins*
b. Adjustable pan lamp. Typical of lamps used in the German and Swiss Alps. It could have been made in Pennsylvania. *From the collection of William A. Dick, Jr.*
c. Swing lamp with a slanting wick support. Probably a native Pennsylvania product. *From the Skinner Museum*

Fig. 9 — Brass Dutch-Type Spout Lamps
Although used most widely in Holland, such lamps were adopted in near-by countries. Still made extensively for the antiques trade. Usually to be viewed with great caution.
a. Lamp with applied copper ornamentation and brass lion's heads. The spout, it will be noticed, turns up.
b. A handsome Dutch spout lamp.
c. Spout lamp with elaborate repoussé pictorial decoration. Perhaps German. *From the Wells Historical Museum*

mines. In Kentucky, and generally among the Southern negroes, the crude hanging saucer lamp became a distinct type that was a sort of hybrid between the betty and the crusie. Such lamps may be found, it is said, in occasional use today. In other parts of America, from French Canada to the Spanish South and the pioneer West, the betty lamp was relied upon for light by the earliest dwellers, as well as by some of the latest.

A third kind of lamp, undoubtedly used in early times in parts of the colonies settled by Germans and Swiss, is the pan lamp. This often bears a close resemblance to the crusie and the betty, but it is adapted to the burning of fat or tallow, and seems to have been little used outside of the Alpine regions of central Europe. The pan lamp sometimes has the conventional curved hanger of the crusie and the betty, but it also occurs with a vertical standard, on which it may be slid up and down. The pan itself is always shallow, seldom over a quarter of an inch deep. The hanger form usually approximates an oblong in shape, enlarging at the inner end. In the other form the shape varies greatly: the pan sometimes three-lobed, sometimes octagonal, very often pointed, occasionally round. The earlier examples are usually of wrought iron, and the pans have upturned edges. Sheet-iron pans are also common.

In the eighteenth century cast iron and brass were often employed for such lamps. Wick supports were not used (though I know of two exceptions to this rule). Instead, the wick was laid in the grease in the pan and lighted. Since the grease tended to congeal, especially in cold weather, little shovels or scrapers are sometimes part of the pan lamp's equipment. These were used to keep the unmelted fat pushed up toward the wick. Of fairly common occurrence is a partition in the pan to keep the grease from spreading over the entire area when only one wick is in use. The standards are usually very nice examples of wrought-iron work. In view of the number of these lamps which have been imported by antique dealers, it is impossible to obtain any idea of how widely they were used here in early times.

Our last category of colonial lamps is that of the spout lamp. How early or in what quantity spout lamps were used again we cannot know. The Germans of Pennsylvania made them in all sizes and shapes, while the fishing people of Cape Cod fashioned a spout lamp all their own. In Europe the spout lamp was known at least from the Middle Ages, and probably from early Christian times, when the *lucerna*, that most elegant of lamps, must have evolved from the multiwick form of the traditional Roman lamp, whose nose or noses grew increasingly to resemble spouts. A precise tracing of development may be impossible, but certainly the spout lamp existed in many forms by the time America was settled. The Dutch had a type more or less their own — though it penetrated other parts of the Continent, as well as England. It was usually of brass, and had a removable reservoir and a straight spout, which projected over a semitubular drip catcher. An excellent example may be seen in the painting *The Lost Thread* by Gérard Dou (*1613-1675*). If the comfort-loving Dutch settlers of New Amsterdam brought lamps with them to America — and early inventories say they had lamps of brass[1] — then this type of spout lamp was among their possessions.

The ingenious tinsmiths and ironsmiths of Pennsylvania, however, so altered the spout lamp from the European forms that by the nineteenth century it had become a highly varied native American device. In the colonial period, however, spout lamps, if there were any, would probably have been either similar to the Dutch types, or would have had upward-curving spouts.

The Cape Cod spout lamp is a New England species of the north European type, and there is no knowing when it evolved. It is perhaps the earliest of our mechanical lamps, for its distinction lies in its having a charcoal brazier to heat the oil and the air in the reservoir, so that the oil, kept fluid, would flow under

Fig. 10 — Tin Spout Lamps

a. Cape Cod spout lamp. The lower part is a brazier for heating the fluid in the reservoir above. *From the collection of Mr. and Mrs. Quentin L. Coons*
b. Small hanging spout lamp. Probably English, nineteenth century. *From the collection of Mr. and Mrs. Earle E. Andrews*
c. Pennsylvania lamp with flat spouts for burning lard. The Dutch spout lamp figures in the ancestry of this device, though it has here become distinctly Americanized. Nineteenth century. *From the collection of Stephen Van Rensselaer*
d. Portable double-spout lamp. Probably a ship's lamp of foreign origin. *From the collection of Mr. and Mrs. William A. Harriman*

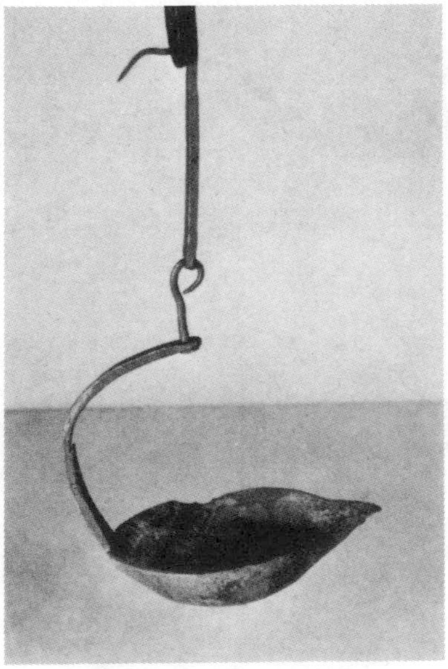

Fig. 11 — Kentucky-Type Hanging Saucer Lamp

Lamps like this were, and occasionally still are, used in the South by negroes and poor whites. *From the Wells Historical Museum*

pressure to the wick. One may conjecture that English spout lamps were used early in New England, and that some colonial Cape Codder, troubled by congealing oil in his lamp, conceived the idea of placing a heater beneath it.

Whether it was the slut, the phœbe, the betty, or the spout lamp that predominated among our early lamps will probably always remain a mystery. But like other articles of colonial days, lamps were probably imported mostly from abroad, though they were made here in small quantities. The impetus to home manufactures occasioned by the break in trade relations with England during the Revolution doubtless changed all this. The Revolution, indeed, made a cleavage line in our national history, dividing things and ideas into those which were dependent on Europe for their inspiration and those which a great political, social, and economic change generated into being. Certainly by the 1820's the talents of our tin- and ironworkers were focused on creating the distinctly native lighting contraptions that appeared in such abundance for the next fifty years. It is only of this later period that we may speak with precision when we talk of "American lighting."

REFERENCES

1. Esther Singleton. *Furniture of Our Forefathers*. Doubleday, Page & Co., New York, 1913.
2. *Probate Records of Essex County, Massachusetts*, Vol. II.
3. Mr. L. L. Thwing has informed me that in the Middle West he has seen a common saucer filled with grease and used, with a rag wick, for a lamp by an old lady who called it a *slut*. A French Canadian told me a similar story in describing the source of light in his childhood Quebec home, which could not afford candles. He could recall, however, no name for this makeshift device.
4. J. Seymour Lindsay. *Iron and Brass Implements of the English and American Home*. The Medici Society, London and Boston.
5. Mrs. N. Hudson Moore. *Old Pewter, Brass, Copper, and Sheffield Plate*. Frederick A. Stokes Company, New York, 1905.
6. Walter Hough. United States National Museum Bulletin 141, *Collection of Heating and Lighting Utensils in the United States National Museum*. U. S. Government Printing Office, Washington, 1928.
7. Howard Herschel Cotterell. *Old Pewter: Its Makers and Marks*. B. T. Batsford, Ltd., London, 1929.

Notes on Early Ohio Lighting Devices

By Rhea Mansfield Knittle

FIGURE 1. Combination rush and candle floor light fashioned during the frontier period of Ohio's settlement. The wrought-iron standard is supported by a rough, hand-hewn base, made from the burl of an ash tree. The adjustable fixture is dexterously forged into a combination of candle cup and clip rushlight holder. This fine specimen was used in Trumbull County, and it is in original condition.

During the opening of the trans-Allegheny country suitable tallow for candles and material for wicking were very difficult to obtain. Fortunately, however, rushes abounded in swamp and swale. The pithy parts of the rush stems were pressed together and soaked in bear grease (or that of some other wild animal). The rushlight was, of necessity, employed in this section of the country a century or more after its use was discontinued along the Atlantic seaboard. As late as the 1840's the inhabitants of wild and sparsely settled sections of Ohio carried pitch-pine flares at night.

Figure 2. An unusual wrought-iron rushlight floor device that does not conform to any type of early fixture with which I am familiar. The slender perpendicular rod terminates abruptly at the top, and at the base is supported on a low tripod with expanded, circular feet.

The bracket is an oblong platform from which rise two iron tubes hollow from top to bottom, with openings only sufficiently large for a rush. No candle sockets of any sort have been attached to these tubes, which are original. The inner section of one side of the adjustable frame is missing.

Note. All of the objects here illustrated were found in Ohio. It seems probable that the majority, if not all, were, as tradition insists, made in that state, which almost from the beginning of its settlement boasted a surprising number of competent craftsmen among its inhabitants.
— *The Editor.*

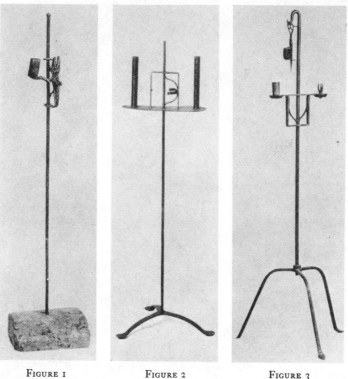

FIGURE 1   FIGURE 2   FIGURE 3

FIGURE 4   FIGURE 5   FIGURE 6

The piece came from the descendants of the original owner and was forged about 1800–1810 in the Muskingum Valley, where malleable bog iron was found prior to 1805. This valley became a mecca for proficient pioneer craftsmen, among whom were many ironworkers well versed in "the art and mistery" of blacksmithing.

Figure 3. An excellent example of a Pennsylvania-Dutch blacksmith's ingenuity as practiced in Lancaster, Ohio, in the early days of Ohio's statehood. Candles were so scarce that this device was contrived as a partial remedy for the situation. The platform holds both a deep candle socket and a three-pronged pricket, upon which the stub of the candle could be stuck and completely consumed after it had burned to the socket level. The tripod base is extremely wide and high, and the shaft, terminating in a crook at the top, is set through the base and strengthened at the joining by an iron ring. This specimen of early wrought iron was in Lancaster County until 1931, at which time moldy tallow was still adhering to it.

Figure 4. Ratchet-type of wood candlestand. Apparently both jackknife and plane were used in its construction. The parts are pinned together by both wooden pegs and early, short wrought-iron nails. Socket holes for candles extend through the platform. The latch that regulates and holds the ratchets is attached to both sides of one upright bar. This piece came from the environs of Tiffin.

Figure 5. A Mid-western frontier oak floor candlestand. Notice the octagon form of the lower portion of the shaft; the finely cut screw, which still operates perfectly; and the construction and balance of the arm with its metal sconce — made to hold a very slender candle — projecting through the base. Two of the three splayed legs, doweled into the oaken ball, are original. Standing where it was exposed to the elements, this sturdy little light survived the neglect. It came from Carroll County.

Figure 6. Uncommonly tall and somewhat light standard made of wood and tin. Its height was necessitated by the use to which it was put. The first communist settlement in the United States was established in Tuscarawas County in 1817 by the Separatists Society of Zoar, who migrated in the spring of that year from Germany. Among the community undertakings was weaving, and there was a weaving room, where material for clothing, blankets, and coverlets was produced on hand looms. This light was used by the side of a loom.

The shaft resembles an elongated broomstick. In it oaken pegs are inserted at regular intervals, for supporting the adjustable wooden arm, into which the little standard slides and is firmly held in position. The cup of this standard is badly charred. It still holds a small tin receptacle for grease or fluid of some sort. The burner or wick tube is missing; so also is the handle which was attached to the side of the vessel. A unique specimen, of interest both as an antique and as an historical item.

Figure 7. Wrought-iron open grease lamp of the frontier era, a type known variously as "slot," "slut," and "open betty." In this particular example, which came from Tuscarawas County and was probably fashioned from local bog ore, the sides are deeper, the handle is longer, the bowl is more circular, and the spout is more adequate than one sees on most lamps of the type. Bear or other animal fat was used in these little lights, a twisted rag wick emerging over the spout. It was better than no light at all, and was easily carried.

Figure 8. Iron betty lamp embodying every good feature that a lighting device of this kind should have. Each part is perfectly

FIGURE 7

FIGURE 8

wrought — hanging staple, handle, chain, and wick-pick (used for removing the constantly recurring carbon or soot from the end of the wick), sliding cover with thumbpiece, the vessel itself, the trough, the spout, and the wick tube. The oak stand or pedestal was at some time stained a dull red. Betties were made in Ohio from various metals — iron, tin, brass, and copper. This example was made in a section of Ashland County when it was still a part of Knox County. The stand came from the Amish district in the adjacent county of Holmes.

Figure 9. Primitive pottery grease lamp, built up by hand from coarse local clay and glazed with chocolate-colored slip of inferior character. The well for grease, oil, or some kind of animal fat has a central circular aperture through which it was filled and two spoutlike openings for the wicks. The base is sufficiently capacious to hold the drippings. This crude device is as sturdy and strong as the backwoodsmen who probably modeled and used it. It came from the vicinity of Winesburg, and is very early. It may have been fashioned by two Swiss potters who erected a pothouse in the near-by wilderness prior to 1818.

Figure 10. Another earthenware fat lamp, potted at least a quarter of a century later than Figure 9. This device and similar contemporary forms are attributed to the Routsons of Doylestown and Wooster, Wayne County, potters from Pennsylvania. The clay has been pugged and built up more carefully than that of the preceding example. The glaze resembles Albany slip, which it may be, for this slip was brought into Ohio in the 1840–1850 decade and was used to glaze the interior of Dutch or apple-butter crocks. The bulbous bowl has two wick spouts, and a generous handle is attached to the standard.

Figure 11. This lamp is similar in body, texture, and glaze to Figure 10. The shape is more sophisticated, and the handle is unique in so far as Ohio pottery lamps are concerned. The bowl is very wide and shallow, and only one spout occurs. The saucer is greater in diameter than that of any similar light that I have observed. This

FIGURE 9 (*above*)
FIGURE 10 (*left*)
FIGURE 11 (*right*)

FIGURE 12

FIGURE 13

FIGURE 14

example is attributed to the hand of an experienced and efficient potter, Curtis Houghton, who migrated from the Vermont pottery district in the 1840's and settled in a rich clay centre now known as Dalton. *Pottery lamps similar to Figures 10 and 11 are now being reproduced; also iron floor stands somewhat resembling Figure 3.*

Figure 12. Tin oil lamp of a type frequently found in Ohio. The cylindrical chamber is capped by a double wick burner and is set into a larger lipped standard. The panlike base and the handle are soldered to the standard.

Figure 13. Three metals enter into the composition of this choice lighting device: The open top reservoir is of copper, and swings on two side pivots. The supporting arms branch out from a slender stem, of iron, sunk into a tin pedestal, which in turn is attached to a tin saucerlike base. A delicate chain containing more than the usual number of little links is attached to one of the arms, and a slender pick is fastened to the other end of the chain. This light came from Portage County.

Figure 14. Tin oil lamp with small detachable triple burner and prominent tubular opening through which to pour the fluid. The chamber is covered with a slightly convex stationary top. Footless, very thin tin snuffers hang by a little hook. The blade end of these snuffers is curled in an unusual manner. Even the box is scalloped around its edge. The ensemble will interest our lighting-device collectors, some of whom may know who patented it. It was found in Coshocton County, where it had been in use.

Figure 15. Pewter swinging lamp made by Homan and

FIGURE 15

FIGURE 16

Company of Cincinnati between the years 1857 and 1872, for use in the home and on Ohio River boats. The original wholesale price was twelve dollars per dozen.

This type of lamp is a development of the New England whaler's lighting device. Although such devices were manufactured as late as 1872, a perfect specimen is now difficult to find.

Figure 16. Tin lard-oil lamp made for a broad, flat wick. The wick holder has three narrow parallel openings in one side whereby the wick could be conveniently "picked up." A slide in the top of the lamp covers a good-size circular aperture for filling. The handle is not in evidence in this picture.

An interesting circumstance in connection with this lamp is that, with five identical brothers, it was found, in 1932, in the attic over an abandoned tin shop in central Ohio. Neatly wrapped in a cobwebby box were the separate parts, cut and marked, ready for shipment — to be assembled at a destination which they never reached. So they were soldered together in 1932, and, as the photograph shows, the tin is almost as shiny as when it was first rolled and cut.

Figure 17. Wrought-iron combination snuffers and wick-pick. This piece has never had feet, or rests, and the handles taper to a delicate thinness seldom found in iron work. The blacksmiths of Ohio's pioneer period wrought not only for utility and durability but also for grace.

The devices pictured, while somewhat crude and homely, are, nevertheless, proof of definite skill and of a desire to combine good workmanship with utility.

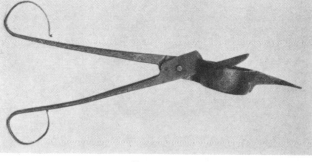

FIGURE 17

American pottery lamps

BY LURA WOODSIDE WATKINS

Fig. 1. Lamp of unglazed red earthenware made at Morgantown, West Virginia, by John W. Thompson, probably before 1840. Height, 5 inches. *The Smithsonian Institution, United States National Museum.*

EVERY LARGE COLLECTION of American lighting devices includes one or more pottery grease lamps. These are primitive affairs, usually with a simple open reservoir on a standard, a saucer base, and a handle or handles. The greater number have a slight beak in the bowl-like reservoir where the wick may rest, others have spouts, while a very few have wick supports.

Such fat lamps are now comparatively rare, but in their day they were probably rather common. They were fashioned by local potters who made a business of supplying household utensils of whatever clay was available. Redburning clay was the material most often used, but lamps were also made of stoneware. Most surviving specimens date from the first half of the nineteenth century.

Almost all the lamps of this type have been found in areas of German settlement, principally in Pennsylvania and Ohio, among the Moravians in North Carolina, and to some extent at a late period in Tennessee. It is more than probable that all American pottery lamps, even when made by potters of British descent, originated among the German settlers. This theory is bolstered by the fact that no pottery lamps of any kind were made by the hundreds of clayworkers of English descent in New England. Neither do they appear to have been produced by any of the numerous English and Irish potters whose histories have been recounted by Arthur E. James in *The Potters and Potteries of Chester County, Pennsylvania.*

Judging by the probabilities alone, the German settlers would have made the style of lamp familiar to them in their homeland. That they actually did just this we know for the reason that similar lamps were in use among the peasants of northwestern Europe, in Hungary, and in Sweden. Continental lamps differ in the respect that they usually have a pouring lip in the saucer base, but they show the ancestry of our American examples.

The lamp shown in Figure 1 is referred to by Walter Hough in his *Collection of Heating and Lighting Utensils in the United States National Museum* as having "English ancestry." By this he probably means that it was descended from an English lamp type known as a "Cornish chill," examples of which are to be found in the Penzance and Truro museums in Cornwall. One of these

Cornish specimens has the lip in the base found on Hungarian and Swedish lamps. There is evidently a relationship between the Cornish and Continental types, but the latter, brought to us by German immigrants, are more likely to be the originals of our own clay lamps.

Hough obtained the lamp shown in Figure 1 in Morgantown, West Virginia, from a daughter of John W. Thompson, the potter who made it. Thompson's father had taken his family over the mountains from Bel Air, Maryland, in 1785, and John became an apprentice in the first pottery west of the Alleghenies, founded by one Foulk at the very beginning of the settlement. This pottery supplied the demand for household wares then so expensive to obtain from Baltimore or other seacoast sources of supply. Thompson succeeded to Foulk's business and continued to make redware until about 1840, when the manufacture of stoneware was begun. The lamp illustrated must have been made between 1800 and 1840. Hough surmises that it may have been a potter's lamp. Although it was perhaps designed for the potter's own use, we now know that it is a type often repeated in the middle Atlantic states. It is most primitive in construction, being simply a lipped saucer on a stand with saucer base and a handle.

A similar example, made in Tennessee of stoneware clay, was illustrated by H. C. Mercer in *Light and Fire Making.* He says of it: "From the boat-shaped earthen lamps of ancient Rome, from the green majolica ones of candlestick shape used by the Moors of today, to this miniature boat-shaped one of stoneware set upon a stemmed dish, in which opossum or 'coon' fat might have burnt for the Tennessee moonshiner, where I found it two years ago in the hill country of White County, Tennessee, there is no change of character or make." He further adds: "There J. T. Goodwin baked it for me of blue clay in 1895."

Such instances of a lamp by a known maker are rare. A lamp that was sold at the auction of the Alfred B. MacClay collection in 1939 was marked on the base, *J. L. Blaney, Cookstown, Pa.* This lamp must have been made between 1825 and 1854, since Cookstown had different names before and after those dates. Needless to say, such a marked lamp is a priceless rarity.

Fig. 2. Stoneware lamp glazed with Albany slip, found in Ohio. Height, 5½ inches. *Author's collection.*

Fig. 3. Lamp with globular reservoir, glazed red earthenware, attributed to Pennsylvania. Height, about 5 inches. *The Smithsonian Institution, United States National Museum.*

Fig. 4. Lamp with two handles and spouts, dark brown glaze. Height, 6⅞ inches. *Henry Ford Museum.*

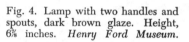

Fig. 5. Lamp with a true spout, dark brown glaze. Height, 5¾ inches. *Henry Ford Museum.*

Fig. 6. Lamp with fully developed spout, glazed red earthenware. Height, 2¼ inches, length, 4¾ inches. *Author's collection.*

At the pottery centers of Bethabara and Winston-Salem, North Carolina, Moravian potters were working as early as 1756 and as late as 1830. Lamps from this area have a light red earthenware body and are decorated with a combination of brown, black, cream, and green slips on a yellow-brown ground.

The large stoneware lamp in Figure 2, with a lipped open reservoir and an Albany slip glaze, was found in Ohio. John Ramsay illustrates an almost identical example in his *American Pottery* (page 158). Albany slip glazing on stoneware was a nineteenth-century technique, and these lamps may have been made about 1840. A pair of lamps of a similar shape were made and used in a rural community in Tennessee as late as 1905.

A number of grease lamps have reservoirs of globular form. The one shown in Figure 3 has a slight lip for a wick rest. It is attributed to Pennsylvania and is distinguished by a rudimentary decoration of tooled straight and wavy lines. Some globular reservoirs are slightly closed in at the top, and have chunky projecting spouts to serve as wick channels. An example with two handles and two spouts is in the Ford collection at Dearborn, Michigan (Fig. 4). The spouts, of triangular shape, are simply contrived. A similar lamp, owned by Mrs. Rhea Mansfield Knittle, is shown in John Spargo's *Early American Pottery and China* (plate 31).

Lamps with true spouts are great rarities, probably because they were difficult to make. Since the reservoirs of all these lamps were turned on the potter's wheel, they are fundamentally cups or bowls adapted to the purposes of illumination by the addition of lips or spouts. A lamp with a true, albeit rudimentary, spout is shown in Figure 5. This displays the novel feature of a reservoir partly closed to prevent the spilling over of oil or grease. A more fully developed spout may be seen on the lamp in Figure 6, which has the wick opening on the upper surface of the beak. Here, as rarely, no stand was provided, and the result is a lamp as primitive as those of ancient Greece or the Near East and not much different from some of them. A lamp of this type, provided with a carrying handle, was illustrated in an article by William J. Truax in ANTIQUES for May 1940. Mr. Truax also showed an example with a deeper reservoir, which might possibly have been intended for a lamp filler.

Another class of pottery lamps is equipped with tubular or gutter-shaped wick supports, which allowed any surplus grease to drip back from the wick into the reservoir itself rather than onto the outside of the lamp. A notable example of this type is that shown in Figure 7. Its wick tube is a perfect cylinder at the outer end, but is opened and spread apart towards the center of the bowl. The lamp with rudimentary spout in Figure 8 has a ceramic trough or channel (the more usual form) inside.

At least four examples of pottery Betty lamps with interior wick supports are known, all from Pennsylvania. One, illustrated in the article by Mr. Truax, has a handle and was not designed for suspension. The lamp in Figure 9 has a punched opening in the tab at the back for the accommodation of a wire or string. Two others of unique form appear in the group shown by Mr. Truax. One is complete with the regular type of twisted iron handle and hook so familiar on iron Bettys; the other has been pierced at the sides in a wholly original manner for an iron suspending wire and hook.

The Bettys are the aristocrats of American pottery lamps and must have a strong appeal for those who like to reflect upon old customs and ways. They represent the successful attempt of their makers to provide a wanted necessity when the usual materials were not at hand. All these lamps, in fact, must give us added respect for the ingenuity of those masters of the wheel.

Fig. 7. Lamp equipped with pottery wick tube in bowl, the standard partly hollow, red earthenware with dark brown glaze. Height, 7 7/10 inches. *Landis Valley Museum.*

Fig. 8. Lamp with pottery wick trough in bowl leading to spout, red earthenware with rough reddish-brown glaze. Height, 5½ inches. *Henry Ford Museum.*

Fig. 9. Betty lamp with pottery wick trough, glazed red earthenware. Diameter, 4½ inches. *Author's collection.*

FIG. 1 — HEART-SHAPED SAUCER LAMP. Attributed to David Spinner, who plied his trade at Melford in Bucks County from 1800 to 1811. This lamp is a mere three inches long, with a single wick channel. Its heart shape suggests that it may have been a wedding present

FIG. 2 — SPOUT LAMPS. Of the same red-brown tone as Figure 1. From Berks County. *Left*, quite apparently copied from a mug; three inches tall; spout of the same length. *Right*, probably modeled after a teapot or jug; stiff, straight spout. Height, 4 5/16 inches; spout 3 1/2 inches long

EARLY POTTERY LIGHTING DEVICES OF PENNSYLVANIA

By WILLIAM J. TRUAX

PENNSYLVANIA pottery occupies an unquestioned place in the domain of antiques. Indeed, since much of it has been unmistakably earmarked by time, we may be sometimes inclined to look upon the whole colorful category as a survival from the distant past. Yet Jacob Medinger, the last of the old-school Pennsylvania potters who were responsible for much of the ware that collectors prize today, died but a decade ago. The craft of making redware pottery in the early manner survived in Pennsylvania because of the rather astonishing fact that the people, though in constant communication with other parts of the changing continent, clung tenaciously for over two centuries to many early methods, customs, and superstitions. Yet, while they perpetuated the customs of their forefathers that seemed to them sound and good and appropriate, they shrewdly adopted new designs that came to the pottery kiln, and sometimes the happy combination of old and new lifted the products of their craft into the realm of art. One writer has observed that almost any antique found in any one of the original states has its counterpart in the Dutch country of Pennsylvania, but that the counterpart always reveals the characteristic local touch.

FIG. 3 — CANDLESTICK. An amusing example in lighthouse form, whose wide saucer might support a betty lamp. Incisions in the sides form the letters *ISI* so that this combination candlestick and lamp stand might be classed as a signed piece. So many potters claim these initials, however, that they are not an exact identification. This piece was made in Lebanon County. The glaze is very dense, with green and dark-brown spots running through it, and slip of yellowish brown. Height, 7 1/8 inches; top diameter, 4 15/16 inches

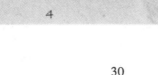

FIG. 4 — BETTY LAMPS. In pottery, with wire hangers; both have pottery wick channels. The hanger of the right-hand example springs from the back, as in metal lamps of the type. This lamp, 4 7/8 inches long, is of dull brown pottery. It was once displayed in the Berks County Historical Society. *Left*, 3 3/8 inches long; bright, yellowish-brown glaze

Though the Pennsylvania potter spent the greater part of his days in making more or less standard commercial products such as pie plates and crocks, he expressed his individuality in the fashioning of numerous odd objects that are to us utterly delightful. Whistles in the form of birds — a whistle could hardly be caged more appropriately; small houses to be used as children's banks; flowerpots with fine pie-crimped edges, designs on their sleek sides, and often an inscribed date; and tremendous dishes for the bride-to-be, abundantly and happily adorned with a medley of tulips and love birds and inscriptions, all in rich, bright colors — such varied objects we find today, a persistent monument to the play spirit of the industrious potter of yesterday.

Lighting devices seem to have offered a special invitation to the personal touch. That the Pennsylvania potters produced lamps of almost every conceivable design is evident from the great variation in extant specimens. The majority of these are of redware glazed in plain colors. Their lack of elaborate decorations may be due to the small surface of the pieces. Occasionally fine specimens turn up with variegated or speckled glaze or with ornamentation in slip. Others, though lacking distinctive coloring, are unusual in form, and sometimes excellently proportioned. No two are alike, and the forms were frequently copied from unrelated objects that caught and pleased the potter's eye. Most of them embody the simplest principles of illumination, providing a receptacle for grease and a channel for holding the wick in place. Still, as some of the illustrated examples testify, more complex devices are to be found.

To the collector of old lighting fixtures the matter of date is important. Yet, in the case of these pottery devices, unless a piece is dated or bears the individual and unmistakable mark of a certain potter, it is difficult indeed to say when it was made. And such identifying marks are rarely found. According to John Ramsay's *American Potters and Pottery*, the eastern Pennsylvania counties of Chester, Montgomery, and Bucks became a pottery-making center before the middle of the eighteenth century; the first recorded pottery in the district was built in 1740. It is generally accepted that the earliest potteries were in Chester County, and several collectors and dealers with whom I have discussed the subject feel that pottery was being made there soon after 1700, if not before that date. So far as I know, however, there is not one existing example of Pennsylvania pottery earlier than a platter inscribed *1733*.

While some of the lighting devices here pictured are of a type used in this early period, I am not credulous enough to believe that any of them can boast an age of two centuries and more. The persistence of old patterns, and the primitive character of many late pieces that were turned out simultaneously with superior work, make the task of dating with any accuracy almost impossible. It is safe to say, however, that the lamps here illustrated represent the century of potterymaking between the years 1770 and 1870. The forms are characteristic of what the collector may expect to find, though the condition of the members of this group is above the average.

Pottery lamps are being copied today, but the discriminating collector will soon learn to differentiate between old ones and new. The latter have a lighter, more porous body, and lack the patina that comes only with age. The fact that old lighting devices in Pennsylvania pottery are not half so numerous as specimens in metal or glass only adds zest to the collector's chase.

FIG. 5 — GREASE LAMP. The molding of the standard resembles linen-fold paneling; three small knobs decorate the handle. Height, 7 ¼ inches; base diameter, 4 ⅞ inches. The color is light brown. This lamp has the characteristics of Berks County production

FIG. 6 — GREASE LAMP. Short, open-top, saucer-base example covered with a glaze almost black in color. Though discovered in western Pennsylvania, it may be an Ohio piece. Height, 4 ⅛ inches; diameter of base, 5 ¼ inches

FIG. 7 — CANDLESTICK. While not particularly appealing in design, this piece has the distinction of an inscription, incised in the base: *W.A. and A.D. No. 22, 1866.* The known list of potters fails to throw light on this bold marking. This stubby specimen was found in Montgomery County. Height, 2 ½ inches. The scalloped saucer base is 5 ¼ inches in diameter. The glaze is speckled brown and green

FIG. 8 — THREE-WICK LAMP. Shape possibly inspired by a quill holder and ink pot, which it resembles. The wick tubes, and the known fact that the well once contained oil, not ink, prove that it is a lamp. The other lighters here illustrated could have been outfitted with wicks made from a piece of oil-soaked rag, but this piece calls for the solid round wick used in camphene lamps. Discovered in Berks County. Height, 2 inches; diameter of bowl, 4 ⅞ inches

On the Trail of the Betsy Lamp

By J. Neilson Barry

"DOES you-all call dem dar lamps bezzy lamps? We-all calls dem grease lamps."

So, then, this delightful little antique, always indelibly associated with old New England days, with Puritan peaked hats and long capes, with Salem witches and Plymouth Rock, was also known in the Land of Dixie. In fact, it was an important utensil there, since by its dim, weird light the slaves "befo' de wah" used to gather in their quarters, and it is probably on its account that the modern lamp in the kitchen never boasted a chimney, the older colored people seeming to feel that lamp chimneys were for "de white folks"; and for themselves preferring a flame open and smoky.

That simple Betsy lamp,* which could be made by a blacksmith, and which was virtually indestructible, belonged essentially to a certain stage in human progress, and for centuries was widely used the world over. It is, in fact, no less than the ancient classic Grecian lamp, with a long, curved handle connected, by a swivel, to a short bar of iron. This device enabled it, therefore, to be carried in the hand, or hung from a rafter or a chair back. Again, it could be placed upon a table, or stuck into the wall or a crevice of the chimney. As its prototype of

---

*In *Colonial Lighting* Arthur H. Hayward traces the origin of what he calls the *Betty* lamp back to the dawn of civilization. Certainly lamps of this general form, but made of clay, were used in the heyday of Babylonia and Assyria. But why *Betty* or *Betsy* lamps? Mr. Hayward does not tell us. Can there be in the term implication of an Elizabethan origin for the metal type with its swivel attachment and ingeniously balanced handle? But if there is, then why is a similar lamp, which is provided with a kind of drip cup beneath the main receptacle, known as a *Phoebe*?

Grecian days has become an emblem of enlightenment, so the Betsy lamp may be accepted as the emblem of advancing civilization, for it constitutes the highest development of the Grecian lamp.

I obtained my first American specimen from an old darkey who had just used it; but not for light. Instead, he had taken it to his Sunday-school class to illustrate the parable of the Ten Virgins. "Yo' jes' skum de grease offen de soup, an' put it in de lamp, wit' a rag fo' wick, an' dar yer war." It was essentially the lamp to be used under primitive conditions. Candles required more elaborate preparation, and necessitated either wax or tallow, but the Betsy lamp required only grease or olive oil.

It was kerosene that caused this humble, but useful, article to become obsolete. As an old darkey told me, "My ole Modder done hear dem talk o' kerry-seen bein' so good, so she don' took an' put some in de grease lamp, and it cotch afire and blaze all up, an' skeerer her, so she grab de tongs and cotched de lamp, and chuck it in de fire. An' she never had no use, no more, fo' no kerry-seen. She war afeared it would *go off* like it had."

The Betsy lamp has ever been a pioneer utensil. After its use in the east had lapsed, save among the southern colored folk, the adventurous invaders of the newer regions of western America found the lamp so invaluable that when an orthodox specimen was not obtainable its place was supplied by means of a tin can cut down to a height of perhaps an inch, provided with a lip and fed with grease in which a twisted rag served as wick.

Fig. 1 — AMERICAN BETSYS
Specimens belonging to the Oregon Historical Society These were brought by the pioneers who crossed the plains in ox-wagons, a journey which took four months.

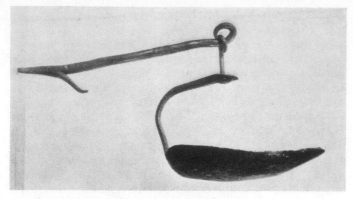

Fig. 2 — SLAVE LAMP OF THE SOUTH
Type of grease lamp used by the slaves in the South "befo' de wah."

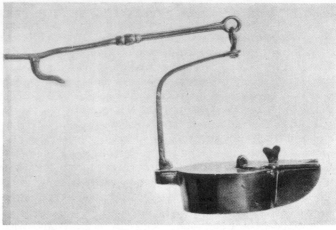

Fig. 3 — A LAMP WITH A HISTORY
Heavy brass "chaliel" supposed to have belonged in the château at Vals les Bains, torn down during the religious wars, about the time of the first settlement in Virginia.

Europe used the Betsy lamp long before the early pilgrimages to America began. Not a few specimens still survive. During the late war, for example, when kerosene was virtually unobtainable in France, the old French Betsy lamps, discarded for half a century or more, were hunted up and again came into common use.

It was during this time that I was passing through an ancient French village just after nightfall, when I noticed a ruddy, flickering light on the crumbling walls, and there discovered an aged peasant lighting his way with one of these lamps. It was a weird and romantic experience. I found, however, that it was difficult to obtain any such lamps for myself, as the country people needed them for light,— since ordinary lamps would not burn the cooking oil which alone was obtainable. In fact, without introductory propitiation of cigarettes and chocolate they could not be purchased. But as the dearth of tobacco and sugar made those luxuries a means of approach, after a free-will gift of such desirable delicacies it became possible to open negotiations, although not always with success.

In Ardeche the only examples which I saw in use were

of iron. One type was hung on a string, but most were of the usual type, sometimes of wrought iron, sometimes of "white" iron. Some more modern ones were machine made. Occasionally a cheap one of tin would be found. I once was in charge of a group of sight-seers, nearly every one of whom obtained one or more lamps as souvenirs. We returned like the Virgins of the parable, bearing our lamps, to the amazement of the country people, who must have imagined that we were disciples of Diogenes. In this instance, indeed, our apparent desire for such souvenirs caused them to be offered at each farmhouse that we passed, so that when finally a woman offered two for sale, all fourteen soldiers declined. They had had enough; so I collected them. I never let one escape.

During the religious wars a famous castle at Vals les

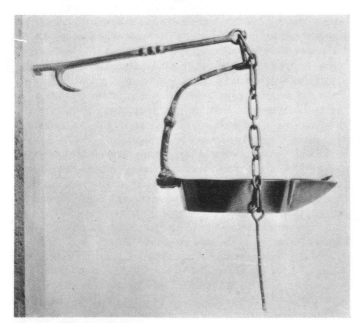

Fig. 4 — A FRENCH BETSY LAMP
Type of brass "chaliel" found in Savoie, France. The wire on the chain is used for picking the wick.

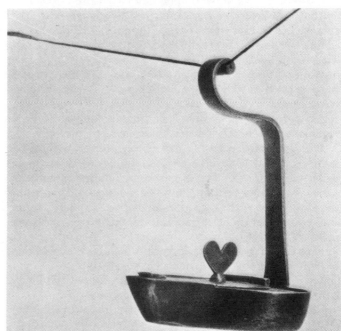

Fig. 5 — ANOTHER FRENCH LAMP
Type of "chaliel" from Ardeche, France. Virtually all are of iron.

Bains was torn down after much fighting. Apparently the brass lamp here illustrated must have figured in some tradition of the place. Anyway it had disappeared, and only turned up three centuries later when I had begun to create a source of revenue for such antiques. When I took it to my lodgings, my host, an aged veteran of the Crimean war, and his wife became almost hysterical, kissing their hands to the lamp and talking so rapidly in their excitement that I could understand nothing of what they were saying. Finally I persuaded one of them to write: and with trembling hand she scribbled, "It is verily the lamp of the old Chateau." But what mystery was connected with its earlier disappearance I could never learn.

In Savoie the Betsy lamp is usually of brass and without a cover. One very small one must have been made for the child of a nobleman, but it was so broken and encrusted with verdigris that only the bowl remained, so that it was impossible to tell whether it had once possessed a handle, or whether it was the toy of some child when the Roman legions occupied that section.

The names used for these lamps were in patois, and do not appear in any dictionary. "Chaliel" seemed to be the term in Ardeche,—with variations. No one seemed to know how the word was spelled, and no two wrote it the same way. In Savoie the term used sounded like "brulay", but, when asked to write it, the people would shrug their shoulders and say it was merely patois.

At a delightfully quaint oil mill near Aix les Bains, the fat, jolly little miller owned a lamp which his ancestors had used for centuries. When I would take parties of sightseeing soldiers to visit the ancient castle and the "Gorge," and this charmingly primitive mill, where cooking oil was made from rape seed, the soldiers were always delighted when the fat little veteran of Verdun would light the brass lamp. A whispered suggestion that some American girl would like it as a souvenir would always result in an attempt to purchase, and then the lamp would be wildly waved as the chubby little miller would frantically gesticulate, with many shrugs, while talking French, two hundred words to the minute, that it was an ancestral heirloom, inseparable from the mill.

Today I went to the Oregon Historical Society to borrow some specimens of pioneer Betsy lamps for the photographer. The aged Curator told me that, nearly seventy years ago, when he was one of the first settlers, he had made a lamp on this same principle, scooping out a turnip and fastening it to a stick; and by its feeble light, as a boy he had read Gibbon's *History of Rome*.

Lights of the Centuries

THREE years from now we should be celebrating the one hundredth anniversary of the invention of the friction match. Before 1827 our progenitors, if in need of fire, were obliged either to borrow a brand from a neighbor or to fall back upon a device quite as primitive as that employed by mankind in earliest ages—the spark struck from metal by impact with hard stone.

But the friction match had been long in use before mankind produced any notable improvements in its apparatus of illumination. The lamps which are supposed to have done service in the *Mayflower* might quite as well have been used in Noah's Ark. There was not much opportunity for evolution in lighting fixtures so long as the burning medium was oil of some kind. Hence it was, after all, —even with due respect to gas—but a step from the Betsy lamp to the incandescent electric bulb.

The collector of lamps, therefore, and of other early means of lending visibility to darkness, possesses an almost limitless field wherein to ride his hobby. Bounded on one side by the threshold of today, its farther verge is obscured in the mists of pre-history. Nowhere else among the crafts is discoverable so great a variety of designs within so narrow a range of fundamental types.

This is true even when the consideration is confined to lighting devices of early American days.

In *Colonial Lighting** we have early iron and tin lamps, later tin, pewter, and brass lamps, lanterns, candles and candle holders, early glass lamps, astral and lustre lamps and ornamental candle holders. These topics, together with an introductory chapter on ancient lamps, and a concluding section of "random notes," furnish the material of the book. Illustrations are numerous, for the one hundred and fourteen illustration plates show many times that number of examples, and, on the whole, show them well. The general method of treatment is sound without being overwhelmingly scientific: for the author allows himself digressions into realms of collateral interest when necessary to seek material for a complete background. Thus readability is maintained throughout. Dates are sparingly assigned to examples illustrated—wisely perhaps—for old types had a way of persisting in manufacture long beyond the earlier years of their origin. But enough well-marked signposts are set up to prove of considerable assistance in any more precise process of identification.

To write a book on a subject hitherto avoided, not because of its lack of interest but because the way to it is lined with pitfalls, requires more than ability and courage, it requires altruism of a high order. Too many collectors are so afraid of exposing their points of ignorance that they are unwilling to share their special knowledge. Mr. Hayward has proved an exception to the rule. What he knows he offers: for the probability of error he apologises. *Colonial Lighting* is, so far as known, the first book of its kind. Whatever on the subject appears in subsequent years must be based upon it and must recognize its primacy. To produce such a book is an achievement. Now that it has been produced it becomes indispensable to the library of the collector.

*COLONIAL LIGHTING. By Arthur H. Hayward. Boston; B. J. Brimmer Company. Illustrated. $7.50.

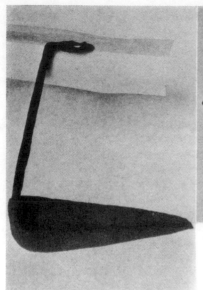

Figs. *1, 2, and 3* — Old Type of Slot, or Slut, Lamps
Untidy affairs that spilled grease when carried about and
dripped it from overcharged wicks when fixed in place.

Further Light on the Betty Lamp

By Charles L. Woodside

Illustrations from the author's collection, except as otherwise noted

IT was with much pleasure that I read the communication from the correspondent of Antiques, G. A. R. Goyle,* on the subject of the betty lamp and the derivation of the name by which it is known. The information contained in his letter provides a valuable and unexpected help in the solution of this interesting problem.

In my article entitled *Early American Lamps* I gave a reason why the betty lamps were so called,† but lack of space prevented any extended explanation. That, as I have stated, the word *betty*, as applied to the betty lamp, was derived from the English word *better*, I have no doubt; nor do I doubt that, did we but know it, the same tradition has been handed down in many families other than my own.

I feel that I can speak with some assurance on this topic, for it so happens that the tradition has come down in my family from ancestors both of English and of French blood. My maternal grandmother, Mrs. Henry Marquand, referred to in my article, was born, in 1802, of old English stock. She lived in Boston, and was eighty years old at the time of her death, in 1882. When I was a

Fig. *4* — The Better Lamp
Of tin, with lid lifted to show wick tube with its aperture well within the lip of the reservoir. Such lamps were clean and neat, and in all respects a great improvement over the open type.

boy she had one of these betty lamps among her prized possessions and brought it out now and then to show as a relic of the past, just as we show similar things of our own today. It was a lamp such as her mother had used, and she always called it a "betty lamp." I especially remember this because our common lamps in use at that time were called *kerosene* lamps. My grandmother used to explain that the old-time device received its name because people who had used the old and greasy slot lamps,* which always spilled the oil when carried about, called these newer ones better than the old, and that *betty* was simply a corruption of *better*. She kept this lamp until late in life, but I have never been able to learn what became of it.

All of these slot and betty lamps were in common use, along with candlesticks, in my grandmother's childhood days. I do not know whether the one she had came from her mother, but it is quite likely that it did — and perhaps from her mother's mother, together with the tradition concerning it.

A further confirmation of this tradition now comes from Doctor H. Hommel,

---

* See Antiques, Vol. XIV, p. 219.
† See Antiques, Vol. XII, p. 498.

* The term "slot" in this connection may well be a euphemism for the word "slut" of untidy connotations. — *Ed.*

35

Figs. 5, 6, 7, 8, 9, and 10 (left and right) — VARIOUS EXAMPLES OF THE BETTY LAMP
Whatever the derivation of the word, it should be noted that the term betty lamp is now
applied indiscriminately to both open and closed types.

Librarian of the University of Würzburg, quoted in G. A. R. Goyle's letter. Doctor Hommel, after a study of words kindred to *better* in Murray's *New English Dictionary*, concludes that *betty* was derived from the verb *beet* or *bete*, an old form of *better*, now obsolete and surviving only in dialect. Its meaning is to make better, to better, and also to kindle and sustain fire. The substantively used present participle of this verb was *beeting*, and there occurs a variant *bettyng*, used in 1581 in the sense of fuel or material for fire. "This reference Doctor Hommel considers sufficient evidence to make it appear plausible that betty lamp is merely another expression for grease lamp, perhaps used dialectically in old England and brought, by early settlers, to America, where it has survived to this day." Thus it would seem that the origin of *betty* might be from *better*, a better lamp, or from *bettyng*, a fuel or material to use in the lamp, or both.

My maternal grandfather, Henry Marquand, was of old French Huguenot stock, born in France, in 1795. He died in Boston, in 1880. As to him, I cannot remember that I ever heard him call the lamp a betty, although I have seen the lamp in his hands. But of this I am certain — he never called it or referred to it as "la petite lampe" or as "la petite," as would be quite natural if that term were customary in France, for French

was his native tongue and he spoke it more or less constantly, as his English was somewhat imperfect. Today, in France, one might very properly speak of small or little (*petites*) lamps, for they are of all sizes, large and small; but in the days of the betty practically all household lamps were small, and therefore such a designation as *petite* would have had little or no significance.*

Moreover, *lampe* is of the feminine gender and therefore requires the feminine form of the adjective *petite*, in which case the final *t* is to be sounded, the pronunciation then being like the same word in English — petite, pronounced pẽ-tēt′ (accent on the last syllable). And while the final *t* may be somewhat elided in ordinary conversation, enough of it remains to distinguish it from the masculine *petit*, which, of course, would not be used in this connection. It would hardly appear, then that the word *betty*, as applied to the lamp, could have come from the French.

So, after much thoughtful consideration of all the evidence in the case, including my own contribution to it, I have come to the conclusion that the explanation of the derivation of *betty* from *better*, whether adjective or verb, is the correct one. But if still further light can be thrown upon the subject from any source, it will be a welcome addition to our present knowledge.

* See ANTIQUES, Vol., XII, p. 211, G. A. R. Goyle.

Fig. 11 — BETTY LAMPS OWNED BY
THE OREGON HISTORICAL SOCIETY

Fig. 1 — VARIOUS LAMPS
    a. Single-burner tin Betty on standard.
    b. Traveling curling tong heater, in brass.
    c. Petticoat pewter lamp on candlestick. Shown also as *c* in Figure 2.
    d. Probably a filler transformed into a lamp.
    e. Modified tin Betty lamp with three wicks.

Some Old Lamps

By ARTHUR H. HAYWARD

Illustrations from the author's collection

IN many branches of collecting, after a certain amount of technical information and a considerable familiarity with designs, patterns, methods of craftsmanship, and so on, have been acquired, it is a comparatively simple matter to assign its definite place and time to any new item which is encountered.

With lighting devices, however, there seem to be no fixed rules for guidance. Each artisan was a law unto himself. Certain general forms and styles were made and used in some parts of the country long after their abandonment in others. Lighting appliances in general were the expression of the taste and skill of the individual maker, rather than the outgrowth of a developed style. Hence, in the collecting of such appliances, there is always the stimulus of the possible discovery of some new type, or some unusual adaptation or adjustment of an old one, to keep the collector on the alert. The thousand and one discoverable variants in form and feature fascinate and baffle while they urge one on.

Generally speaking, all lighting appliances in the Colonies, for the first two hundred years, were one-man affairs. That is to say, a blacksmith, iron-worker, tinsmith, pewterer, glassblower, carpenter, or whatever the craftsman might be, would — either quite unaided, or perhaps with the help of an apprentice or two — make a few lamps for local distribution. Perhaps no two would be exactly alike. Form or design would change as new ideas or suggestions came, but each specimen always exhibited, to a marked degree, the maker's own individuality. And this accounts for the amazing variety of very simple things.

Let me illustrate a few which I have recently added to my own collection, each of which, I think, may claim to be something out of the ordinary.

I happened one afternoon to visit a shop in the country where I had now and then found something of interest. The dealer picked up a small metal box, black with age, and asked me to identify it. The type was new to me, but, after examining it carefully, I concluded that it must be a pocket lamp for heating curling-irons, and that it was probably used in the early days of the Republic, when both beaux and belles sported elaborate powdered and puffed coiffures. Conveniently small to slip into a pocket or satchel, it was no doubt used, while traveling or at social functions, to repair such damage as may have been caused by winds or weather. (*Fig. 1b.*)

After liberal applications of polish and elbow grease, I found that I had a beautifully made brass box with rounded ends, on the top of which were two folding hinges. On these, when upright, was placed the curling iron, the business end of which would then be directly over the

Fig. 2 — VARIOUS LAMPS
  a. Folding lantern in tin.
  b. Dutch lamp, of the seventeenth century, in pewter.
  c. Petticoat pewter lamp detached from its standard, which appears at the right.
  d. Oil lantern, single wick. The oil container is of pewter instead of tin.

two rows and all perfect. The wooden frame, too, is sound, but what makes the piece particularly valuable is the fact that the top shelf, from which the pewter tubes hang, is covered by a brass plate and has the name of the maker and the place stamped on it.

I have a friend in New York who specializes in candle molds. His collection includes a number of rare pewter molds, and a very few of what is scarcer still, molds of pottery instead of pewter, and in the same sort of wooden frames. I wrote him of my find and he replied that he was particularly attracted to this purchase of mine, both for its small size and the fact that it was a marked piece; and that if I cared to exchange, he would give me for it another pewter mold and one of his rare pottery ones. I shipped it to New York, and the two molds in Figures 5 and 6 are the result. They are each for twenty-four candles, and are in almost perfect condition.

Several of the pewter tubes show slight signs of oxidization, but the pottery ones, of common unglazed red clay, are in proof condition though the wood of the frame is somewhat worn. I do not think that these were made in New England, as the type is rarely or never found here. This specimen, I feel sure, came from Pennsylvania or adjacent territory. (*Fig. 6.*)

At the same auction sale I secured the swinging brass grease lamp on a tall standard, with the curved handle at the side, shown in Figure 3 at the extreme right. This is beautifully made, with two open wicks protruding from the flat top like the wicks of Betty lamps. Because the lamp itself is pivoted, swinging freely, I feel that it was intended for use on shipboard. The handle might easily be slipped into a socket on the wall. This lamp is unmarked,

broad wick of a whale-oil burner, which, in turn, when not in use, was covered by a tightly fitting brass cap. I surmise that there must be similar lamps about, but I had never happened to see or hear of anything of the sort before, nor have I since; so I treasure this one in my lamp collection as rather unusual.

Not long ago I was in the shop of a friend, a dealer of long experience in one of the Cape towns of Massachusetts, and he brought out the lamp shown in the center of Figure 1. It was a whale-oil, two-wick petticoat lamp in pewter, resting in the top of a well shaped pewter candlestick. The two formed so perfect a whole that it seemed evident that both were made by the same hand and were meant to go together. Unfortunately neither piece was marked, so I do not know the name of the pewterer, but the proportions of the pieces show that he had a good eye for balance and design.

Now petticoat lamps in tin, of which I have several, are not uncommon, but this was my first meeting with a pewter example. Perhaps some of my readers may own a pewter petticoat lamp, but I doubt if a more graceful combination of lamp and its candlestick mate can be found than this one of mine. The lamp lying on its side to show the "peg" beneath the petticoat may be seen in Figure 2, beside its pewter candlestick.

While recently attending an auction of the collection of a dealer who had died, I purchased, among other things, a pewter candle mold. Now candle molds in tin are frequently found in the antique shops, though they are growing scarce, while ten years ago they could be had in abundance. But molds of pewter in a wooden frame are rare.

This mold is in excellent condition, with twelve tubes ranged in

Fig. 3 — GREASE BURNERS
  a. Crude iron grease lamp on standard. The saucer has a lid pierced for wicks.
  b. Brass Betty lamp, probably of Pennsylvania origin.
  c. Tin Betty lamp.
  d. Brass grease lamp for two wicks. Probably English, and perhaps for ship use.

Fig. 4—LANTERNS
  a. Wooden lantern with tin bottom and top. On the wooden door in the rear are three mirror reflectors.
  b. Half-round tin lantern.
  c. Tin lantern, of usual type but interesting for its completeness of oil font and chimney.

but its very fine workmanship and the quality of the brass may indicate an English origin.

Another item of interest which I secured was the hanging, three-candle chandelier, all of pewter, pictured on the cover. This is one of the most charming pieces of my collection, and the simplicity and grace of its design become increasingly apparent day by day. I thought at first that the chains connecting the top with the candle-band were of pewter like the rest, but, upon cleaning off the corrosion, I found that they were of brass. I realized then that pewter was much too soft a metal to make into chains which would have to withstand considerable wear. The rest of the chandelier, even the candle-holders, are of the finest quality of pewter.

Candle-holders of similar design were now and then used in the early meeting-houses, but they were usually of tin and sometimes of iron. Pewter is unusual for this purpose, and a hanging chandelier of so graceful a design is an acquisition which almost any collector would be proud to own.

The quaint little wooden lantern in Figure 4 is a birthday gift to me from my wife. Now, while wooden lanterns are occasionally found, they are so uncommon that one marks the day when he discovers a really good one. Most of them are rather large, clumsy affairs; but this one is small and daintily proportioned, with delicately turned finials to the corner posts. Three sides of the lantern are of glass; the bottom and the top, with its little round ventilator, are of tin; the unusual feature is the wooden door forming the fourth side. In the center are set four small pieces of looking-glass, all at slightly different angles so

that each may reflect the flame from the single candle which furnishes the light. This piece, perhaps, originated in the brain of some bright young farmer, who put his idea into practical form in the winter days when there was not much that could be done out of doors.

Of the other two lanterns in Figure 4, the half-round one, in the center, which may have been a shop lantern, has interesting piercings at the sides and over the tin door in the center of the back. Such pieces were usually painted on the outside, but left bright within, the surface of the tin reflecting the light of the single candle in front. Some late owner "improved" this lantern with a heavy coating of cheap gilt paint outside and in. An original, hand-molded tallow candle, half burned, in the holder, increases the charm of this piece, which, while not extremely rare, adds a quaint touch to my lighting collection.

The remaining lantern, one of the more familiar, square, tin variety, owes its chief charm to the quarter-circle shaped oil-font which is attached to its door — swinging with the latter as it is opened — and the little bottle-shaped glass chimney, resting on the tin shelf above the burner and held in place by the tin smoke conveyor above. This lantern is, of course, of a much later date than the other two.

Betty lamps, the origin of whose name has been lost, but about which many purely speculative theories have been advanced, are among the most fascinating of all the varied members of the lamp family, partly because they were the first type of lamp used by the Pilgrims and partly because of the many variations in design and material which they displayed as the early Colonial artisans commenced making them for the settlers. They were originally of iron, but it was not many years before the tinsmiths, who had developed a really remarkable proficiency in their medium, replaced the heavier and generally more clumsy iron lamps, with lighter, cheaper, and equally effective Bettys in tin. I do not know why, but a good, early, tin Betty is harder to find at the present day than an iron one.

I have been fortunate to have had sent to me within the past year several particularly good specimens. The first (and probably the oldest one) is the third in Figure 3. About the size and shape of the iron Bettys from which the first tin ones were copied, it is complete in having the wick-pick and the swivel hook to enable suspension of the lamp from a convenient peg or chair-back. It also has a sliding cover hinged on the projecting wick-spout, which shields the filling hole in the center of the top. I was interested to find this lamp half-filled with tallow

Fig. 5 — CANDLE MOLD
Pewter tubes, twenty-four in all, in a wooden frame.

or grease of some kind, now hardened and yellowed with age; and this I allowed to stay, as it had been, undisturbed for many years.

The other two tin examples, modifications of the Betty idea, are of later date and are set on a central column or stand, with a deep saucer base, which was usually weighted with sand or gravel to prevent its being easily tipped. The extreme left-hand one in Figure 1 is quite crude, a half-decked open body, very similar in shape to that of the tin hanging Betty just described, with a circular wick-tube sticking up from the bottom in the open space. Its large curved handle and wide base make this a safe lamp to carry about the house. The one at the right is a modified form of Betty. Circular in shape, it carries three open wicks in the top which has an opening for the grease. A crude attempt at ornamentation is seen in the raised pattern about the sides of the top.

This lamp is in better condition than the one at the left, on which the coating of tin has entirely disappeared in spots. When I received it the lamp had recently been decorated with a thick coat of green, yellow, and brown paint which it took some hours to obliterate, and there remain traces which it was impossible to wipe off wholly.

Besides being made of iron and tin, Bettys are occasionally found in other metals. In Figure 3 the second lamp is beautifully made in brass. It was picked up in Ohio, whither it had been taken from Pennsylvania, where it was

probably made. It has a well designed hanging hook and a very ingeniously arranged spring on the bottom of the hinged cover, which holds the cover shut. While, as I have said, this lamp is of Pennsylvania origin, I know of another quite similar, which came from Vermont, showing that the making of Bettys in various metals was not confined to any one section of the country.

The tall, black, rather awkward iron lamp at the left of Figure 3, looking more ungainly in contrast to the polished elegance of the brass beauty at the opposite side, is nevertheless of much interest. The round cast-iron top, about the size of half a small orange, has a flat cover with holes through which wicks may be thrust. The picture does not show it, but the top swings on side pivots exactly as in the lamp on the right. Sticking straight out is the handle, while the three flat legs are cut from a single piece of iron, bent and held fast under the round flat skirt by the tip of the central shaft. This is very early and evidently homemade.

Figure 2 shows two little lanterns, which, while not particularly valuable, are a bit out of the ordinary. The tin one at the right with the barrel-shaped glass, is a graceful little hand lantern and has a small whale-oil lamp in the bottom, made of pewter instead of the customary tin. The other, while comparatively modern, is a traveler's folding, pocket, hand lantern. The candle-holder, which slides up into the body of this lantern when not in use, has one of those concealed spring arrangements for keeping the lighted end of the candle at the top of the holder.

Fig. 6 — CANDLE MOLD
Earthenware tubes. A type apparently unknown in New England. Probably from Pennsylvania.

The small brass hand-lamp in Figure 1 with the long spout is rather a puzzle. Originally it may have been a simple oil filler which was afterward converted into a lamp, or it may have been made just as it is. I am inclined to think its original use was for filling. The small brass cap near the handle now covers a single whale-oil wick tube.

A few weeks ago I received a letter from a dealer friend in Ohio, who always writes me of any unusual discovery in the way of lighting appliances. She wrote "am sending on approval two Betty lamps, one very small and early, the other a perfect whale. Never saw one of its size before." In due course the pair arrived. The "whale" was indeed well named. Made of sheet iron, with a tin cover hinged in the middle and raised by a riveted loop of tin, it is in perfect condition, and includes a hanger and a wick-pick. After a coat of rust had been removed, it proved to be one of the best of its kind, and the largest Betty that I had ever seen, measuring fully eight inches in length and about the same in height. (*Fig. 7.*)

Its companion, which, of course, we at once dubbed "Jonah", is a diminutive affair, some three and a half inches long, beaten from a single piece of wrought iron. Jonah is of the early open Betty type, with an open trough in the nose for the wick. Mr. Whale looked as if he could assimilate little Jonah without much difficulty. This friend, to whom I am indebted for several of the pieces on these pages, wrote, further, that the "whale" formerly hung in the first schoolhouse built in Crawford County, Ohio.

Concerning the remaining lamp in this little group of mine, the tall pewter one in Figure 2, there is quite an interesting story. For several years, a group of the residents of that classic section of Boston known as Beacon Hill, has staged, each summer, a pageant for the benefit of some charity. Homes filled with beautiful ancestral furnishings are opened to the public. Special exhibitions of heirloom pewter, glass, china, and silver are held. Around the sacred green of Louisburg Square are erected small booths from which are sold flowers and fresh vegetables, candies and toys for the children, and various articles, artistic, useful or otherwise, such as are usually found at church and society fairs. One table at least is devoted to antiques. There is a parade of some sort and all those in attendance, and in fact many of the people living "over the hill", are costumed in the elegant garb of their forefathers and foremothers. The whole affair is most picturesque. Thousands of spectators wander along the narrow streets lined with ancient houses, and view through eyes of a century ago, the goings and comings of their fellow citizens.

I strolled there at noontime on the day of the fete. It had been showery during the morning, delaying the out-of-door features, and I found most of the booths just start-

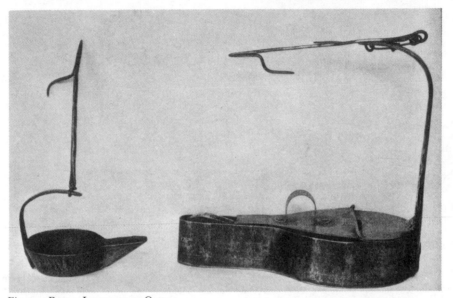

Fig. 7 — Betty Lamps from Ohio

That at the left is beaten from a single piece of sheet iron. That at the right, of unusual size, formerly lent its aid to educational enlightenment in the first schoolhouse of Crawford County, Ohio.

ing to unpack and display their goods. The antique table had only a few articles arranged and nothing which interested me, so I wandered about the streets, admiring the groups posing on front steps, paying my fee to enter some of the fine old homes opened for the public's inspection. Just before leaving, I decided to make one more circuit of the Square. As I approached the booth labeled *Antiques* I saw that the attendants had been busy and that the display had been much increased.

Quite a gathering of people had assembled and, as I edged my way toward the table, I caught a glimpse of this old pewter lamp at the far end. As quickly as possible, I wormed my way out and around the crowd at the other side, fearful that some more fortunate collector would secure the prize before I could reach it. At last I succeeded in reaching the table and picked up what I found to be an old pewter double-base lamp resting on a tall, graceful column rising from a saucer base. It was in fine condition, of a superior quality of pewter. The little lamp, with its tiny hinged cover, could be lifted out of its snugly fitting case, and was perfect except where the flame from the small wick had melted away a bit of the soft metal at the tip. There was no mark on the lamp, but I judged it to be of Flemish or Dutch make and dated it well back toward the seventeenth or possibly very early eighteenth century.

I asked the charmingly attired young attendant if she knew anything of the piece, which was simply tagged "old lamp, 3 dollars". She could give me no information, and when I had tendered my money and tucked the lamp under my arm, she seemed pleased that she had so quickly made a sale. She was not more pleased than I.

I have since seen, in an old portrait by one of the Dutch painters of the sixteen hundreds, a pictured lamp almost the exact counterpart of this of mine. So I feel that my judgment of it is approximately correct. It is such totally unexpected finds as this that makes "antiquing" such a fascinating pursuit.

Fig. 1 — THE UNCHANG-
ING LAMP
The iron betty lamp at
the left and the tin lard-
oil lamp beside it — the
one of the eighteenth
century, the other of the
nineteenth — are, to all
intents and purposes, the

same devices as the an-
cient Roman clay lamps
that are illustrated at
the right. *This and other
illustrations, except as
noted, from the Galpin
Collection in the Buffalo
Historical Society Mu-
seum*

The Light of Other Days

By ROBERT WARWICK BINGHAM

THE birth of the lamp was undoubtedly accidental. Possibly the falling of a lighted fragment into a container of grease suggested the idea to some inventive mind of prehistoric times, and the first lamp, with the floating or partially submerged wick, was constructed. The primitive containers were of natural formation or an artifact of stone, such as may be found among the archæological remains of the Kanakas, the aborigines of Hawaii. From such crude beginnings developed the clay lamps of Egypt, Assyria, Rome, Greece, and the great ancient empires of the Far East. These pottery lamps of the ancients are found in various shapes and sizes, all following the primitive usage and indicating advancement only in the shaping and decoration of their containers. Some early forms resemble a shallow saucer with its edges curled up into lips for holding the wick. The more familiar design, as illustrated, is covered and boasts separate

Note. The reader will find in *Early American Lamps*, by Charles L. Woodside (ANTIQUES for December and January 1927–1928), a step-by-step consideration of the development of lighting devices. Likewise, ANTIQUES has published, from time to time, more specific articles on various types of early lamps. *Further Light on the Betty Lamp* appeared in April 1929; in July 1932 were illustrated and described several pewter lamps by Dunham and the Porters; and so on. The following notes, however, offer a convenient general summary of the subject. — *The Editor*.

openings for introducing the oil and for holding one or more wicks. While the potters turned out such vessels of clay in countless numbers for the masses, the wealthy folk of Rome, and those of like station in other lands, used lamps of brass, bronze, and other metals, highly embossed and tooled, but in general form corresponding with the simpler lamps of clay. The light was poor, unsteady, and smoky; but it was the light of Plato and Aristotle, and, by its flickering rays, the Roman generals planned their imperial conquests.

It is almost unbelievable that, from a period previous to the dawn of the Christian era until the middle of the eighteenth

Fig. 2 — STANDING LAMPS OF CONTINENTAL TYPE
Both are of continental form; the first a Dutch specimen of brass; the second, of pewter. Each has an oil reservoir and a wick spout. Their gleam was feeble

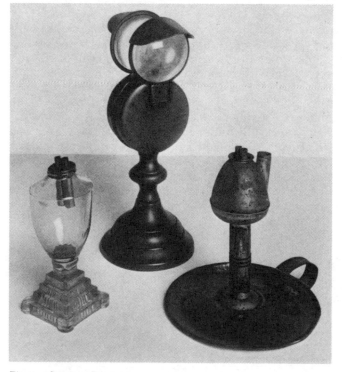

Fig. 3 — SIGNS OF PROGRESS
Double-wick whale-oil lamp (American, nineteenth century); bull's-eye lamp (late eighteenth or early nineteenth century); tin upright lamp with Franklin burners, placed at an angle (nineteenth century)

century, the advancing peoples of the world continued to struggle along with a quite primeval form of illumination. It is true that candles were used, and that by massing their light a certain intensity of illumination could be obtained; but the lamp to all intents and purposes remained the light of the ancients.

In an accompanying illustration (*Fig. 1*), with the clay lamps will be found a lamp burning lard oil, and, to the extreme left, the betty lamp of the period of early American colonization. This last may well be called the pioneer lamp of the New World; it was found in the cabins of Plymouth colony and in the homes of New Amsterdam, and it accompanied the pioneer into the golden West. I have found such lamps dated as late as 1830, with an oil container and a simple floating or partially submerged wick. Their form is much like that of the ancient lamps of clay, proclaiming that, up to within a century of the present day, man's knowledge of lighting had not progressed materially beyond its status in the cave period. The lamp that sufficed the followers of John Carver and Peter Minuet still continued to serve the brave pioneers whom Daniel Boone led to the west of the Blue Ridge.

The flowing sands of time had marked the middle of the eighteenth century before science set to work in the interest of improved illumination. It was Benjamin Franklin who devised properly placed burners for whale oil and a wick of superior capillary attraction. At the close of the century the Swiss inventor Argand made still further helpful alterations. The item to the right in Figure 3 is a tin upright lamp fitted with Franklin's

Fig. 4 (left) — Pewter Lard-Oil Lamp (*c. 1840*)
Such pewter lamps are apparently a late device. Mr. Woodside states that he finds no evidence of their production previous to 1825. The majority are of later date

Fig. 5 (right) — Brass Lamps with Camphene Burners (*c. 1840*)

burners. In the centre of this same illustration will be seen an English double bull's-eye lamp of about 1773. This marks early attempts to concentrate light for reading by means of lens and shade. Picture your colonial ancestor on an August evening in the year 1774. He places the lighted bull's-eye on the table, draws up his favorite Windsor, and, after seating himself comfortably, focuses the light on the *Pennsylvania Packet* and reads Shippen's *Open Letter to King George III*, the advertisements for runaway slaves, and the thrilling news that "on Wednesday last Captain Giddings arrived at Portsmouth in nine weeks from London." Such were the "good old days." The later eighteenth century, however, took upon itself to atone for the backwardness of the past. Inventions literally rolled into the patent offices, both in America and in Europe. The flat wick, such as that shown in the lamp of Figure 4, the circular wick, the chimney, and the wick control, which prior to this time had been nothing but a pin or other sharp instrument — all these inventions thoroughly revolutionized the problem of illumination.

Though improvements without number were made in the lamps themselves, whale oil

Fig. 7 — Candlesticks with "Adapters" (*nineteenth century*)
Left, whale oil; right, patent fluid. These "adapters" are usually known as peg lamps, because of the peglike member that fits into the socket of the candlestick

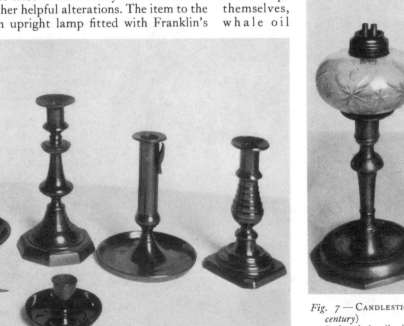

Fig. 6 — Brass Candlesticks (*dates uncertain*)

Fig. 8 — CRYSTAL CHANDELIER (c. 1850–1860)
Originally intended for gas lighting. The far from appropriate globes are part of the "improvement" associated with electric wiring of the fixture

interesting nineteenth-century contrivances we find "adapters" of glass, some arranged for whale oil, others for camphene, but all made to fit into a candlestick and convert that utensil into a lamp.

When, in the 1860's, kerosene appeared on the market as a lamp fuel, the death knell of small lamps using whale oil and similar fluids was sounded. The crowning triumphs of lamp construction — the chimney, circular and flat wicks, the toothed control wheel, plus kerosene — provided what our fathers generally considered an ideal illumination. Kerosene meant larger lamp

Fig. 9 — DESIGN FOR "GASELIER — GOTHIC" (c. 1850–1860)
From *The Universal Decorator*, published in London

long remained the favorite burning fluid. It was in the decade before the drumbeats of the Mexican War began to throb that several patent burning fluids appeared upon the market. Among them was the so-called *camphene*, extremely dangerous, but capable of yielding a more brilliant and steady light than former fluids. Its use required lamps with special burners and extinguishers.

Whatever might be done for and with lamps, candles were the mainstay of household lighting, from the founding of the first colony until well beyond the dawn of the nineteenth century. And candles of course required holders. There was the brass candlestick for the desk, similar to the smallest one shown in Figure 6; the slide candlestick provided with a flange for raising the candle as it burned; and the stick with the daintily curved handle for lighting the way to bed. We find candlesticks in every imaginable material — brass, copper, pewter, tin, iron, silver, glass, and porcelain. And the costly candelabra, generally of silver or Sheffield plate, must not be forgotten, for these remained in vogue for the dinner table long after their more humble brethren had been laid away.

But to return to lamps: among the

Fig. 10 — KEROSENE LAMPS
The lamp at the left was sold as a souvenir of the Centennial Exhibition of 1876. That at the right seems to be of similar date

reservoirs than had hitherto been possible, and stimulated the designing of new lamp forms, some good, some rather horrid. In any event the revisions embodied in these lamps enabled a man, at last, to read his papers with some degree of comfort. The light afforded was fairly steady, its brilliancy far beyond that of previous devices. If properly cared for, the lamp was virtually odorless. With these advantages in its favor, for a period, kerosene reigned supreme.

Experiments in incandescent gas lighting were begun by Henry Drummond as early as 1826; but the use of illuminating gas for reading purposes did not seriously encroach on the realm of the kerosene lamp until the advent of the Welsbach burner in the early 'eighties, which, in its turn, yielded to the electric bulb. Old gas burners have not become collectors' prey; yet they are almost as obsolete as the betty lamp. The latter, however, stands for us as a souvenir of some thousands of years of inventive stagnation; the latter is but a marker in the late swift race from darkness made visible to darkness banished. This somewhat staggering development in the science of illumination took place in little more than one hundred and fifty years.

II Oil Lamps

The nineteenth century produced a plethora of lighting devices unlike any seen before. The development of new fuels, a resulting flood of patented devices in which to use them, and the birth of mass-production methods combined to produce a profusion of lamps and other artifacts now prized by collectors. By the end of the nineteenth century—the terminal point for most lighting collections—the centrally served systems of gas and electricity rendered all previous lighting technology obsolete. It was a century of unprecedented progress.

Just as the slanted wick support, typical of the betty lamp, marked a major improvement over the crusie, so John Miles' 1787 English patent of an agitable lamp with a threaded burner and sealed upright wick tube brought an end to widespread use of the betty and its allies. The use of a vertical wick tube supported by a metal disc isolated the flame, and this made possible the entry of the glass blower and his heat-sensitive product in the lamp business. He could produce the glass fonts to be filled with whale oil. But how to affix the wick tube and burner?

Since glass, unlike metal, can not be threaded, the first and simplest approach to this problem was the drop burner, a wick tube supported by a concave tin disc that merely rested on a flat opening in the glass font. Inasmuch as the drop burner was held in place only by gravity, the lamp obviously was not really agitable. Need for a secure lamp led to use of the cork burner, usually one or two wick tubes soldered to a rimmed top plate with a wafer of cork secured underneath by a small tin washer. A slot in the wick tube just above the plate allowed adjustment of the wick by careful use of a wickpick. Since burners are often missing today, glass lamps intended for drop burners can be recognized by the absence of any neck or flare at the opening, while a lamp made for a cork burner had a short recurved neck which accepted and gripped the cork wafer much like the neck of a bottle.

The final improvement in whale oil burners for glass lamps was the threaded metal collar attached to a more or less straight neck formed on the glass font. This collar, seldom missing, permitted burners to be used interchangeably with metal lamps. Collars were made in three standard sizes, and nearly all subsequent burners, including modern electric adapters, conform to these standards.

This interchangeability of burners allowed the owner of a whale oil lamp to modernize by taking advantage of newer, better, or cheaper fuels, or of the latest patented improvements. This feature, unfortunately, may cause confusion for the collector who has a lamp that is in fact older than the burner, or one that has been "enhanced" by the substitution of an earlier whale oil burner on a lamp intended for kerosene. Because of this feature, burners do not furnish hard evidence for dating collared lamps. Since most of these early burners were intended for whale oil which is somewhat viscous and has a high flash point, they were designed to bring heat *from the flame to the oil* by making the wick tubes short above and long below the burner plate.

The rising cost of whale oil led to the substitution of lard or lard oil as an illuminant. Primarily an American fuel, it was safe and inexpensive. At normal summertime temperatures, lard oil, sometimes called "prairie whale oil," burned well in any whale oil lamp but during colder winter temperatures tended to congeal more than whale oil. To overcome this deficiency, hundreds of ideas were patented, all the way from simply making the wick tubes of copper for better heat conduction to Zuriel Swope's weird contrivance illustrated in Arthur H. Hayward's article, "Lard-Oil Lamps" (pp. 129-130). Many lard oil burners typically used one or more wide, flat wicks capable of producing a greater amount of light, as well as the necessary heat. While most of these lamps used in the common homes were small humble affairs of tin, the elegant solar lamp, in many handsome models produced by such prestigious makers as Cornelius of Philadelphia and Starr of New York, graced the homes of the wealthy.

As early as 1830 various formulas were tried in an effort to produce a better lamp fuel which would give a brighter light. Known as "burning fluids," these formulas usually consisted of mixtures, in various proportions, of spirits of turpentine, which by itself tended to smoke, and alcohol. Ambitious inventors added all sorts of trace adulterants presumably for the sole purpose of securing a patent. Regardless of the mixture, however, such burning fluids invariably were highly volatile, possessed a low flash point, and were, consequently, extremely hazardous.

Many explosions and fires resulted from their careless use.

To reduce the hazard, the basic fluid burner, unlike that for whale oil, was designed with the wick tubes long on the outside and short or nonexistent on the lower side of the burner plate. This was done, simply, in an effort to keep the heat of the flame *away* from the fuel. Also, because of the fluid's volatility, a small cap for each wick tube was provided, usually attached by a fine chain to the burner plate. The caps are often found to be missing, but usually a small hole in the plate where they were fastened remains. There seem to have been as many patents issued to keep heat *from* the fuel to make fluid lamps safe as there were to conduct heat *to* the fuel to make lard oil lamps practical.

By the Centennial year, 1876, kerosene had largely replaced the older illuminants, only to be outmoded in turn by Edison's invention of the incandescent electric lamp in 1878. Unappreciated by early collectors and writers alike, the lamps and lighting devices of the kerosene era, having met the one hundred year definition of "antique," are now receiving the attention they have long deserved.

The Whale-Oil Burner: Its Invention and Development

By C. Malcolm Watkins

HISTORIANS of lighting devices have been careful to avoid discussion of the invention of the enclosed upright wick tube burner, popularly known as the whale-oil burner. Perhaps it has never occurred to them that, in the history of lighting, this invention is possibly the most significant development since the creation of the saucer lamp some three thousand years before Christ. Perhaps, again, it is easier to dodge the subject, and when questions arise concerning the origin of the wick tube burner to cite Benjamin Franklin as the probable inventor. But no documentary evidence has ever been presented to support such an assumption. Hence it seems well to attack the subject and try to determine the facts concerning the beginnings of the wick tube burner.

At the outset we must realize that the change from the betty lamp, and its allied types with slanting wicks, to the reservoir with enclosed upright burner did not occur in one leap. The betty lamp, as everybody knows, is distinguished from its even simpler predecessor, the saucer lamp, by a slanting wick support of metal, one end of which was attached to the oil reservoir while the other end protruded slightly beyond the spoutlike nose of the lamp. Lamps evolved from the betty type always had such a slanting wick channel fastened to the bottom of the oil reservoir, although sometimes partly tubular in shape. But it was by a stroke of genius that some lampmaker, whose name we shall probably never know, conceived the idea of setting the wick channel perpendicular to the bottom of the oil reservoir. This idea revolutionized lamp design and encouraged innumerable new forms and types.

The Pennsylvania iron swing grease lamp in Figure 1 exhibits one of these early upright wicks. The cylindrical reservoir is entirely open at the top, though the tubular wick channel is almost sophisticated enough to be called a burner. Figure 4a shows an early tin peg lamp, also from Pennsylvania, with an upright wick support. This support is virtually the same as the kind found in betty lamps, except that tabs are bent around at the top to hold the wick in place. The transition toward the enclosed burner may be seen here, since the reservoir is equipped with a top. However, an opening an inch in diameter, around the wick, is retained. In Pennsylvania this type of lamp continued in use well into the nineteenth century.

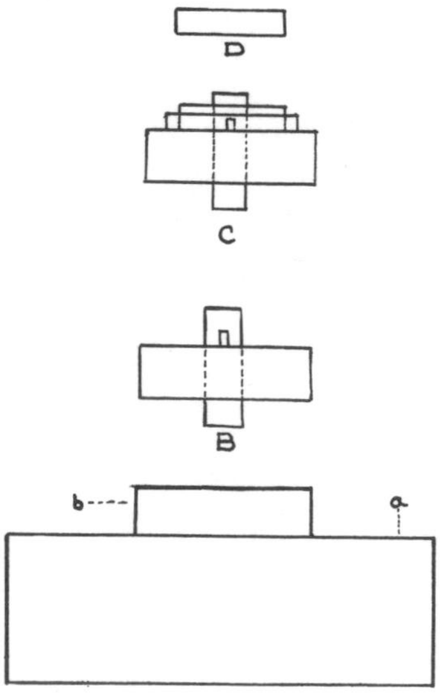

The next step, obviously, was completely to cover the reservoir. But the old-fashioned wick support, still a heritage from the betty lamp, made this a difficult operation. Thus it remained for someone to invent a new type of burner. This, of course, was accomplished; and, though Franklin may have been responsible, there is good evidence that another claimed the invention.

Fig. 1 — PENNSYLVANIA GERMAN CAST-IRON SWING GREASE LAMP Showing upright wick support in open reservoir. A transitional step from the betty lamp to the enclosed upright wick tube burner.
From the Charles L. Woodside collection

The British Registry of Patents furnishes this evidence, for on February 12, 1787, a resident of Birmingham named John Miles entered the statement that "His Most Excellent Majesty, King George the Third . . . did give and grant unto me, the said John Miles, during the term of years therein expressed, should and lawfully might make, use, exercise, and vend within England, Wales, and Town of Berwick upon Tweed, my Invention of 'Making Lamps in Different Forms, and of any Kind of Metal or Metallic Substances, to be Used without Inconvenience on Horses, Carriages, Breasts of Men, or any Body under Motion, so as to give Perfect Light though ever so much Agitated, or to be Used in Halls, or Staircases, Tables, Desks, or other Purposes where Motion is not required.'"

As one reads further concerning this patent he soon perceives that here, indeed, is the earliest record of the enclosed upright wick tube burner. Miles sets forth "to cause a particular description of the said invention." The "said invention" is not the burner under discussion, but, instead, the enclosed reservoir. It is, however, almost so obvious as to be a certainty that Miles likewise invented the tubular burner, since such a burner is entirely dependent for its existence upon an enclosed reservoir. He states: "I take any kind of metal or mixture of metals or metallic substances that can be cast, rolled, drawn, or pressed into the form I wish and the purpose requires." But, then, since "the most simple form is the most easily understood," he proceeds to describe the lamp diagrammed in Figure 2. No drawings are included with the patent papers, but Miles' description is sufficiently clear to permit an accurate reconstruction. The reservoir *A* is drum-shaped and covered. The cover *a*, which is permanently affixed, has a hole large enough for rim *b*. *B* is the simple burner unit.

For the moment it may be well to recall the two types of whale-oil burner, so called, best known to lamp collectors. Cne of these burners consisted of one wick tube (occasionally two) which passed through two metal discs separated by a layer of cork. The lower disc, of course, was smaller than the upper, the cork being for the purpose of holding the entire arrangement secure and leak-proof when it was inserted in the opening at the top of the lamp reservoir. Oftener, however, brass and pewter collars were provided in the openings of the reservoirs, and the burner, having then only one disc of brass or pewter, screwed into the collar air-tight. The latter type became standard, and is familiar to everyone. It was filled with one or two, and sometimes three, wick tubes. In both types of burners the wick tube was provided with a slot at the base of the external part, and the disc or discs with a small hole. The purposes of these slots and holes are fully explained by Miles, for they are important details in his patent.

Miles' burner is far more elaborate than its successors. In

Fig. 3 — A GENUINE MILES LAMP The burner is of a later type than that called for in Miles' patent.
From the collection of Doctor Edward A. Rushford

Fig. 2 — DIAGRAM OF MILES' LAMP, AS DESCRIBED IN PATENT *A*, reservoir; *B*, burner; *C*, burner with outer rim, or "preserver," and inner rim on which fits extinguisher cap, *D*

the diagram (*Fig. 2*) it will be noted that burner *B*, which is a tin disc with a rim attached and a wick tube passing through, is just large enough to fit into rim *b* on top of the reservoir. This may be equipped, Miles says, either to squeeze or to screw air-tight. The slot in the wick tube just mentioned must be provided so that excess oil may return to the wick. *C* shows the burner complete. Here two rims have been fastened around the edge of the burner, one inside the other. The outer rim, called a "preserver," is for the purpose of preventing excess oil from running over. The inner rim is for securing cap *D*, which is screwed or squeezed to it. When the lamp is not in use, the rim prevents any possibility of spilling oil. This is designated as an extinguisher. The small hole in the disc mentioned above is a necessary feature, and Miles explains his reasons:

"As they [the wicks — Miles allows for one or two] continue to burn the oil or spirits when they get warm will naturally swell, and as the reservoir is every way air-tight, and the oil or spirits having no other way for expansion, the liquid will flow superabundantly up the burner tube or tubes, so as to over charge the preserver, and afterwards, as the oil or spirits diminish by burning, the air will press the same way to supply the vacancy occasioned by the diminution of the oil or spirits, and to retard the oil or spirits in rising to supply the burners, to prevent both which inconveniences I make a small hole through the top of the reservoir." This careful explanation should satisfy those writers who have held that this hole was for the purpose of "ventilation," or the "escape of gases," or for allowing excess oil to return to the reservoir.

Since it was an unspillable lamp that concerned Miles in this patent, the creation of a new type of burner was only an incidental matter; and Miles goes on to describe an enclosed reservoir lamp that would employ an Argand, or air-tube, burner. Three years previous to Miles' invention, Ami Argand had designed his well-known internally ventilated wick, and had patented it in England. It is, therefore, a fair assumption that this type of burner was first used in open reservoir lamps. So far as this phase of Miles' patent is concerned, however, there is little point in discussing it further here.

But it is perhaps worth while to digress in another direction, for in the same patent Miles describes a "lamp that will continue to burn without trimming for a long space of time." This lamp, operating "upon the same principle as a bird-cage water fountain" consists of a vertical cylindrical oil reservoir from which a tube runs to a "bason." When the "oil or spirits have found their just medium" in it, after having flowed down from the reservoir, a quantity of fine wire is placed in the centre of the basin in such a manner that it will stand upright. This wire, which constitutes the burner, is then heated until the oil catches fire, "and it will burn (if defended from any sudden impulse of air) so long as it is properly supplied." Why this specification should have been included in a patent for a lamp which is "to be used without Inconvenience on Horses, Carriages, Breasts of Men, or any Body under Motion" is something of a mystery.

It is the first part of the patent that is of great significance, however, for it presently resulted in a great outburst of lampmaking. Lamps of tin, glass, brass, and pewter made their appearance in forms hitherto impossible. Made at first in England under the conditions of Miles' patent and exported to America, they met with popularity and were imitated by local lamp makers. A Miles lamp is shown in Figure 3. In Figure 4 *b* and *c* may be seen two lamps made in this country in imitation of the type. The frequent occurrence of these lamps in present-day collections indicates how widely they must have been used. How long production of the lamps continued is not known; but advertisements at the turn of the century show that they were manufactured as frank imitations of Miles' lamp. The *Columbian Centinel* of Boston for February 8, 1800, for example, printed the following advertisement for Joseph Howe, a Boston tinsmith:

"AGITABLE LAMPS,

"Which are so constructed as to prevent the oil from spilling although the Lamp should be overturned, or thrown in any direction; made after the much

approved ones called 'MILES' Patent Lamps,' and warranted to be equal to them in every particular, by JOSEPH HOWE, *near the Boston Stone*, and for Sale, Wholesale and Retail, either plain, polished, or japanned, and of any form.

"N.B. All kinds of Tin Ware, plain and polished, as usual."

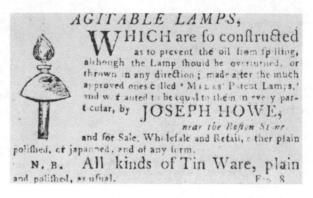

Another advertisement, in *J. Russell's Gazette* for February 24, 1800, announces *Patent Lamps*, with the comment, "The lamps are so

constructed as not to spill the Oil when overset." The *New England Repertory* for November 23, 1803, printed an advertisement for Ebenezer Stedman: "Miles' Pocket Lanthorns, some with cases and slides." In his patent, Miles says, "in order that lamps made on this principle may continue to burn in all sorts of weather, I place or fix them in a lanthorn made for that purpose in any form or shape I think proper."

Every collector knows the development of whale-oil lamps from this point on, and the large quantities in which they were produced. In all of them the principle that John Miles discovered and patented is employed. It was this principle alone that made possible the æsthetic advance in lamp design and the wealth of beautiful brass, glass, and pewter lamps turned out during the first half of the nineteenth century. Similarly mechanical improvements were the outgrowth of the enclosed upright wick tube burner, whose modified forms made possible the successful use of volatile oils and lard oil.

It is strange that John Miles should have remained in obscurity for nearly a century and a half, in spite of his epoch-making contribution to the development of lighting. Perhaps the distinctively American term "whale-oil burner," derived from the use in this country of whale oil for these lamps, has led to the assumption of American origin. But even if Benjamin Franklin was the actual inventor of this burner, as legend persists in assuring us, it was nevertheless Miles who placed the device before the world and put it to practical use. It is to Miles that available documentary evidence points.

(*To Miss Barbara Epstein the writer wishes to express his gratitude for her valuable assistance in research for this article.*)

Fig. 4 — TIN PEG LAMPS
a. Pennsylvania lamp with upright wick support and partly covered reservoir. *b* and *c*. Lamps made in this country to imitate Miles' patent lamp.
From the Charles L. Woodside collection

Early American Lamps*

By CHARLES L. WOODSIDE

Illustrations from the author's collection

Part II: Closed Lamps

ONE of the causes of the Revolutionary War was the restriction placed (by the Mother Country) on manufacturing in the colonies; but toward the close of the century, after independence had come and the new nation had established itself, conditions once more became settled and a great revival of industry set in. And although this industrial activity was seriously interrupted by the War of 1812, it soon recovered, and thereafter continued with increasing vigor.

THE WHALE OIL TYPE

This industrial development brought about many changes. The steam engine had proved successful, and new machinery of various kinds, the result of American ingenuity, was applied to industrial processes. The individual craftsmanship of former days had gradually given way to mass manufacturing. No longer were utensils and other articles made singly to order, but by special machinery in quantities of hundreds and thousands. It was during this period that the closed lamp, as exemplified by the whale oil type, came into active being. Who invented it and when and where, and whether it had been in use to some limited extent before this time have never been definitely determined; but when it was put on the market, its immediate adoption by the public and its immense popularity were unquestioned.

The American whale oil lamp with its distinctive burner was a great innovation, entirely different from anything of its kind that had preceded it, a lamp "of a form peculiar to the country."† It was probably a production of the inventive genius of our own Benjamin Franklin; and, while the evidence is somewhat obscure, the invention is very generally attributed to him by all well-known writers on the subject. The matter is one in which he would naturally be greatly interested, partly because of its general importance, as evidenced

Fig. 7 — EARLY GLASS LAMPS

Blown and fashioned by hand for the tin and cork burners. *a*, with welted foot; *b*, blown oil bowl and pressed base, acanthus pattern, Sandwich; *c*, candlestick with fixed peg lamp top, welted foot; *d*, four-part mold; *e* and *f*, one wick.
Heights range from 1¾″ to 6¾″; capacities, from 1¾ oz. to 4½ oz.

by his improvement in the street lights in Philadelphia, and partly because of the fact that his own father was a maker of candles in Boston. Moreover, his active and alert mind was constantly engaged, even while important matters of state were under consideration, in observing and improving just such things as these which appertained to the comfort and convenience of daily life.*

I think we can truthfully say that, whenever it may have

*It would not be surprising to learn some day that the whale oil lamp had its origin in a cork stopper and a bottle in the hands of this wise philosopher and genius. Corks and bottles were in common use in those days. What could be more easily accomplished than to thrust a small tube through the length of such a stopper, to insert a wick in the tube, to fill the bottle with oil, and to put the stopper in the bottle? It simply remained to apply a flame to the wick and behold, a lamp! And furthermore, what could be more natural at the time this event may have taken place than that Franklin should have gone to his friend and neighbor, Richard Wistar, maker of glass in Philadelphia, where they both lived, and shown him his bottle lamp and asked him to make a good and properly designed lamp for his new cork burner. For Richard Wistar was not only a maker of glass bottles and glassware in general, as his father, Caspar Wistar, had been before him; but he was also the maker of Franklin's electrifying globes and tubes, and of the panes of glass for the square lanterns which Franklin devised for use in lighting the streets of Philadelphia — a form of lantern which has remained in use to this day; and later he was the maker of Franklin's glass lamps. Franklin improved the street lantern in 1757, and it may well be that the smoky lamp it contained caused him to consider what improvement could be made in this utensil.

I doubt very much if Franklin fully realized the true value and significance of his invention, although he never appears to have missed anything. Apparently he did not consider it of any particular importance, for he has never mentioned it except in connection with the use of two wick tubes instead of one. It does not appear to have been adopted for use in any general way, partly, perhaps, because new inventions did not make a strong appeal in those days, and partly because Franklin went to England immediately after, remaining there more than five years. Wistar however, appears to have designed a lamp of proper form, and in 1769 it is recorded that he "united the two branches [of his business] at his house in High Street, above Third, where he made glass lamps

Fig. 8 — WHALE OIL BURNERS

a, *b*, and *c*, tin and cork; *d*, pewter, early form; *e*, brass, early form; *f*, pewter, later form; *g*, brass, later form; *h*, brass, later form; *i*, pewter, later form.

and bottles, and brass buttons." [Bishop, *History of American Manufactures.*] Wistar closed his factory in 1780 and died in 1781, while Franklin was in France; and Franklin died in 1790, soon after he returned home, not having seen Wistar since 1776. With the passing of these two men, so intimately connected with this affair, the light of the lamp went out and even the

---

*Continued from the December number of ANTIQUES.

†H. J. L. J. Massé, in *The Pewter Collector*, page 101, says, "Boston was the chief seat both of its [pewter] manufacture and also of the distribution of English pewter. The use of whale-oil necessitated the introduction of lamps of a form peculiar to the country."

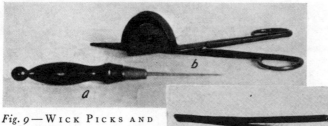

Fig. 9 — WICK PICKS AND
SNUFFERS
a, iron wick pick with wooden
handle; *b*, wrought iron hand-
forged wick pick and snuffers
combined, for lamps and candles; *c*, Sands' improved lamp wick adjustor,
marked *Patent Intended*. Boston, 1866.

been invented, the real introduction and adoption of the whale oil lamp were largely due to the establishment of the factory of the New England Glass Company at Cambridge, Massachusetts, in 1818; and to that of the Boston & Sandwich Glass Company at Sandwich, Massachusetts, in 1825. Both of these factories put out an immense quantity of these glass lamps, of all sizes and designs and of many colors, blown, molded, and pressed, whose attractive appearance, combined with their cleanliness, at once brought them into favor. So popular did they become that pewterers, tinsmiths, brassmongers, and even pottery makers hastened to join in the effort to supply the demands of the public, and incidentally to enhance their own profits.

The whale oil lamp consisted essentially of an oil bowl, or receptacle for the oil, and a detachable burner for holding the wick. The oil bowl was made with a circular opening at the top, into which the burner was fitted. The burner could readily be removed when filling the oil bowl, as occasion might require. The burner was the really new and distinguishing feature of the lamp. It was characteristic of this type of lamp and was never used with any other.

CORK BURNERS

The first type of whale oil burner consisted of a cork stopper placed between two tin discs, the upper one larger in diameter

than the lower one, through all of which passed the tin tube for the wick, the whole being securely soldered together. The wick tube had a slot on one side through which the wick could be picked up as it burned away. It was made in two sizes: small, with one-wick tube; and large, with two-wick tubes placed a little apart. It was fitted into the opening of the oil bowl just as one fits a stopper into a bottle. The upper disc was turned up around the edge to prevent the overflow of the oil in case the wick overfed — that is, drew up the oil faster than it could be burned; and a small hole through the disc and cork allowed such surplus oil to run back into the oil bowl.

In the larger burner the wick tubes were usually one quarter of an inch in diameter at the top, a little larger at the bottom, and one and three quarters inches long. The upper disc was one and one quarter inches in diameter, and the tubes, which extended three eighths of an inch above it, were separated by a small space of about one eighth of an inch. In both sizes the upper disc was sometimes stamped with the word *Patent*, but was devoid of further information as to when and to whom the patent was issued. I presume the patent referred to the arrangement of the wick tube and the tin discs, which was probably an improvement on Franklin's original invention. It is well known that Franklin never took out any patents, though he made many inventions. For, as he said, "we should be glad of an opportunity to serve others by any inventions of ours; and this we should do freely and generously."

Fig. 10 — TYPES OF LAMPS
a, tin hand lamp, painted red, tin and cork burner; *b*, brass peg lamp, to be used in a candlestick; *c*, pewter chamber lamp — the smallest regular lamp known to the author; *d*, Sheffield plate peg lamp; *e*, tin hand lamp, japanned, with tin and mica chimney; *f*, brass table lamp, cast and turned; *g*, tin hand lamp, japanned; *h*, pewter table lamp, made by Rufus Dunham, Westbrook, Maine, 1837-1876, pewter burner — a very fine specimen.
Heights range from 1¾" to 8¾".

Fig. 11 (left) — PORTER'S ORIGINAL PATENT BURNING FLUID
Porter's advertisement in the *Portland Transcript* of April 3, 1852.

Fig. 12 (below) — FLUID BURNERS
a, pewter, with brass wick tube and pewter cap; *b*, brass, with brass wick tubes and caps; *c*, brass, with brass wick tube and cap; *d*, pewter, with tin wick tubes and pewter caps; *e*, brass, with brass wick tube, extinguisher, and cap, marked *E. F. Rogers Patent, Jan. 30, 1866*.

lamp itself temporarily disappeared. Meantime, owing to the disturbed condition of the country, the manufacture of domestic glassware had diminished to a considerable extent and was not revived and successfully prosecuted "until long after the period of the late war (1812)," [Joseph D. Weeks, *Report on the Manufacture of Glass*] which brings us close to the beginning of the great era of industrial development. Then, with its coming, the whale oil lamp was brought forth and relighted in full glory.

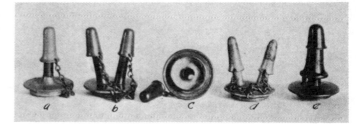

The use of this burner required that the opening at the top of the oil bowl should be made round and smooth, with the edge turned up slightly to form a short neck, into which the cork could be readily and properly inserted. All of the lamps that were used with this type of burner were of blown glass shaped by hand — from the little courting lamps, (so-called, though in reality chamber or retiring lamps) to the larger ones of fine design and workmanship. After glass pressing was invented and perfected, about 1830, oil bowls were blown in a variety of shapes and then fused to pressed bases. These lamps continued to be made until the eighteen forties; and occasionally, some of them may still be found having the lacy glass pressed bases of that period from the Sandwich factory. Cork burners were always used with these blown oil bowls except in the few instances where they may be found in tin lamps. Some of these early lamps are shown in Figure 7.

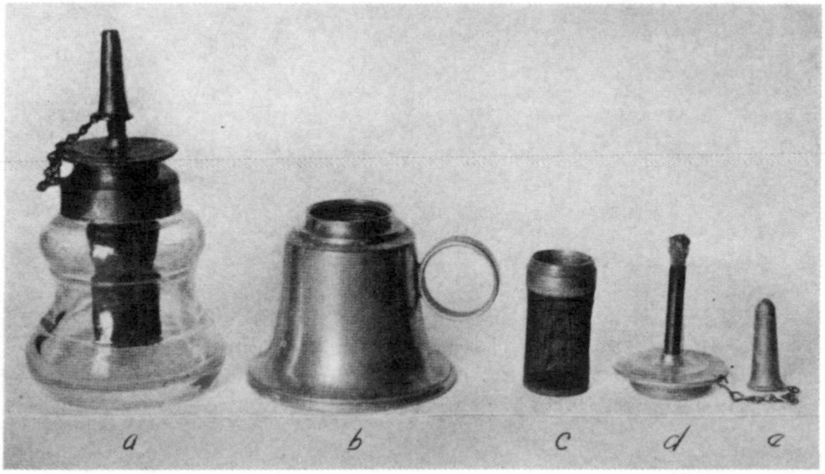

Fig. 13 — FLUID LAMPS

a, glass, molded; *b*, pewter; *c*, glass, pressed, Sandwich pattern. In pressing this lamp the plunger entered at the bottom. After it was withdrawn the bottom was reheated and closed up tight. *d*, glass peg lamp, for candlesticks and chandeliers; *e*, pewter lamp.
Heights, excluding burners, range from 2½" to 5"; capacities, from ¾ oz. to 3 oz.

Of the great output of lamps during the whale oil period from the time of the introduction of the pewter burner, the far greater proportion was made wholly of glass, with molded or pressed oil bowls fused to pressed bases, or with such oil bowls attached to metal stands with metal or marble bases. Of these lamps there was an almost endless variety. Many were of excellent design, very attractive and satisfactory, while others were simply good, bad, or indifferent. Pewter lamps, too, were greatly in vogue. Of these, as to quality and appearance, the same thing may be said. Some fine brass lamps were also made, and quantities of cheap lamps in tin, plain and japanned. Figure 10 shows some of these lamps.

SCREW THREAD BURNERS

The cork burner was eventually superseded by the well-known pewter burner, since it could better withstand the wear due to the constant removal of the burner for filling the oil bowl. The pewter collar, screw threaded on the inside, was cemented to the opening at the top of the glass oil bowl, and the burner, similarly threaded, was screwed into it. The use of tin for the wick tubes was continued. Burners and collars of brass with tin or brass wick tubes were also made. Pewter lamps with brass screw threads and brass burners are of later make than those with pewter screw threads and pewter burners. Figure 8 shows the general appearance of all of these burners.

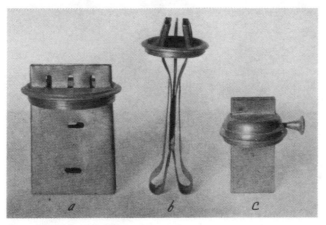

Fig. 14 — FLUID SAFETY LAMPS

a, glass, with safety tube inside; *b*, pewter, with safety tube inside; *c*, additional safety tube which screws on burner *d* and fits inside of safety tube *b*; *e*, cap for wick tube, and cap chain. Lamp heights range from 2½" to 3", exclusive of burner.

Fig. 15 — LARD OIL BURNERS

a, pewter and copper burner, length 2¾", width of wick, 1¾"; *b*, pewter and copper burner, length 3¾", width of wick, ¾", stamped *Southworth's Patent, July 1842* on the collar; *c*, pewter and tin burner, with wick regulator, width of wick, ⅞".

DATES OF PEWTER LAMPS

It seems to be generally believed that pewter whale oil lamps were made and used during Colonial days, or, at least, during the later seventeen hundreds; but, after an exhaustive search, I have been unable to find any evidence to support this view. Of course, it may be correct; but it may be said with certainty that no maker of pewter lamps who marked his wares has yet been discovered as working earlier than 1825.

The whale oil lamp, if perfectly trimmed, gave an excellent light with little or no smoke or odor. The oil consumed with an ordinary two-wick burner of medium size was approximately one quarter fluid ounce per hour, the amount varying according to the condition of the oil, the wicking, and the wick trimming. It required comparatively little care other than filling, picking up the wick, and trimming the latter from time to time when it became encrusted with carbon.

The utensils for this purpose were the wick-pick and the snuffers, as shown in Figure 9. Snuffers are usually associated with the candle, but they were also used with whale oil lamps and the earlier Betty and grease lamps.

SOURCES OF WHALE AND SPERM OIL

The whale oil lamp derived its name, of course, from the oil that it consumed. This oil, commonly and commercially known as whale oil, came chiefly from the blubber of the Greenland right whale. Sperm oil, on the other hand, came from the cavity in the head of the sperm whale, and was of a much superior quality and therefore much more valuable. Sperm oil was burned only in those lamps where the best obtainable light was demanded, as in public halls, in naval vessels, lighthouses, and the like; but its greater cost limited its use in most homes,* where ordinary whale oil was commonly burned.

Fig. 16 — LARD OIL LAMPS

a, tin, with brass claw feet, two wicks, each ¾″ wide; the oil holder may be tipped forward as shown, as the oil burns low. *b*, tin, with cast iron base, original gold lacquer; brass plate on oil bowl says *S. N. & H. C. Ufford, 113 Court St., Boston. Kinnear's Patent, Feby. 4. 1851*; two wicks, 1¾″ and ¾″ wide. *c*, pewter, unmarked, one wick, 1¾″ wide; burner shown in Figure 15 *a*. *d*., glass hand lamp, two wicks, each ¾″ wide; burner shown in Figure 15 *b*.
Lamp heights range from 5½″ to 8″; capacities, from 2½ oz to 5 oz.

The whale oil lamp continued in general use well into the eighteen seventies, long after coal oil and kerosene had made their appearance. I can just remember that, when I was a young boy, a pair of handsome Sandwich lamps, relics of former days, stood on the mantel, and that they were always lighted on special occasions.

PORTER'S BURNING FLUID

While the whale oil lamp was enjoying its well merited popularity, continuous efforts were being made to produce a still better light, either by means of a new oil or a new burner. The introduction, in 1834, of a new *burning fluid*, as it was called, with its brilliant white light, was, therefore, hailed as a great advance and perhaps a real solution to the lighting problem. This fluid was the invention of John Porter of Boston, and was universally known as *Porter's Original Patent Burning Fluid*, as he called it, or *Porter's Fluid*, or simply *Fluid*.

Experiments had been made with oil of turpentine as an illuminant, but the smoke from the rosin which this material contained rendered its use out of the question. Porter discovered that, by adding quicklime to the

*It may be of interest to note here the prevailing Boston prices of these oils at various times in past years. In 1835, whale oil sold at 35 cents per gallon; 49 cents in 1850; 71 cents in 1855; 49 cents in 1860; $1.45 in 1865, and 65 cents in 1872. The rise in price in 1865 was due largely to the destruction of the whaling fleet during the Civil War. Sperm oil, owing to its superior quality, sold at 84 cents in 1835; $1.20 in 1850; $1.41 in 1860; $2.25 in 1865; and $1.45 in 1872. The higher price of the sperm oil, it may be said, was due to some extent to the demand for its use as a lubricant and in the manufactures.

oil of turpentine and distilling the mixture several times in succession, the rosin would be eliminated and the resulting purified oil would burn without smoke. From further experiments he found that, by adding two or three parts of alcohol, by volume, to one part of the distilled and purified oil of turpentine, the flame was considerably increased in size and the light much improved.

The lamps in which this fluid was burned were universally known as *fluid lamps*. In later years, however, when camphene was also burned, they were sometimes referred to by the latter name. Porter's advertisement in the *Portland Transcript* of April 3, 1852, a copy of which is reproduced in Figure 11, is interesting as showing the date of introduction of the new fuel.

As this fluid gave a very white and brilliant light, it was almost immediately put into extensive use. There was no smoke and no odor, and the wicks needed almost no attention. But, unfortunately, the fluid turned out to be very explosive; and, therefore, could not be used with whale oil burners, through which the flame might readily communicate with the gases which formed in the oil bowl, so as to produce an explosion.

To obviate this danger as much as possible, a new type of burner was eventually evolved. It consisted essentially of a metal base about one and one quarter inches in diameter, threaded to fit the collar on the oil bowl; of one or two tubes for the wicks; and of caps for the tubes. The tubes, about one and one quarter inches long, were much smaller in diameter than those of the whale oil burner, and were set near together at the base and further apart at the top — about one inch — far enough to secure a separate and distinct flame from each. The caps were attached to the base by small brass chains.

At first the burners were made of pewter and tin, but, after a time, of brass only. The caps were generally made of pewter even after the burners were made of brass. As it was considered dangerous to blow out the light, the caps were placed over the flame to extinguish it. At other times they remained in place on the tubes to prevent evaporation of the fluid. In some early burners with a single wick tube, a separate tube was provided, slightly larger, which, when slid upward over the wick tube, would cover the flame and extinguish it. Caps were also used with such burners to prevent evaporation. Figure 12 shows these burners, and Figure 13 some of the fluid lamps.

The wicks for Porter's fluid burners were made sufficiently large to fit tightly in the tubes, so that by no chance could the flame communicate with the gas generated in the

Fig. 17 — WHALE OIL SHIP LAMP

Whale oil ship lamp, such as was used on the ship of Donald McKay and others in the 1850's. This lamp is hung in gimbals; and the bottom is so weighted that it will maintain its vertical position under all circumstances of the pitching and rolling of the ship.

oil bowl. They were usually woven from some coarse loosely spun cotton yarn. When I was a little fellow in school, I remember that at one time all the boys and girls were weaving this material for wicks and other things through the round opening in common wooden spools. These spools had four pins stuck in a square at one end, over which the yarn was woven by the aid of another pin held between thumb and finger.

CONVERTED WHALE OIL LAMPS

In many instances whale oil lamps were converted into fluid lamps by the substitution of the new burner and of the new fluid for the old; and while this arrangement was satisfactory if the oil bowl was small, the accumulation of gas formed in a large bowl, partly empty and therefore liable to explode, was dangerous alike to life and property. Accidents and fires from this cause became so frequent that, about 1850, the fire insurance companies in Massachusetts and some other states inserted a clause in their policies forbidding the use of fluid lamps on pain of forfeiture, unless a special permit was granted and an additional charge was paid; and this clause remains in their policies to this day, although its purpose is now obsolete.

The introduction of the so-called *safety lamp* and the use of small lamps, or those having small oil bowls, remedied this trouble to a very considerable extent, though not wholly. Nevertheless, the danger of explosion, even though greatly diminished, materially limited the use of the fluid lamp. Still it was a great favorite, especially in the form of the peg lamp, shown in Figure 13 *d* (similar to the whale oil peg lamps) for use in candlesticks and chandeliers; and continued in general use, along with the whale oil, until long after the coming of kerosene.

CAMPHENE LAMPS

Of course many attempts were made after the introduction of Porter's fluid to secure a lamp, the safety of which would no longer be a matter of doubt. The fact that purified oil of turpentine would produce a good light without the addition of alcohol led to its use under the trade names of *camphene* and *chemical oil*. But its light was not nearly so brilliant as that from the burning fluid; and since the words *burning fluid*, *fluid*, *camphene*, and *chemical oil* were soon used indiscriminately, no practical change in the situation resulted. Camphene, as such, must have been placed upon the market about 1846, for the earliest advertisements for its sale that I have been able to find occur in that year.

SAFETY LAMPS

Many forms of safety lamps were also devised, among the most notable being those of J. Newell in 1851–1853 (*Fig. 14*). These lamps were provided with a wire-gauze cylinder extending from the collar to the bottom of the bowl, the space between being sometimes packed with cotton. The wick coming down from the burner was enclosed in this cylinder. Sometimes the gauze cylinder was attached to the burner instead, and, in other cases, both cylinders were used together, one inside the other, for added safety. These lamps were "constructed on the principle that flame, in passing through wire meshes, loses heat, and will not explode inflammable gases."

LARD LAMPS

Experiments had been made from time to time with lard as a lighting medium, but the results were not satisfactory. The lard remained in a more or less solid condition, and the wick was unable to draw it up for burning. In 1844 a patent was granted for a "new method of producing lard oil from the solid constituents of fat by hydraulic pressure," and it is stated in Bishop's *History of American Manufactures* that "it proved valuable." The oil was clear and colorless, and remained liquid unless exposed to the cold. As such exposure might occur at any time, artificial means were devised to keep the lard oil warm when in use, generally by the extension of the wick tube down nearly to the bottom of the oil bowl. The heat from the flame was thereby communicated to the lard oil, with the desired result. Figure 15 shows several characteristic lard oil burners, two of which, *a* and *b*, belong in the lamps shown in Figure 16, at *c* and *d* respectively.

Many other devices were tried, with more or less success, such as the arrangement shown in Figure 16*a*. In this lamp the oil holder is attached to the upright by a hinge, and may be tipped forward and downward, if desired, to ensure melting and the consequent free flow of the oil. There are two wicks in this lamp instead of one, each three quarters of an inch in width, placed side by side. Another lamp had the oil holder in the form of a cylinder mounted on its axis, which could likewise be turned downward for the same purpose. A correspondent in the *Scientific American*, of July, 1860, suggested that "a wire placed near the burner and extended down into the oil would accomplish that purpose in a satisfactory manner."

As lard oil was not inflammable or explosive, it was received with confidence, and, in due time, came into use along with whale oil and fluid. It retained its hold for many years, and, even as late as 1865, Bishop states that 249,896 gallons of lard oil were manufactured in Boston during that year. The United States Navy, always conservative in such matters, did not adopt lard oil for use on board ship until 1868, and then "on the score of economy and efficiency" and "in view of the considerably increased cost of sperm oil," as stated in the annual report. The year following, it was stated that "its use has proved quite satisfactory for illuminating purposes," and it "may be used with about equal efficiency and facility and with a considerable saving of first cost."

The burner used with lard oil generally carried a wide, flat wick, and in this respect was different from the wicks which had preceded it. Wicks were sometimes as wide as two inches; and, of course, this added burning surface greatly augmented the amount of light given out. The light was clear, bright, and satisfactory. The wick required picking up and trimming, just as did that of the whale oil lamp. The wide flat wick was characteristic of the lard oil lamp, although narrow ones are occasionally found in them and in some forms of lamps burning fats and grease. Figure 15 shows three characteristic lard oil burners, and Figure 16, several lard oil lamps.

OTHER INVENTIONS

Of course many lamps other than those described were made; but although they were probably used here and there, none of them ever came into general use. Among these was *Dyott's Patent Camphene Solar Lamp*, 1852, described as "the only lamp in use that will burn dry with a short wick;" the *Improved Diamond Lamp*, 1856, "the cheapest, safest and best yet offered to the public;" *Sanford & Kinne's Patent Hydro-carbon Vapor Lamp*, 1860, of which it was claimed that "six jets will burn an hour at a cost of one cent, or two small jets all night for a cent, making a saving of 25 per cent over any other way of burning the fluid;" and many others of various kinds. Besides these there were the Argand lamp and the Astral lamp, beautiful and excellent, but too costly for general use.

Petroleum came in 1859. The first patent for a kerosene burner was issued that year; others followed in rapid succession. Thus the kerosene period of lighting was ushered in. But many of the older lamps continued to be used for many years afterward.

American Glass Lamps

By Lura Woodside Watkins

OUR present lack of definite information about the origin and early manufacture of glass lamps makes an exact chronology of types impossible. Little knowledge can be derived from the lamps themselves; one may only draw inferences from the few straws in the wind of glass history. Such fragmentary bits of evidence are almost exclusively the scant references to lighting devices in bills and inventories, or in glasshouse and other advertisements.

It has been established that closed-reservoir lamps were in use during the last decade of the eighteenth century and were being advertised in America as early as 1800. They were, however, of metal — tin, iron, or brass — and were fitted with burners for whale oil. These burners, screwed into the body of the lamps, were, from the first, approximately the same as the later standard type. Since finding a means of attaching a metal burner to a glass reservoir presented a problem, the manufacture of glass lamps was probably delayed until some years later.

The casual reader may be misled by the mention of glass lamps in eighteenth-century advertisements. A careful survey of the subject quite certainly indicates that such lights were not true closed-reservoir lamps, but were either float lamps or devices constructed on the Betty-lamp principle. Candleholders with glass shades were also known as lamps. The earliest document thus far discovered that points unquestionably to the familiar glass whale-oil lamp is a New England Glass Company bill of sale, May 1, 1822, which lists "3 Doz. Peg Lamps" at six dollars.

In 1816, the Boston Glass Manufactory advertised "entry, street, factory, illuminating and reading Lamps, Lamp Tubes, globe and strait." Although we have no direct knowledge concerning the contemporary meaning of the terms *illuminating* and *reading*, it seems probable that the Boston company's lamps were various kinds of lanterns or Argand lamps fitted with the customary globes and chimneys. Had the factory made peg lamps, it would undoubtedly have mentioned them specifically. At any rate, we may conclude that the peg, or socket, lamp was the first type to be made wholly of glass. Invented originally for insertion in a candlestick of metal or other material, it was found convenient for many purposes, from the worker's light in its homemade wooden frame to the chandelier with many sockets.

Peg lamps were used until after the Civil War and must be dated by general style and shape and by type of burner. The first examples were

probably plain blown. They were fitted with one or more wick tubes held in place by a cork set between two tin discs — the *cork-disc* burner. After 1830, screw-thread burners for glass lamps as well as for those of metal were made practicable by attaching a threaded neck of metal to the lamp font. Once having launched the simple peg lamp, the glass companies proceeded to ornament the reservoirs in diverse ways. Molding, cutting, or engraving was employed to elaborate plain blown surfaces. Figure 1 pictures a lamp fluted in a dip mold before expansion by blowing, and a pair of early waffled and ribbed lamps blown in a full-size mold. At first the pegs were fashioned separately and applied to the reservoir while the glass was still soft. In 1839, William Leighton of the New England Glass Company secured a patent for a device by which peg and body could be blown in one.

It was only a step from the peg lamp, which could not stand without support, to the simple blown lamp with a handle for convenient carrying, and to other larger affairs with standards of their own, either blown or pressed. By the middle 'twenties, the glasshouses were advertising a variety of small lighting appliances, besides the more costly lamps with pendants and shades that were in vogue, both here and abroad, during the early nineteenth century.

On July 22, 1824, the New England Glass Company advertised in the *Boston Commercial Gazette:* "Stand Lamps — Candlesticks with drops — Astral Lamps with cut glass pedestals — Fountain Lamps with cut glass pedestals and founts — cut and plain Socket Lamps — cut, painted, rough and plain Entry Lamps, newest patterns."

The first entries in Jarves's account book at the Sandwich works (*1825*) include "Liverpool lamp glasses, small and large rose foot lamps, tulip lamp glasses, cylinder lamp glasses," and "button stem short lamps." In 1825, he mentions "chamber and high blown stem lamps, lamps on foot and peg lamps"; the following year, "Lafayette Chamber Cylinder Lamps" and "petticoat" lamps.

Three years later (*1828*), Bakewell, Page & Bakewell, of Pittsburgh, were advertising "an Assortment of Astral or Sinumbral Lamps, on Pedestals and for Suspension, Also, Tuscan, Vase, Mantel and Chamber Lamps."

To collectors of American glass lighting devices, the important items in the foregoing lists are the button-stem short lamps, the chamber lamps, and the stand lamps, or lamps on foot. They seem to represent the earliest types with

Fig. 1 — PAIR OF PEG LAMPS BLOWN IN A THREE-SECTION MOLD, AND PEG LAMP BLOWN IN A PART-SIZE MOLD WITH SUBSEQUENT EXPANSION
With the exception of the pair of three-mold lamps belonging to Charles L. Eshleman, all illustrations are from the Charles L. Woodside Collection

Fig. 2 — EARLY BLOWN GLASS LAMPS (*1820–1830*)
The saucers have welted rims

which we are familiar. Petticoat lamps of glass we do not recognize by that appellation. They were possibly hand blown, with a conical dish base, like the example in Figure 2b. This type has occasionally been ascribed to the Stiegel period, perhaps on account of its welted saucer rim; but Stiegel never mentioned lamps in his inventories, although he did advertise candlesticks. Such rare lights as the petticoat form, fashioned by hand and beautifully proportioned, probably represent the first attempts to make a glass standing lamp.

Button-stem lamps were undoubtedly the exquisite small chamber lights with baluster stems, known today as "wine-glass" lamps. Imitating, as they do, the shapes of various wine glasses, they il-

Fig. 3 — BLOWN "WINE-GLASS" LAMPS (*1820–1840*)

Fig. 4 — BLOWN SPARK LAMPS (*1820–1840*)
All but one have cork-disc burners

Fig. 5 — EARLY SPARK LAMPS
a and *e* have blown bowls and pressed bases. *b* and *d* were blown in a three-section stopper mold. *c* was blown in a rib mold and expanded. All have cork-disc burners

type of hollow blown stopper that matches the arched pattern decanters. In making them the ingenious glassblower took the easiest means at hand to give decorative quality, with results whose very crudity makes them attractive to the modern eye.

It seems certain that the first tall whale-oil lamps with pressed feet were devised in the 'twenties. The slender, finely proportioned example in Figure 6b well illustrates the earliest type. The reservoir and hollow bulbous stem are blown separately and united by a disc or wafer, which extends well beyond the oil container. Made separately, also, and joined to the upper portion while both parts were in a semimolten condition, is the square pressed base. This, with its rosette design

lustrate the glassworker's continuance of a long-familiar technique into a new field. It is perhaps not generally known that drinking glasses had been used for years as float lamps. Francis Buckley, in his *History of Old English Glass*, quotes a reference to such an adaptation in the *London Daily Post*, for October 1, 1728. Thus the wine-glass form was quite naturally suggested to the glassblower, who, until pressing was brought to his assistance, was obliged to improvise lamp designs of his own.

Wine-glass lamps and the little blown chamber or spark lamps, shown in Figures 3 and 4, may be considered representative of the early period, although individual specimens may be of later date. Such simple forms were undoubtedly turned out quickly by skilled glassblowers, and could be sold for a small sum. Their convenience must have kept them in demand long after larger and more ornate lighting devices were on the market. Such lamps are often quite tiny, the burners accommodating only the slenderest of wicks. Their illuminating power was less than that of a candle. It is assumed that they were used to brighten the way to bed or to burn as a dim night companion. Occasionally one hears them called "courting" lamps. The connotation is obvious, but the term is probably part of the romantic legend that so frequently grows around ancient things.

The unusual pair of lamps in Figure 5b and d were fashioned by blowing in stopper molds. They present a familiar appearance to collectors of three-mold glass, who will recognize in them a

underneath, is the counterpart of bases that were fairly common on other objects, such as bowls, glasses, sweetmeat jars, caster bottles, and candlesticks. In obtaining the final base form of a square, or square with indented corners, a certain amount of cutting was necessary, in order to remove the overplus of glass from the pressing. The crude base of this particular lamp, although uncut, does not form a perfect square.

Few early tall lamps equipped with their original cork-disc burners have survived. The oldest of them belong to a period before 1830. In specifications for a patent taken out by Deming Jarves July 20, 1828, for a mode of affixing glass chimneys to the cork tops used with glass lamps, we read, "The tops of the glass lamps in ordinary domestic use consist of cork enclosed between two pieces of metal." Thus it would seem that screw-thread burner caps were not then known, although an authenticated Cambridge lamp of the early 'thirties is so equipped.

To the early 'thirties, also, belong the lamps in Figure 6a and c, both of which have their original shades. Both have pewter mountings. The one at the left has an uncommon burner of the Argand type; the other has the standard whale-oil wick tubes, which project only slightly above the reservoir opening, but, in the reverse direction, extend well down into the oil font. The globe, resting on a perforated rim, is held in place by a single pewter screw. This second example closely resembles the Cambridge lamp mentioned above.

The pear-shaped reservoir is typical of the early period, and may sometimes be seen on the exquisite Sandwich lamps with lacy bases. The blown portion is often frosted, as, likewise, were many shades and chimneys of that time.

In Figure 7 is an extraordinary pair of lamps with bases pressed in lacy acanthus design, but with oil fonts of blown, three-section-mold glass in the baroque *horn of plenty* pattern. These are important, not only for their beauty as lighting devices, but also because they point definitely to the Sandwich origin of three-mold glass in this particular design.

The lamps in Figure 8 have blown bowls and charming lacy bases. Two of them have feet contrived from cup-plate molds, with baluster stems attached to the figured side of the pressed part. Actual cup plates were rarely so utilized; these bases are even thicker than are the heaviest cup plates. Such choice specimens are among the most delightful finds that reward the glass-lamp collector. Several patterns may be discovered.

After 1840, lamps of every description were made in the American glasshouses. Most of the patterned types still frequently found belong to the mid-century period. The Boston and Sandwich Glass Company was largely responsible for their prevalence and popularity, as lighting devices formed a great part of the firm's output. It is interesting to note that such lamps, almost unknown in England, were considered an American innovation.

The following quotation from the *Whitworth and Wallis Report on Industry in the United States*, published in 1854, assures us on this point:

The Boston and Sandwich Glass Company make large quantities of lamps peculiar to the country, as being used instead of candlesticks. The exceedingly low price at which these articles are sold creates a great demand for them, as the glass offers facilities for cleaning which no other material presents, the oil being so easily wiped off the surface; whilst a decorative effect is produced at a cheap rate by the adaptation of the forms to the pressed methods of manufacture.

Later on in the report occurs this paragraph:

Whilst upon this point, it may be well to remark, that the lamps alluded to, and which supply the place of the common candle in domestic use, are articles of great consumption, and are manufactured in immense quantities, chiefly of tin and pewter, and even of common glass and earthenware. They are of various sizes, and are adapted to one or more wicks, according to the purpose for which they are required. These are almost universally used, except when wax tapers or gas are adopted. Attempts are sometimes made

to render them more or less decorative, especially the larger kind, with two or more wicks for table use; those manufactured of glass, either cut or pressed, being the most successful in this respect. From the peculiar construction required, however, there can be little doubt that a pleasingly ornamental article might be produced by the combination of metal tubes and glass, — the former being used as a column, and the latter material manufactured as the oil-holder and base, or the column and base might be manufactured out of metal, and the oil-holder alone of glass. At present the article is unnecessarily clumsy and inelegant. It is however, in its integrity, and has not yet been overlaid or disguised by false or crude ornamentation, in which use has been bidden defiance to for the sake of decorative art.

It is customary to speak of the *pressed* lamps of Sandwich and other early factories. As a matter of fact, while lamp *bases* are almost invariably pressed, nearly all fonts were figured by being blown in molds. The two distinct parts were joined during the subsequent process of manufacture. Pressed lamp reservoirs belong to the pattern-glass era and frequently duplicate the patterns seen on tableware.

The greater number of figured spark lamps, also, are molded rather than pressed. Following the first small blown hand lamps, fitted with cork-disc burners, came similar fluted or slightly molded lights having collars for screw-thread burners (*Fig. 9*). These lamps are often pleasing in color, as, for instance, the Sandwich examples of sapphire blue, green, amethyst, or opalescent glass. The forms, too, are good, and delicate, applied handles frequently occur. Later types of the hand lamp are much larger and heavier — hence, as a rule, devoid of artistic merit.

Stand lamps of the same period in solid color are considered extremely desirable by collectors and are rare enough to command high prices. The familiar *loop and petal* pattern is occasionally found in the rich, dark colors of the 1850 period. The bases are made in the same molds as are the *petal and loop* candlesticks. In 1849, the New England Glass Company listed "Gen'l Taylor" and "pillar foot" lamps in canary color, at $1 a pair.

During the heyday of the large whale-oil lamp, reservoirs were pressed in patterns now well known to pattern-glass collectors (*Fig. 10*). Such designs as the *Sandwich star, waffle, waffle and thumbprint, bell-flower, horn of plenty, sawtooth, diamond point, heart,* and *harp* were all adapted to lamp decoration. Bases and bowls were pressed separately and put together in different combinations, so that one type of reservoir may dis-

Fig. 6 — WHALE-OIL LAMPS WITH PRESSED BASES (*1825–1835*)

Fig. 7 — PROBABLY UNIQUE PAIR OF SANDWICH WHALE-OIL LAMPS
The reservoirs are blown in three-mold baroque design.
From the collection of Charles L. Eshleman

play several kinds of bases, or one style of base a number of different oil fonts. At first the joinings were made by hand; later, the ingenuity of moldmakers effected a simpler method for obtaining the same result. Accordingly, punty scars sometimes appear on the inner surface of bases that were attached to their reservoirs by the earlier methods, while there is no evidence of hand workmanship on lamps whose parts were combined by mechanical means. Many small stand lamps of the latter type are to be found. Although they may date as early as 1845, they are ordinarily of simple construction and pattern.

Kerosene came into use in the 'fifties, but was not generally adopted until the following decade. Virtually all glass lamps before 1865 were devised for whale oil or burning fluid, or, less frequently, for lard oil. Lamp design was good and suited to the purpose for which it was intended. Many such lamps continued to be

Fig. 8 — SMALL STAND LAMPS WITH LACY BASES (*1830–1840*)
c has a reservoir blown in a three-section mold. *d* and *e* have bases pressed in cup-plate molds

Fig. 9 — PRESSED AND MOLDED SPARK LAMPS (*1835–1850*)
The short burners are for whale oil; those with extinguishers, for camphene or burning fluid

Fig. 10 — PRESSED AND MOLDED LAMPS OF THE MID-NINETEENTH CENTURY
a, Pressed fluid lamp. *b*, Molded lamp with safety fluid burner. *c*, Pressed whale-oil lamp. *d*, Molded lamp with vapor burner. *e*, Pressed fluid lamp

place with plaster of Paris. This practice frequently resulted in unsuitable combinations of base and reservoir.

The principal merit of the earlier kerosene lamps is color. Amethyst, ruby, green, and blue were supplemented by new and lighter tints of clear, translucent, and opaque glass. Every style of ornamentation was employed in the manner beloved by the Victorians. Cutting, engraving, gilding, and molding are all to be found on these lamps. Pattern glass also was adapted to the requirements of illumination. The *bellflower, buckle, blackberry, honeycomb, ivy,* and many other designs will come to mind. The patterns are confined to the oil containers, which rest on bases of glass, metal, or marble. Such lighting devices have little artistic value.

Several types of base are common. The marble plinth with a brass or bronze column to support the reservoir was doubtless considered elegant in its day, and may

used until well into the gas era, and were later, after temporary retirement, brought forth to be fitted for electricity. Similarly, kerosene burners were made to fit the standard-size threaded necks of the earlier lamps. Lamps constructed primarily for burning whale oil or camphene are usually of glass throughout; those with marble or brass bases are typical of the kerosene period.

It is noteworthy that the pressed whale-oil and fluid lights have reservoirs of modified cylindrical or conical shape, with rounded shoulders; bowls in the form of a flattened sphere came into style with kerosene (*Fig. 9e*). The later lamps are not so pleasingly shaped or so well proportioned as their predecessors. Bowls and bases, sold separately in quantity, were assembled according to the tastes of retail dealers. It was a simple matter to join the upper and lower parts by brass collars held in

have been inspired by the Whitworth and Wallis report. Less expensive were square bases of black or opaque white glass. Glassmakers vied with each other to produce the jettiest black and the purest white for the purpose. A squared base, outlined in cyma curves and supporting a fluted column, must have been extremely popular. Fragments of such bases from the Sandwich ruins have been found in such great variety of coloring that a partial list may be of interest. In clear glass there are sapphire blue, peacock blue, and amethyst; in opaque colors, black, white, bright blue, powder blue, pale blue, turquoise, and violet; in translucent or alabaster glass, light green, light blue, bright blue, powder blue, and violet. Parts of a base in mottled blue and green have also been discovered. In fact, the colors defy classification. It is doubtful that other glasshouses of the time devoted quite so much attention to commercializing lamp production.

Kerosene lamps of cased glass decorated by cutting — popularly known as overlay — were among the most elaborate and highly treasured products of the Centennial period. Many of them were taller than the ordinary stand lamp and had pedestals of bronze and marble, of glass, or, in rare instances, of cased glass to match the bowl, mounted in metal. Colors were so combined that the clear crystal was exposed where darker hues of green, ruby, or blue had been cut away; or a clear tint, such as rose or light green, was allowed to show beneath a surface of opaque white. Under the flame of the light, these reflecting facets were brilliant indeed.

Both tall and hand lamps made entirely of pressed glass are to be seen in antique shops, and command good prices when displaying an unusual color or other striking feature. They are bound to become more desirable with time, as the kerosene lamp gradually passes out of existence. At present, however, the old reliable kerosene burner is still a household necessity in country districts and will doubtless continue to be for many years. Collectors should be wary in buying kerosene lamps, lest they pay collectors' prices for glass that was made only yesterday.

Fig. 11 — HANDSOME KEROSENE LAMP
Of alabaster glass, resembling white jade

Note. In so far as we are aware, Mrs. Watkins' discussion as presented above constitutes the first attempt at a historical summary of American glass lamps with illustrations so selected and arranged as to furnish a guide to the chronology of the successive forms developed by the glass manufacturers. The collector will doubtless find many glass lamps differing in certain details from any of those portrayed by Mrs. Watkins. Nevertheless, he should be able to determine the period of his variants by considering their major outlines and their evidences of technical method in the light of the textual and pictorial demonstration which Mrs. Watkins has so carefully prepared. Thus used, her article should prove to be one of the most helpful contributions to the lore of glass collecting that has yet appeared. It will be observed that very little stress is laid on factory attributions, which, in so far as concerns glass in general, are far less important than many people believe. In the case of lamps — particularly those delightful examples that were produced prior to the era of mechanical pressing — attributions to specific factories are seldom of any importance whatsoever.

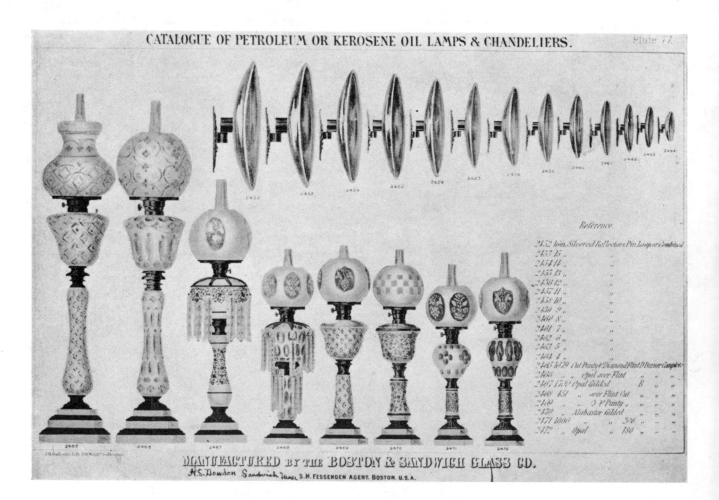

Glass lighting devices

BY JANE S. SHADEL, *Research assistant, Corning Museum of Glass*

IT IS NATURAL to think of glass and lighting together, since for many years during the nineteenth century lighting devices were a mainstay of the American glass industry and glass, with its attractive appearance, reflecting properties, and ease of cleaning, has distinct advantages over other materials used for the purpose.

What is known about lighting in America before 1800 comes mainly from wills and inventories. From these, we can judge that candles were the most important means of illuminating middle- and upper-class homes. Oil and grease lamps made of various materials were also used, but probably few were of glass. An advertisement which appeared in the *Boston News-Letter* in 1719 shows that some glass lamps were in use in the early eighteenth century:

Lately imported from London . . . fine Glass Lamps and Lanthorns well gilt and painted, both convex and plain; being suitable for Halls, Stair-cases, or other Passageways. To be sold at the Glass Shop in Queen Street . . .

Regrettably, we can't be certain what these glass lamps looked like; they may have contained candles, or have been simple float lamps with a wick threaded through a cork. Any wide-mouthed vessel could be used as a float lamp. Wineglasses were used this way in England, and they may also have been so used here.

Both metal and ceramic candlesticks were used in the Colonies, and glass ones were probably in the minority. By and large, those of glass were English—free-blown, mold-blown, and sometimes enameled or cut. In addition to the ordinary single candlesticks there were tapersticks for the smaller candles which were carried to the bedchamber, and multibranched sconces and chandeliers for lighting in the largest rooms. A few candlesticks do exist which were probably made in this country in the eighteenth century: Stiegel advertised "ornamented candlesticks" in the *Pennsylvania Gazette* in 1772 and the Philadelphia Glass Works at Kensington advertised them in the *Pennsylvania Packet* in 1775, so we may assume they were made here. However, no existing specimens can be positively attributed to any American factories, and the great majority of lighting devices used in America were probably imported until well into the nineteenth century.

The most important invention in the lighting field in the eighteenth century was that of Ami Argand, a Swiss, who patented in 1783 a lamp which gave a light equal to that of about ten candles (Fig. 1). This device burned

Fig. 1. *Portrait of James Peale* by Charles Willson Peale, 1822. The Argand lamp has a ceramic base and a glass chimney. There is a lamp closely related to this one in the Winterthur collection. *Detroit Institute of Arts.*

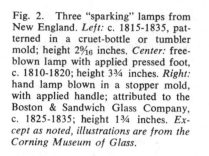

Fig. 2. Three "sparking" lamps from New England. *Left:* c. 1815-1835, patterned in a cruet-bottle or tumbler mold; height 2⁹⁄₁₆ inches. *Center:* free-blown lamp with applied pressed foot, c. 1810-1820; height 3¾ inches. *Right:* hand lamp blown in a stopper mold, with applied handle; attributed to the Boston & Sandwich Glass Company, c. 1825-1835; height 1¾ inches. *Except as noted, illustrations are from the Corning Museum of Glass.*

colza oil (a vegetable oil) or whale oil, and was the first to use a glass chimney to increase the draft and make the flame brighter. Argand's tubular wick drew air up inside, increasing the amount of oxygen feeding the flame. This light was so bright that Count Rumford said of it in 1811, "No decayed beauty ought ever to expose her face to the direct rays of an Argand lamp" (quoted by C. Malcolm Watkins in the *Smithsonian Report for 1951,* p. 395). These lamps were made in a variety of different materials, and were important to the glass industry mainly in that they all used glass chimneys.

It did not take long for the Argand lamp to become popular in the United States. Those who could afford it, and the expensive oils it burned, were quick to adopt this improvement. In a Mt. Vernon inventory taken early in 1800, five lamps and thirteen pairs of candlesticks are mentioned. Though we do not know what kinds of lamps these were, other sources indicate that some were elegant Argand devices. Candles and candlesticks were still much used: in two well-known paintings by the Bostonian Henry Sargent, of about 1820, it is notable that only candles are used to light the *Tea Party* and at the *Dinner Party,* although one lamp is visible on the sideboard and an Argand chandelier hangs from the ceiling, there is at least one candle visible on the table. So candles had by no means been displaced.

More important than the Argand lamp to the less wealthy citizens was the "agitable" burner, one which could be securely fastened to the lamp instead of floating on the surface of the fuel. This lessened the danger of fire when a lamp was overturned, and minimized messy oil leaks. The agitable burner was patented in 1787 in England, and by the turn of the century these cork devices were in common use. The cork fitted tightly into the opening in the lamp, and running through it were one or two parallel short metal wick tubes. Most of the simple glass lamps in use between 1800 and 1830 burned whale oil, were free blown or mold blown, and had the cork burners described above. The smallest of these lamps are those known today

as sparking lamps, from the romantic notion that they were used in the parlor when a suitor came calling, to indicate the brief amount of time convention allowed him to stay. The mundane truth is that these were used in inns and in private homes to light the way to bed, and to insure that the guest didn't "burn the midnight oil" in a wasteful fashion. One had only the amount of time allowed by the few ounces of fuel to undress and prepare for bed. Frederick Law Olmsted, writing of travels through the South, speaks of one of these as a "little bed-lamp, with a capacity of oil for fifteen minutes use" (Watkins, *op. cit.*) (Fig. 2). These small lamps generally had only one wick but the larger ones had two, as two adjacent flames give more than twice the light of one—a phenomenon also observed with candles.

It is difficult to say whether the whale-oil industry in New England led to the popularity of glass whale-oil lamps or whether the popularity of the lamps contributed to the rise of the whaling industry, but in any case the production of whale oil, a major source of income in New England from 1789 until 1865, and the glass industry flourished side by side and undoubtedly aided each other. As early as 1816, the Boston Glass Manufactory advertised in the Boston *Columbian Centinel* "India shades for candles . . . entry, street, factory, illuminating and reading lamps, lamp tubes [chimneys] globe and strait," while the New England Glass Company, in 1819, advertised in *Niles Register* (Baltimore): "Lamp glasses, astral lamp shades . . . Hall or entry lamps . . . Grecian lamps, richly cut . . . Chandeliers for Churches and Halls . . ." It is likely that the "India shades" were what are called today hurricane shades, used to protect candles from sudden drafts. They were used in the eighteenth century and the early nineteenth, but probably more in the South than in New England, as the climate there was more favorable to life with open windows. After the invention of the pressing machine in the 1820's, quantities of lamps were made with blown fonts and pressed bases in a number of different styles and shapes (Fig. 3).

Fig. 4.   Group of pressed candlesticks and lamps
in varied colors. New England, c. 1840-1860.

Fig. 5.   *The Hobby Horse,* anonymous, c. 1840.
The astral lamp on the table in the rear has a circular font
(concealed by its shade).
National Gallery; gift of Edgar and Bernice Chrysler Garbisch.

Fig. 3.   Lamp with modified Argand burner,
designed to use whale oil. Mold-blown and cut
font, blown stem, and pressed foot. The shade
has been ground to minimize glare. American,
c. 1835-1840; height 17 inches.

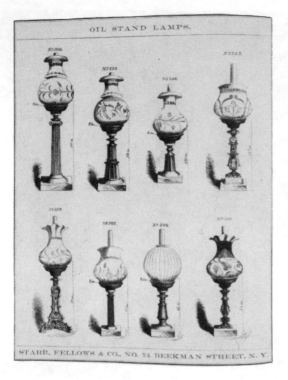

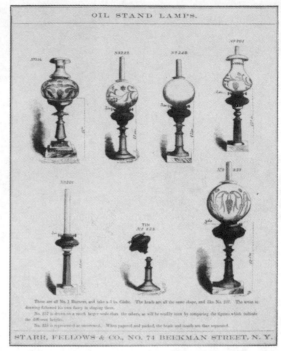

Fig. 6. Solar lamps, from a catalogue of Starr, Fellows & Company, New York City, 1856. Elsewhere in the catalogue is a statement that these will burn lard or whale oil. *Old Sturbridge Village.*

Fig. 7.   Globes and shades for gas and other fixtures from a catalogue of McKee & Brother, Pittsburgh, 1860.

Fig. 8.   Coal-oil and fluid lamps from the McKee catalogue of 1860. In the 1864 catalogue "coal oil" was changed to "carbon oil."

Eventually, by the 1840's, lamps and candlesticks were being pressed in two pieces, sometimes of different colors, and joined in varying combinations (Fig. 4).

Glass was the single most popular material for lamps during the nineteenth century, and the glass industry grew in response to the demand for lighting devices. Around 1809 the astral lamp, originally a hanging light, was invented in France. This worked on the Argand principle and burned oil, but had a circular font to reduce shadows (Fig. 5). Further modifications of this were the sinumbra lamp and the solar lamp; the latter could utilize the very viscous lard oil, which was much cheaper than whale oil (Fig. 6). Lamps of these types were found in the dining rooms and parlors of American homes from about 1820 to about 1850. They were expensive, however. Many contemporary paintings testify to the fact that there was seldom more than one lamp in a room, as does the following excerpt from a diary of 1849:

. . . sitting in the little darkened parlour with bookcases and busts around us, and the fire glimmering in the large fire-place. There by the evening lamp, Downing and his wife read to me by turns from their most esteemed American poets. (Watkins, *op. cit.*)

The reference to "the" evening lamp makes it clear that there was only one. It can be seen from the illustrations that the stems and bases of these lamps were often of metal or marble, but all of them had a glass shade and chimney, or a combination of the two. These were tall lamps, very dignified, and were not so easy to carry from room to room as the simple whale-oil lamps.

The next development was the invention of volatile burning fluids, the first of which was patented by Isaiah Jennings in 1830. The names pine oil, camphene, and burning fluid were used more or less interchangeably; all were mixtures of turpentine and alcohol in various proportions. The price of whale oil was rising and the new fuel was cheap, if often a fire hazard. Many whale-oil lamps were converted to use the burning fluids and are today found with the characteristic diverging tall wick tubes, with metal caps, which kept the flame away from the fuel, rather than with their original burners. By the 1840's, the cork whale-oil burner had been replaced by a more reliable metal screw-on burner which was permanently affixed with plaster of Paris.

In spite of Argand's demonstration that chimneys increased the brightness of the flame, they were not much used with ordinary whale-oil and burning-fluid lamps. No contemporary illustrations have been found showing a chimney in use on a burning-fluid lamp, but chimneys designed for camphene lamps are shown in at least two glass-factory catalogues of the 1850's and '60's (Fig. 7).

"Carbon oil" and "coal oil" are early names for the liquid now called kerosene. This became a practical and inexpensive fuel when it was discovered that it could be refined from petroleum, and since it was cheaper than whale oil and less dangerous than burning fluids, its use grew rapidly. The speed at which kerosene replaced other fuels in public favor becomes apparent when two catalogues of the Pittsburgh firm of McKee & Brother are compared. Their 1860 catalogue illustrates several varieties of candlesticks, a number of peg lamps, hand lamps, and stand lamps all burning fluid or oil, and one "Coal Oil Lamp" (Fig. 8), shown with a chimney. The 1864 catalogue of the same firm shows only "carbon oil" lamps and candlesticks—the oil and fluid lamps have disappeared. Dur-

ing the 1860's 378 lamp patents were granted, probably more than the number taken out in the preceding sixty years (Lowell Innes, quoted in *National Antiques Review* for January 1970, p. 14). As most of the oil fields were found in the Midwest, it is not surprising that Pittsburgh became the center for the manufacture of pressed-glass kerosene lamps; and as kerosene lamps required chimneys, their production became a mainstay of the Midwestern glass industry. In the 1860's there were nine glass factories in Pittsburgh alone turning out nothing but chimneys in a variety of styles.

In spite of the growth of the glass industry in the west, New England factories continued to produce their share of glass lighting devices. One type which is especially associated with the Boston & Sandwich Glass Company and the New England Glass Company is the kerosene lamp with cased font and globe, cut in the Bohemian style (Fig. 9).

The advent of kerosene finally drove candles into ornamental rather than practical use, as the comparative scarcity of candlesticks in art glass indicates. The new fuel suited the pocketbooks of most classes and its use swept the country, gaining adherents which it kept until the advent of cheap electricity in the twentieth century. In the Sears, Roebuck & Company catalogue of 1897 there are several pages of advertisements for kerosene lamps and chandeliers, all made of glass, and only one advertisement for candles. Even in rural homes the modernity of kerosene was preferred to the romantic charm of candlelight.

Although the streets of Baltimore were lighted by gas as early as 1816, this type of lighting did not gain universal popularity until after the invention of the Welsbach mantel in 1885. The necessity for linking gas-lit homes to a central source of supply slowed the growth in popularity of this fuel, and only those living in the larger cities had access to it. Glass shades for gas fixtures and glass "gasoliers" were made in quantity, however, and were advertised by a number of glass manufacturers (Fig. 7).

Most of the glass lamps of the 1880's and 1890's may be found advertised in sales catalogues of the time as vase or parlor lamps, or occasionally as banquet lamps (Fig. 10). They are today popularly called Gone-with-the-Wind lamps, a name which, since it refers to the Civil War period, is very misleading. None of these lamps was made until thirty years after Scarlett O'Hara's time, and they would have been completely out of place down on the old plantation. Parlor lamps were made from various types of art glass, but they are most frequently found with elaborate enameled decoration of leaves, flowers, and sylvan subjects. With heavy cast-brass fittings to enhance the decorative scheme, they were undoubtedly status symbols in many homes.

Lamps of this same general type were also made in the heavy "brilliant" cut glass popular around the turn of the century (Fig. 11). Here the refractive properties of cut glass were exploited to the utmost, and such a lamp, lighted, would have been dazzling to behold. In the early twentieth century some of these were designed for electricity as well, but neither type is as common as the colored, decorated lamps.

Glass today is still a popular material for lamp bases and shades, although its appeal is more aesthetic than functional. The simple glass light bulb, however, is one of the main products of the glass industry, and without it, electric lighting would not exist.

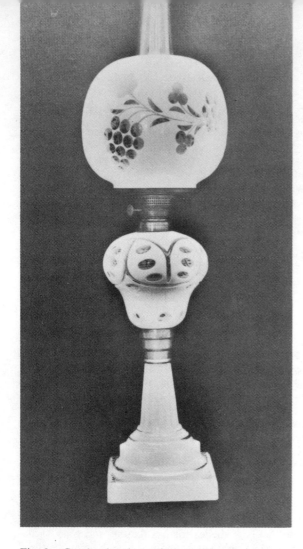

Fig. 9.   Cased and cut lamp with pressed base.
Attributed to the Boston & Sandwich Glass Company,
c. 1860-1870.
Collection of Mr. and Mrs. Kenneth Wakefield.

A COMPLETE CUT GLASS LAMP.

"PRINCESS LAMP."
IN THE "SULTANA" CUTTING.   HEIGHT 18 INCHES.
Strawberry Diamond and Fan Cutting..............$24.00 Each.
Lorraine   "   .... 30.00   "
Sultana   "   .... 36.00   "

USUAL DISCOUNT.

C. DORFLINGER & SONS,
36 MURRAY STREET.   NEW YORK.

Fig. 10.   Decorated parlor lamp, American, c. 1890-1900.
Height 19 inches. *Collection of Pearl V. Jenkins.*

Fig. 11.   Cut-glass parlor lamp from a tradecard
of C. Dorflinger & Sons, c. 1890-1910.

64

Miniature Glass Lamps

By WILLARD EMERSON KEYES

A CONTEMPORARY writer has pointed out that a sharp line separates miniatures that are specimens of a class from those which qualify only as freaks and sports. In the natural world a Tom Thumb is a freak, out of sorts with most of humankind, handicapped in the struggle for life's prizes. The pygmies of the African equatorial forest, on the contrary, by some inscrutable design of providence, are all similarly stunted — to better their chance of survival among their neighbors and near kin, the ugly, long-armed gorillas.

The same distinction may be made in the arts. The dime upon whose surface patient industry has engraved the Lord's Prayer is an example of an abortive talent, a sense misused — little more

Editor's Note. Perhaps the best guess as to the *raison d'être* of the miniature lamp of the 1820's and early 1830's is that whale oil, the burning fluid employed, was fairly expensive, and was purchased in small quantities. Lamp reservoirs were correspondingly small. With the advent of camphene as a burning fluid in the 1830's, reservoirs and lamps alike increased in size, and illuminating power was somewhat intensified. The wide adoption of kerosene, which began in the 1860's, further magnified both the lamp and its light. Henceforth the use of chimneys became the rule rather than the exception, and flat wicks, adjustable by means of a wheel, were generally used. Hence it is fair to say that, until the mid-1800's, lamps, except for a few monumental Argand and astral types, were, of necessity, relatively small. Miniature lamps of the later period were made to serve specific purposes calling for small dimensions. Some were employed to furnish the necessary heat for vaporizing aromatic fluids supposed to relieve asthma, whooping cough, and sundry disturbances of the breathing passages. They burned whale oil. Others served as sickroom lights. Doubtless in this late period not a few small lamps were made for children. Small glass lamps consuming alcohol have long been in use among certain of the medical fraternity and have performed various useful functions in domestic establishments. The novice may easily mistake these modern devices for the tiny whale-oil lamps of a prior era.
— *H. E. K.*

than an idiot's delight. On the other hand, a whole world of manufactured miniatures responds to a well-defined need. The after-dinner coffee cup — to say nothing of the spoon that goes with it — is a familiar example. Made small to be of larger use, it is as legitimate as a miniature portrait by Peale or the exquisite embellishments of fine fans, and snuffboxes, and table china. In this class may properly be included those tiny lamps whose faint sparks once helped to make darkness visible throughout New England. They are authentic miniatures.

A hundred years ago the manufacture of glass lamps in America was a flourishing industry. But one who looks over any considerable collection of early examples will be struck by the number that are of diminutive size. Seeing that hardly one is even of single-candle power, it is natural to ask whether they were mere playthings—bibelots for bucolics—or were designed for some particular and special use.

An answer may be found, perhaps, in a study of the extraordinary collection of miniature lamps owned by Walter B. Snow of Malden, Massachusetts. Having cultivated a nice appreciation of our colonial and early-republican arts, Mr.

Fig. 1 — MINIATURE LAMPS ON BASE
The first in line is reputed to have been made to match the furnishings in the Middleboro, Massachusetts, home of General Tom Thumb, the famous dwarf exploited by P. T. Barnum. This would seemingly place it in the 1870's.

The second lamp, with blown reservoir and cast or pressed base, is probably a Sandwich product of the late 1820's or early 1830's. The next is a camphene burner of the late 1830's or early 1840's, of pressed glass. Camphene was a distillate of turpentine, highly explosive and necessitating a close-fitting metal collar, long wick tube, and an extinguisher, which served for quenching the flame and as a cap to prevent evaporation of the highly volatile fluid. The last lamp in the row was fashioned like a wineglass until a final manipulation drew the top of the bowl together, leaving a small aperture for the cork-shod wick holder. Date, about 1825.

These and other lamps illustrated are so-called miniatures, from the collection of Walter B. Snow, of Malden, Massachusetts

Fig. 2 — MINIATURE LAMPS
The first in the row is a mold-blown and expanded peg lamp with lengthened knopped stem attached to an inverted pressed cup plate serving as base. An unusual and interesting specimen. (Compare Fig. 8, *p. 145*, ANTIQUES for April 1936.) The lamp at the extreme right is another wineglass lamp similar in time and technique to that in the preceding illustration. The three camphene lamps in the centre (*1835–1850*) are pressed items of the so-called salt-shaker type. They are the smallest items in the Snow collection, with a capacity of about a tablespoonful of fluid. The centre lamp carries an inner cylinder of brass gauze extending from the burner into the reservoir, probably as a safety device

Fig. 3 — EARLY BLOWN SPARK LAMPS *(1820-1830)*
The lamp at the extreme right was blown in a three-part mold for decanter stoppers. The stopper stem was then sheared off, and the aperture shaped to accommodate the burner. Flattening the original top of the stopper to constitute a base and adding a handle completed an interesting process of transformation. Similar metamorphoses occur throughout the early history of molded and blown glass

Fig. 4 — VARIOUS LAMPS
The first exhibits a curious gash or fissure in the upper part of the reservoir. Presumably this was intended to assist ventilation. The second and fourth items appear to have been blown in dip molds and subsequently drawn together at the top. They are perhaps abbreviated cruets of the early 1800's. The blown lamp at the extreme right exhibits an unusual handle

Snow found that he could hardly compete with famous antiquaries in the better-known fields of trophy hunting. He determined, therefore, to concentrate on miniature lamps. In the course of years of travel up and down New England, he has accumulated a store which, he maintains, includes every lamp of the kind ever catalogued and many not catalogued. The collection embraces all the American precursors of glass lamps back to the tallow dip.

Though the present consideration is limited to the glass lamps in the Snow collection, the number indicates that the trade in them must once have been large and profitable. Not improbably all or nearly all the examples in the Snow collection came from one or another of the few glassworks in New England. To be sure, it is difficult to trace any glass lamp to a particular time or place. Few bear any trademark or maker's imprint. Not one lamp in the collection betrays the secret of its birth. On the brass burners of some may be deciphered the word *Patented.* Nothing more. The connois-

seur, from his knowledge of certain telltale characteristics, may be able to make shrewd guesses as to date and source. But these will be tentative, for caution is nine points of connoisseurship. Perhaps it is enough to know that miniature glass lamps were extensively made and sold for domestic uses in the years between 1820 and 1850.

Arthur Hayward, in his *Colonial Lighting*, published in 1927, remarks that good specimens of peg lamps are hard to find. Peg float lamps of rich ruby-red glass, hardly larger than an eye cup, are probably scarcer still (*Fig. 6a and b*). Nor are there many to be found like the later cylindrical camphene peg lamp pictured in the same group. It is of emerald-green overlay on clear crystal. The light given by the two ruby float lamps must have emphasized rather than dissipated the encircling gloom. Perhaps they were used for sickrooms to yield a faint yet faithful glimmer all through the night.

The little blown "sparking" lamps pictured in Figure 3 were hardly more effective. Their handles show that they were meant to

Fig. 5 — OPAQUE GLASS LAMPS, PLAIN AND DECORATED *(1835-1885)*

Fig. 6 — Lamps in Colored Glass
Two ruby float lamps; a small pale-green pressed kerosene lamp (*c. 1870*); a peg lamp, green overlay on crystal (*1840–1850*); a
reservoir in salmon-pink and white glass on clear base, camphene burner (*1835–1850*)

be carried about the house like candles — useful, like the modern hand flashlight, for exploring dark corners in closets, cellars, and attics. But is their name properly "spark" lamps or "sparking" lamps? A "spark" lamp would ordinarily be one affording a light like a tiny spark — and many of these miniature lamps did little more. A "sparking" lamp suggests charming connotations. The feebleness of its flame was as grateful to lovers as dim moonshine. It was a luminary countenanced by stern parents because it was timed to flicker and go out at a seemly hour — at the very moment when parting becomes the sweetest sorrow. It was the monitor warning the enraptured twain that the courting time was over.

The aura dispensed by these miniature lamps could not adequately illumine a room or even a table. It was insufficient for sewing or reading. It could never have suggested to our sires the luxury of reading in bed. If all the miniature lamps in the Snow collection were primed and lighted together, their combined effulgence would hardly equal that of a present-day 60-watt electric bulb. It is interesting to ponder why, in the average household whether in town or country, these miniature lamps should ever have been preferred to candles. Perhaps their novelty was an attraction. Perhaps they were recognized as frail beacons of progress by folk who felt the stirrings of the spirit forecasting the machine age.

Most of us recall that the first automobiles were anything but an improvement upon the horse and buggy. These glass lamps may have been less efficient than candles. But their makers were, perhaps unconsciously, responding to an urge to make the world a pleasanter place to live in. Something new was in the air. All at once men were developing a faculty for industrial invention which had been virtually latent since Noah launched the Ark. The shallow betty lamps of Daniel Webster's youth, the oyster-shell lamps of Eastern Shore negroes in Maryland, the grease pots for theatre footlights, still used within the memory of living men, were as primitive as those borne by the foolish virgins of Jerusalem in the days of Herod. Walter Hough of the National Museum in Washington remarks that float lamps were found in the tomb of Tut-Ankh-Amen — lamps which had lighted that monarch to dusty death. More than three thousand years later our New England forebears were, in the main, groping their way through the world by the light of lamps no better than those of ancient Egypt. Such inadequacy must have fretted the generations of a hundred races through the intervening millenniums. Yet, not until the almanac makers were preparing to shift their numerals from the 17's to the 18's had anybody mustered enough gumption to ponder and tinker and ultimately to evolve something distinctly better. The miniature glass lamp has its place in the evolution of lighting devices.

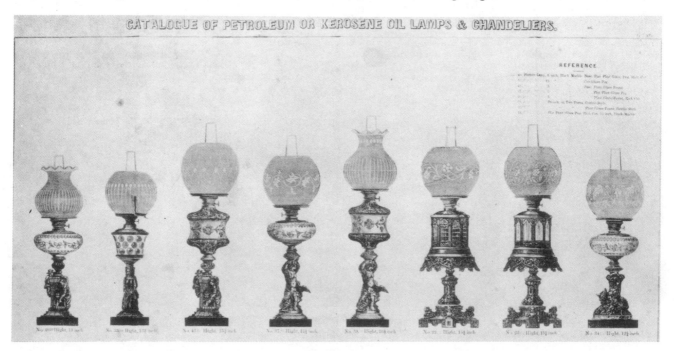

A REGIONAL COLLECTION OF GLASS LAMPS

By MALCOLM WATKINS

IT IS increasingly difficult to ascertain with exactitude what types of nineteenth-century glass were used in any given region of the United States. The latter-day processes of trading and collecting have largely dispersed from their original places of use those pieces of glass which have survived. Thus much significant information about local tastes, as well as about the distribution of glass made in our early glass factories, has been lost.

To anyone interested in these ramifications in the study of glass, therefore, a group of lamps collected from original sources in the region around Hallowell, Maine, will prove of particular interest. The collection, made by Doctor James D. Nutting of Hallowell, on whose notes this article is based, comprises about one hundred thirty lamps, all but a few of which date from earlier than the kerosene period. The lamps are such as one might find in any good collection of glass lamps; yet their associations with the central Maine region give them more than ordinary importance.

As a young man Doctor Nutting, in the late 1800's, took over his father's medical practice and thus had access to the homes of many of the established families in the region of Hallowell. In the earlier part of the century, it had been the most prosperous town on the Kennebec River, including as it did Augusta, Farmingdale, and Manchester. Located at the head of navigation, it became a business center for the surrounding communities.

After the founding of the glassworks at Cambridge and Sandwich Hallowell naturally became a center of distribution for glass that arrived by ship from East Cambridge and the Cape. Some of the best of this, the evidence shows, was purchased by the wealthy residents of Hallowell, while the remainder was picked up by peddlers who sold it through the countryside.

As their source of manufacture, most of the lamps in the Nutting collection suggest one of the two leading Massachusetts glasshouses. Very often the lamps of these factories are indistinguishable, particularly the early examples, and such is the case here. There are no colored lamps in the collection.

FIG. I — GLASS LAMPS. 1. Blown font. Pressed hexagonal base. Fitted with fluid burner. 2. Blown font. Pressed base of type generally attributed to Sandwich. Designed for use with cork-disc sperm-oil burner like that in 3, fitting into the opening like a stopper. 3. Lamp made in three sections (one of a pair). The blown font, fitted with a cork-disc burner, is separated from its base by a hollow blown knop, which is joined to the rest of the lamp by flat wafers of glass. The base is of the primitive pressed type that was first used in the late 1700's by English and Irish glass factories, and by the New England Glass Company during its early period. 4. Pear-shaped blown fonts are common to both factories. The base of this lamp, however, is of the same supposed Sandwich variety as that of 2. Fitted with a fluid burner, but it may originally have had a sperm-oil burner which screwed into the same pewter collar. 5. This lamp may have been made at either factory. The stepped base is square with waterfall fluting inside. 6. Similar in construction to 3, this lamp is probably a Cambridge piece and may date as early as 1815. The edges of the square base have, as usual on these crude bases, been smoothed with the cutting wheel. Its original burner was doubtless of the cork-disc variety. The ungainly brass collar was probably added later so that the lamp could be converted to use with a fluid burner.

7. Blown font and pressed lacy acanthus-pattern base. Sandwich. 8. Again similar in construction to 3 and 6, but the base here indicates a somewhat later date. The fluid burner in this case may well be original with the lamp. 9. The engraved font (other things being equal) would suggest a Cambridge attribution, since this kind of decoration was much more common there than at Sandwich. The lacy base, however, identical with that of 7, quite surely points to Sandwich. 10. Blown font on high pressed base. Pewter sperm-oil burner. 11. The base is a slight variant of those of 2 and 4. 12. This may have originated either at Cambridge or at Sandwich, although the base resembles those of two lamps illustrated in Lura Woodside Watkins' *Cambridge Glass*. 13. A late descendant of the "wineglass" lamp (c. 1840–1850). Heavy and massive, the glass here is all hand-shaped. 14. The pressed base of this lamp is externally like that of 2. Inside, however, it is fluted.

FIG. II — GLASS LAMPS. 1. Hexagonal hand lamp. 2. Lamp with paneled reservoir and hexagonal base. 3. This lamp with star motive on the font is probably later than most of the others. 4 (*rear*) and 7. *Sawtooth diamond* lamps, probably New England Glass Company products. 5 (*front*). Sandwich *moon and star* hand lamp. 6. Font like that of Figure V, 9, but on a different base. 8. Pewter sperm-oil lamp. 9. Combination brass, glass, and marble lamp, probably designed for use with kerosene. 10. *Tulip* pattern. 11. The pattern here appears to be an *Ashburton* variant. 12 and 14. Again the *lyre* pattern. 13. The hexagonal reservoir has plain panels. Base similar to those on the probable Cambridge lamps in Figure IV. 15. This pattern appears on early Sandwich spill or celery vases. 16. Plain hand lamp.

FIG. III — GLASS LAMPS. 1. Pressed glass font and base. *Star and punty* pattern, which was made at Sandwich. 2. *Heart* pattern. Lamps such as this, with pressed fonts and heavy six-sided bases, were probably made in both factories. 3 and 5. Pair of sperm-oil lamps with blown and engraved fonts, blown-knop stem, and pressed base. These constitute a more elegant variant of Figure I, 2 or 11, and probably date from the same period (*c. 1845*). Retention of the blown knop as a device to increase the height of the lamp lingered for some

time, and it is even seen, though rarely, on lamps designed to burn kerosene. 4. Horn of plenty pattern (one of a pair). Pressed font; heavy six-sided base slightly higher and more elaborate than that of 2. Pewter sperm-oil burner. Said to have come from the family of Hallowell's first settler. 6. The dolphin stem of this lamp furnishes evidence of Sandwich origin. Its use in this manner is rare: it is more commonly found supporting a candle socket.

7. Again a pressed base and pressed reservoir. 8. This one varies from the others in having a font which was blown in a mold. 9. The vertically-paneled font here is pressed. The base is evidently from the same mold as that of 4. 10. *Lyre* pattern, a Sandwich design. 11. This *Ashburton* pattern lamp is probably a Cambridge product. The font appears to have been blown in a mold.

FIG. IV — GLASS LAMPS. 1. This mid-century period specimen has been adorned with pendants suspended from a metal collar. It was probably intended for use with kerosene. 2, 4, 6, 8, and 9 have identical bases and cut fonts. These are probably Cambridge products. 4 and 6 have elegant knops ornamented with medallion-like cutting. 3, 5, 7, and 10 are sperm-oil lamps converted to kerosene use. The disproportionately large shades and chimneys are, of course, consequences of the lamps' modernization. 11. This has a cut font and is probably Cambridge glass. 12. This, like 1, was probably a kerosene lamp. The base of the lamp in Fig. II, 13, though smaller, is similar to those shown here.

FIG. V — GLASS LAMPS. 1. *Tulip* pattern font. 2 and 4. Pressed *waffle and thumbprint* pattern fonts. 3 and 5. Again pressed fonts, this time in *star and punty* pattern. 6. Solar lamp with marble base, brass column and reservoir, and frosted and etched glass globe. This type of lamp was made in the 1850's by Cornelius & Sons Company of Philadelphia and by W. H. Starr of New York. 7. The mold used for the pressed font of this lamp was frequently employed to make hand lamps. Then the design would be inverted, a flat bottom would take the place of the domed top, and the burner opening would appear where the reservoir of this lamp joins the stem. 8 and 10. The Sandwich *Lyre* pattern reappears here. 9. Fonts like this are known to have been made at Sandwich by blowing in molds. 11. *Arched leaf* pattern.

All illustrations from the collection of Doctor James D. Nutting

Three Maine Pewterers

By Charles L. Woodside and Lura Woodside Watkins

Illustrations, with the exception noted, from the Woodside collections

Fig. 1 (*above*) — Lamp Marked "a. porter" (*1830–1835*)
Of pewter, for burning whale oil. Mark reproduced at
right below.
Height: 5 inches

Fig. 2 (*right*) — Lamp Marked "a. porter" (*1830–1835*)
Of pewter, for burning whale oil.
Height: 6 inches

THE story of American pewter-making is still so far from complete that nothing more is known of many of the pewterers than the names of the towns where they worked; and, in some instances, even those locations have been wrongly assigned. The three men whose histories we here bring to light are Allen Porter, Freeman Porter, and Rufus Dunham. Information concerning them comes, for the most part, from Frederick Dunham, one of the sons in the old-time firm of Rufus Dunham & Sons, of Portland, Maine. Mr. Dunham has further given us a picturesque tale of a group of pewterers, tinsmiths, brush and comb-makers, and tin peddlers — not in Southington, Connecticut, or in Westbrook, Connecticut, where the Porters are supposed to have worked, but in Westbrook, Maine, now a part of the city of Portland.

Because the story of Allen Porter and his brother Freeman antedates that of Rufus Dunham, it is important to relate first the few facts we have been able to obtain about this earlier pair. It is thought that Allen Porter came from Connecticut to Westbrook, Maine, a township about three miles west of Portland, incorporated in 1815. At that time the place included a district — later set off as the city of Deering — that was annexed to Portland some thirty years ago. In this Deering section of Westbrook, in a village known as Stevens Plains, Allen Porter settled about 1830. It is possible that he manufactured pewter somewhere in the Nutmeg State before his departure for Maine, but we have been unable to find any evidence to that effect. Mr. Dunham further assures us that, though he has consulted records in Southington, Connecticut, he has found no reference to Porter or to any other pewterer.

Fig. 3 — Pewter Pitcher Bearing F.
Porter's Mark
Height: 6½ inches.
In the collection of Mrs. Watkins

deaths. The place Mrs. Porter lived to just before 1900. Of his further relation- nothing more is thirties he was in met and talked with Forbes, whom he persuaded to go to Westbrook as a foreman in Freeman Porter's factory. The daughter of Mr. Forbes believes that Allen never thereafter returned to Westbrook. According to Mr. Dunham, he sold out to his brother, and probably returned to Connecticut. Freeman Porter continued the business until the Civil War. During his later years he suffered ill health, a circumstance that may account for his abandonment of pewter-making. In 1868 he was a town selectman.

Freeman Porter first appears as his brother's bookkeeper at Westbrook in 1832 or 1833. From an article on Westbrook by Leonard B. Chapman in the Deering *News* of July 25–28, 1900, we learn that this younger man was born in Colebrook, New Hampshire, July 1, 1808 — though because of the lack of early records in Colebrook the date cannot be verified. Freeman was only twenty-four or twenty-five years old when his connection with the pewtering business began. Two years later — March 16, 1835 — a partnership between the brothers was announced, and in the *Eastern Argus* of Portland on April 20, 1835, appeared the following notice (*Fig. 11*):

"Allen Porter has associated himself with his brother Freeman Porter, under the firm of A. & F. Porter, for transacting Mercantile and Manufacturing Business, at his old stand on Stevens' Plains, Me."

On July 1, 1835, Freeman Porter married Mary Ann (Buckley) Partridge. The couple began housekeeping in a dwelling on Stevens Avenue, where they remained until is still standing. a ripe old age, dying Allen Porter and ship with the firm known. In the late Hartford, where he a certain Elizur B.

Rufus Dunham

The account of Rufus Dunham begins with his birth in Saco, Maine, May 30, 1815. He was of the ninth generation in descent from John Dunham, who came to Plymouth in 1630. At the age of nine, compelled to earn his own way, he went to live with a farmer, who beat and otherwise illtreated him. One day, in a drunken frenzy, the man gave the boy an unusually hard flogging with a harness strap; whereupon the lad ran away to Portland. There he found a job in the United States Hotel as handy boy about the billiard room and bar. Young Dunham had something fine about his make-up. The atmosphere of drinking and gambling that surrounded him made no unfortunate impression on his character. He was always looking forward to better circumstances. Meanwhile he attended night school and in that way managed to obtain a rudimentary education.

Concerning his father, Frederick Dunham says: "One Sunday with a companion he strolled in the country to Stevens Plains, Westbrook, three miles from Portland. At that time the place was very much alive, since it was the headquarters for one hundred or more peddlers whose markets were in northern New England, Canada, and along the coast of Maine, New Brunswick, and Nova Scotia. The windows of the different factories where were made high-back horn combs, brooms, tinware, decorated japan ware, brushes, and pewter ware so fascinated him that, in the following week, he asked for time off so that he might see the works in operation.

"On this second visit he bound himself as an apprentice for three years to Allen Porter. His wages were to be two suits of clothes per annum, his board, and fifty dollars in cash. This was in 1831. At the end of two years, he broke his contract on the ground that he had not received the pay due him for overtime work."

Boston was his next goal. Since there were no railroads or steamboats, he made his way by sailing packet. Once in the city, he secured work in Dorchester with the pewterer Roswell Gleason. Here, and in Poughkeepsie, he spent the time between 1833 and 1837. By the latter year he was making plans for a business of his own, and the attraction of Westbrook drew him once more. He had saved eight hundred dollars and had secured molds and tools in Poughkeepsie. In 1837 he opened a shop in Stevens Plains with his brother John as helper. The following year he exhibited his wares at the Mechanics' Fair in Portland, and received a silver medal for the best specimen of *block tin ware*, as pewter was sometimes called at that time. The Portland *Transcript* of September 29 thus briefly mentioned him: "R. Dunham of Westbrook presented some elegant Britannia Ware."

For power he at first used a foot lathe. Later, as business warranted, a horse, walking in a circle, replaced foot power. Still later Dunham installed a steam engine. It is said that he had the distinction of being the second man in Maine to use steam for motive power.

"He sold his first product to Eben Steel, a crockery dealer in Portland, and he was very much elated to find that he could *sell* as well as *make* his wares. The winters were long and the highways impassable, save for the road to Montreal via Crawford Notch, Lyndonville, Derby Line, and Coaticook, Quebec, which was kept open by a long line of four- and six-horse vans transporting freight from Canada to Portland, for reshipment by water to Boston. Consequently, the peddlers could do no business, and most of the Westbrook shops shut down for want of trade.

"Rufus Dunham, however, filled a wagon with his goods and went north to barter pewter wares for furs, hides, sheep pelts, yarns, stockings, mittens, oxtails, hogs' bristles, and cattle horns. The hides and pelts he forwarded to Portland — a welcome cargo for the teamsters to spread over their winter loads while on their way to the coast. On arrival these articles were sold to local tanners and wool pullers, the bristles and oxtails to brush-makers, the horns to comb-makers. The furs, yarns, stockings, and mittens were taken to Boston and turned into cash among various merchants of the Hub.

"By thus opening a winter market, Dunham was able to give

Fig. 4 (above) — LAMP MARKED "F. PORTER WESTBROOK NO. 1." *(after 1835)*
Except for the reservoir, similar to the lamp of Figure 1. Mark reproduced at the left.
Height: 6 inches

Fig. 5 (left) — LAMP ASCRIBED TO F. PORTER *(after 1835)*
Though unmarked, this pewter whale-oil lamp is the same as a known F. Porter specimen.
Height: 3½ inches

his men year-round work. As he usually paid cash wages, the best workmen were attracted to his shop. He employed from twenty-five to thirty helpers, many of whom worked for him during their whole lives."

Dunham continued his business in Stevens Plains until 1861, when his buildings were burned and he leased new quarters in Portland. In 1876 his sons Joseph S. and Frederick were taken into the firm, which remained as Rufus Dunham & Sons until 1882, when it was dissolved.

Mr. Dunham was twice married; first, to Emeline Stevens of Westbrook, by whom he had two children; second, to Emma B. Sargent of Portland, who became the mother of nine little Dunhams. His home was on Stevens Avenue, almost directly opposite that of Freeman Porter. After the second Mrs. Dunham's death, the house was purchased by the Bishop of Portland, and is now used as the rectory of Saint Joseph's Church. Rufus Dunham was always a highly respected citizen in his community, and one who was accustomed to extend lavish hospitality to his friends and to notables who passed through the town. It is said that, on one occasion, he entertained thirty-two persons in his home overnight. For many years he was a trustee of Westbrook Seminary. The All Souls Universalist Church of Portland is a memorial to him and to his wife.

Stevens Plains

The statement that one hundred or more tin peddlers were congregated in Stevens Plains suggests to the imagination a scene of

Figs. 6 and 7 — WHALE-OIL LAMPS MARKED "R. DUNHAM"
The mark is shown at left.
Height: 6 inches and 8 inches

enormous activity. What with the shops turning out the useful and decorative articles that filled the peddlers' carts, the arrival and departure of the vans, and the sorting of the goods taken in exchange, it was the centre of a varied and colorful life.

The decoration of tinware was in itself an industry. This work was done almost entirely by women. Trays, teapots, matchboxes — all the many objects japanned and painted in gay colorings — came forth from the shops of Westbrook. The tin box illustrated in Figure 8 was purchased from Mrs. O. H. Perry, granddaughter of Zachariah B. Stevens, a tinsmith, who sent out many cartloads of gaudy tin to be bartered for rags. The long building where these rags were sorted remained standing until nearly 1900, when it was pulled down and its only remaining cart was destroyed. Thus vanished the last vestiges of the once-flourishing industries of the Plains.

A note in the Deering *News* mentions Thomas Brisco as another decorator of tinware. "He was a peddler and the driver of his own horse and cart. His goods consisted of japanned tin ware, japanned and ornamented by his wife, aided later by five orphaned nieces. Undoubtedly, he was the first tin ware manufacturer and peddler of the Plains." Rufus Dunham bought a share of Brisco's property.

Walter B. Goodrich and his son Walter F. Goodrich are named as tinsmiths by Miss H. A. Forbes. The term is applied indiscriminately to makers of pewter, britannia ware, and tin. It would be interesting to know whether any real pewter, other than the products of the Porters and Rufus Dunham, came from Stevens Plains. Further research might reveal the names of additional makers. At least one clockmaker — Enoch Burnham — belonged to the community.

Wares of the Porters

Mr. Kerfoot briefly dismisses Allen Porter, saying that the only specimen of this pewterer's work that he has seen is a lamp belonging to Louis G. Myers of New York. This is presumably one of the two shown in Mr. Myers' *Some Notes on American Pewterers*, opposite page 46. No comment concerning them occurs in the text. It will be observed that these lamps have flat wicks, such as were used for lard oil. Miss Forbes states that her father — the Elizur B. Forbes who came to work for Freeman Porter in the late thirties — was the inventor of this type of burner, with its little toothed barrel wheel for turning up the wick.

The only known pieces of Porter's pewter are lamps. It is interesting to note that the three examples in the Woodside collection have stems that must have been made in the same mold. Freeman Porter, no doubt, continued to use his brother's molds when he took over the business.

Mr. Kerfoot mentions lamps, candlesticks, water pitchers, and coffee pots by Freeman Porter, who "shares

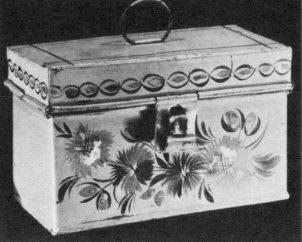

Fig. 8 — Tin Box from Westbrook
Made in the shop of Zachariah B. Stevens. Bright yellow, with red and green flowers

with R. Dunham and William McQuilkin the task of keeping American collectors supplied with open-topped pitchers," of which he made at least a third of the number now in existence. A pitcher (*Fig. 3*) brought from Maine by Mr. Woodside's grandmother, bears the mark *F. Porter Westbrook No. I*. It was always spoken of as the britannia pitcher, though it is of pewter. The significance of the *No. I* and *No. II* in Freeman Porter's marks is unknown.

Wares of Rufus Dunham

In a letter from Frederick Dunham to Mrs. Samuel G. Babcock, published in the Boston *Evening Transcript*, Saturday, March 19, 1927, some interesting sidelights are thrown on nineteenth-century methods of pewter-making. Speaking of his father, Mr. Dunham says:

"He bought his first metal of James Ellerson of Boston — tin, copper, antimony, and bismuth. The mixture when melted was cast in molds — the body of the pot, cover and bottom, spout and handle. After being turned, using a hand lathe, the parts were soldered together, the handles japanned, and they were ready for market. So far as I know, all pewter was cast in molds. With the advent of rolled metal, the word pewter was dropped, and Britannia was the new name adopted.

"In the 1860's there was a revolution in the pewter business. Teapots and what is called 'hollow' ware were made from rolled metal and spun on lathes into shape and called 'white metal.' For the more particular trade such articles were electro-silver-plated. The unplated goods were known as Britannia ware. [The beginning of rolled britannia ware antedates 1860, however. The first sheet of such metal was produced with a pair of jeweler's hand rolls in Taunton, Massachusetts, as early as 1824.]

"About 1870 there was a demand for copper bottom teapots, as . . . they were more serviceable than those made entirely of pewter. These wares were usually stamped *R. Dunham & Sons, Portland, Me.*"

Rufus Dunham manufactured Communion ware, coffee and tea urns, rolled and cast metal coffee and teapots, ale and water pitchers, ale mugs, both plain and with glass bottoms, soup tureens, soup ladles, teaspoons, tablespoons, castor frames, salts, peppers, and mustard cups, whale-oil and fluid lamps, candlesticks, and other small articles.

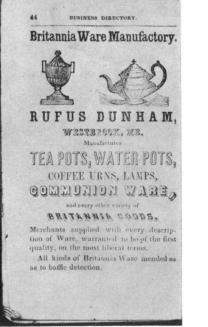

Fig. 9 (left) — Portland Directory Advertisement (*1844*)

Fig. 10 — Portland Directory Advertisement (*1866–1867*)

Fig. 11 — Partnership Notice, "Eastern Argus" (*April 20, 1835*)

A LAMP DEALER ILLUSTRATES HIS WARES

A Gallery Note

By MALCOLM WATKINS

Illustrations from plates in the collection of Arthur Sussel

IT IS always a source of satisfaction when contemporary documents are found which authenticate or provide information about existing antiques. Particularly is this true with regard to early lighting devices, where it is often difficult accurately to establish the dates of certain forms or the relationships of these forms to technical details.

In the possession of Arthur Sussel of Philadelphia is a group of nineteen lithographed plates, 9 by 11 inches in size, which were published as advertising material or as part of a catalogue for a mid-nineteenth-century American lamp dealer. They illustrate several simple types of pewter and glass lamps familiar to present-day collectors, as well as a wide variety of so-called *solar* lamps. The latter are most important in revealing, through the forms and details of bases and glass globes, the range of early Victorian design.

One of the plates illustrates a solar lamp with spherical globe bearing the name W. H. STARR. Starr was a New York lamp dealer who was in business on Beekman Street in the 1840's. In 1846 he took out a patent on a *Compound Capillary Burner*, a variation on the Argand burner as applied to solar lamps. It should be explained that the common type of solar lamp had been patented in 1843 by Robert Cornelius. This was an Argand lamp over whose burner was placed a convex disc with a hole in its center. The flame of the lamp, impinging on the inner surface of the disc, was forced by the air current — basic to all Argand burners — through the opening so as to produce a tall white column of light. The lamp burned either lard or sperm oil.

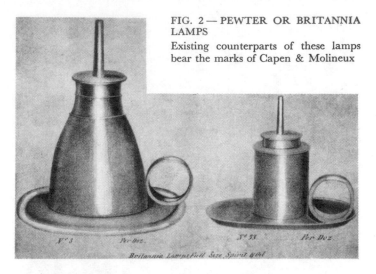

FIG. 2 — PEWTER OR BRITANNIA LAMPS

Existing counterparts of these lamps bear the marks of Capen & Molineux

Starr ran the following advertisement in Wilson's *Business Directory of New York City* in 1848:

STARR'S
Lamp and Chandelier Manufactory
No. 67 Beekman Street, New York.

Dealer in Solar Oil, Globes, Glasses, Wicks of all kinds, Prisms, Stained and Painted Glass, Britannia Lamps, Lamp Tops, Lamp chains, etc., etc. W. H. S. takes pleasure in offering at exceedingly low prices and of his own manufacture, Improved Solar lard and camphene lamps and chandeliers, a most extensive variety with all the latest and most valuable improvements. He is constantly manufacturing his Patent Capillary Burner, Camphene, Doric, Oriental and Parlor lamps, Brackets, Side, Hanging, Gothic, Shadowless and Acorn lamps, of various prices and qualities; also, the Universal Ladies Lustral Miniature Solar Lamps, a

FIG. 1 — PEWTER LAMPS

Left, a lamp like this (but with addition of a handle) by Capen & Molineux appears in Kerfoot's *American Pewter* (Fig. 258). *Right*, "Segar" lamp. The columns were kept filled with burning fluid. The knobs were attached to rods which, wet with fluid, would be thrust into the flame of the lamp to get a "light"

FIG. 3 (right) — GLASS BEDROOM LAMPS

Or, according to the title of the plate, *Etherial Oil, Composition Fluid and Oil Glass Lamps*. These are commonly seen in collections today. They are identified as: (*top row, left to right*) Bed Lamp, Gothic Cone, Bed Lamp, and (*bottom row*) Engraved Handled, Cut Flute. Pressed, cut, engraved, and molded

new article, combining beauty and convenience with exceeding economy. Camphene Patent Burning Fluid, Ethereal and Chemical Oils, fresh from his manufactory wholesale and retail. Dealers supplied on the most favorable terms. Please call and examine cards of patterns and prices.

The types of lighting devices here mentioned correspond fairly closely to those illustrated in the plates. One cannot say positively that the plates were published for or by Starr, but it is probable that they are the "cards of patterns and prices" to which the advertisement refers.

Eight pewter lamps are illustrated. "Spirit and oil" are indicated for them, since sperm oil and fluid burners were interchangeable. These were evidently manufactured by the New York firm of Capen & Molineux: most of them are identifiable either by similar existing marked specimens, or (in the case of two) more tentatively by details of the cast shafts like those found in other lamps made by this concern (*Figs. 1, left, and 2*). Capen & Molineux worked in William Street from 1848 to 1853, according to Kerfoot (*American Pewter, p. 156*), who describes them as appearing "to have been the leading specialists in pewter lamps."

It is perhaps worth noting that the plates designate the lamps not as pewter, but as *Britannia Lamps*, and that the advertisement also mentions britannia lamps, but none of pewter. This brings up the point that the distinction between pewter and britannia has been and often still is rather thin. The point is elucidated by Kerfoot, who says:

"Britannia" was a trade name given to a superfine grade of pewter by some English makers along about the middle of the eighteenth century . . . It looks as though the name may have been more of an advertising dodge than indicative of a metallurgical innovation. And it may not be altogether a coincidence that this advertising name was adopted just at the time when pewter's monopoly of the tableware business was being first seriously threatened by the growing use of china . . . Actually . . . the tin-copper-antimony alloys that are indubitably fine, and to be called "pewter," merge into those that are progressively less fine, until they come to coincide with our later-day notions of "britannia," so gradually that no hard-and-fast line of differentiation exists between them.

All Capen & Molineux lamps that I have examined may justifiably be called pewter, since they by no means possess the objectionable tinlike qualities found in objects cast aside by today's collectors as "britannia," but on the contrary have the best characteristics of good pewter. Even if the lamps under discussion were not made by Capen & Molineux, Starr's use of the term

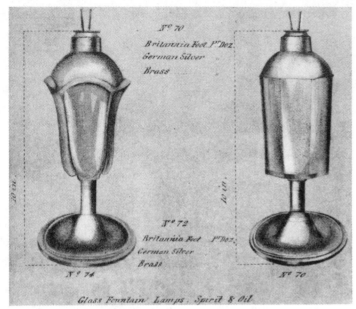

FIG. 4 — GLASS LAMPS ON METAL PEDESTALS
Lamps of this type, often found detached from their original bases, are not peg lamps, as sometimes erroneously described, but were secured to their bases in the manner shown. The designation britannia was probably used by the manufacturer to mean what collectors now call pewter; the distinction between britannia and pewter is rather vague and often confusing. These lamps were also made in brass

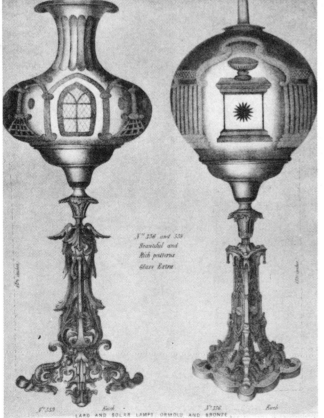

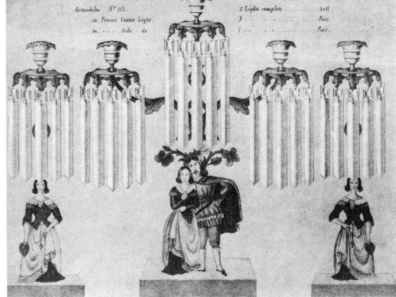

FIG. 5 (*left*) — SOLAR LAMPS
Described as possessing "beautiful and rich patterns," these lamps illustrate the lamentable result of combining mixed gothic and renaissance design with machine techniques. They reflect some of the deplorable aspects of early Victorian living

FIG. 6 — THE LAST WORD IN MID-CENTURY GIRANDOLES
A glaring example of misapplied design, even worse than Figure 5

FIG. 7 — TIN "SIDE REFLECTOR" SOLAR LAMP

The convex disc with flame hole in center, which characterizes the solar lamp, is distinguishable

FIG. 8 (*right*) — SOLAR LAMP

Characterized by Spartan simplicity and admirable directness

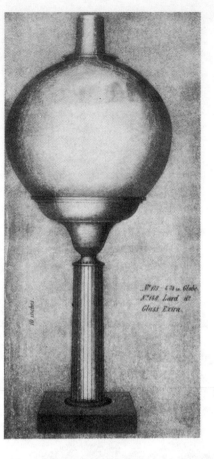

with an overlay glass reservoir mounted on a brass standard, and an unidentified brand of "patent" burner. Two hanging lamps evidently employ the principle of Horn's patent.

All these plates illustrate the best examples of American lamps in use just prior to the introduction of kerosene. They show that the lamp around 1850 was characterized by well-developed technical devices, the use of mass-production methods of manufacture, and the frequent application of inappropriate motives of design. They are expressions of early Victorian taste and techniques.

britannia was probably for purposes of enhancing the sale of his lamps, rather than to indicate any essential contrast between those and lamps frankly designated as pewter.

To return to the subject at hand, two plates are devoted to small glass lamps of fairly common type (*Figs. 3, 4*). These are perhaps from different sources. Lamps of the type shown in Figure 4 are sometimes erroneously called peg lamps because of the small pegs that protrude to secure them to their metal bases, which are often missing in examples found today.

Solar lamps predominate in the plates. One can see that such lamps gave designers great liberty to exercise ingenuity. Unless intended to hang from the ceiling, solar lamps were usually supported on pedestal bases. These bases, having no other function than that of support, afforded a tremendous temptation for adornment. What happened when the designer yielded to the temptation may be seen in the examples shown in Figure 5. Similarly, the eager virtuosity of the glass engraver sometimes led him into executing decoration like that of their shades. These are perhaps the "Gothic" lamps mentioned in Starr's advertisement.

On the other hand, an appreciation of simplicity and directness still survived, as exemplified in the lamp of Figure 8. Here the plain globular shade, which may have been colored, but was probably of white translucent glass; the simple inverted-bell-shape reservoir, designed to provide a minimum of depth but a maximum of fuel capacity and supporting area for the shade; and, finally, the austere column on the heavy marble plinth, all combine to create a lamp that answers without deviation the demands of its function. Solar lamps of any description are sufficiently uncommon today to be called rare.

Less successful are some of the other devices — the girandoles, the terrifyingly ornate chandeliers, and the octagonal hall lanterns engraved with gothic arches and funeral urns. The variations among other devices shown in the plates from those here illustrated occur principally in ornamental details of bases and shades for solar lamps. Two or three types of fluid lamps appear, one

The Etiquette of Nineteenth-Century Lamps

By MAJOR L. B. WYANT

Except as noted, illustrations from the author's collection

IT HAS not been long since our grandmothers put away on the shelf, for the last time, those odd-looking contrivances whose feeble light once gave visibility to the darkness of the domestic scene, but which now provide little save the substance of conjecture. Almost no evidence of any kind survives to help the antiquarian classify the inexhaustible variety of these alluring articles. Such strictly utilitarian things were seldom mentioned in the records of their day, and were infrequently illustrated in contemporary prints. Hence the student, the collector, and the decorator have difficulty in placing extant examples in correct association with appropriate accessories. Trusting that my effort might encourage further contribution to an obscure subject, I have spent some time in gathering such fragments of published data on lighting devices as I could find, together with a few examples of lamps that might serve to illustrate the text. The references are offered in the full flavor of verbatim extract.

As a beginning I shall ask that versatile American "Benjamin Count of Rumford" to speak briefly on the Argand lamp. These lines are taken from Volume II of his essays, published in London in 1800, not long after the advent of Argand's device.

An Argand's lamp is a fireplace . . . the glass which surrounds the wick (and which distinguishes this from all other lamps) serves merely as a blower. The circular form of the wick is not essential; for by applying a flatted glass tube as a blower to a lamp with a flat or riband wick, it may be made to give as much light as an Argand's lamp; or at least quite as much in proportion to the size of the wick, and to the quantity of oil consumed, as I have found by actual experiment.

Rumford also recites a fact that might later have been useful to other experimenters in the field of improved burners: "Heat cannot be propagated downward in liquids, as long as they continue to be

Fig. 1 — "READING THE SCRIPTURES"
Lithograph by J. Baillie, showing the type or astral lamp common to the parlors of the 1840's.
Courtesy of Leo Wagner

condensed by cold." It was essential, of course, to keep the oil fluid.

While we wish to limit ourselves primarily to lamps of the nineteenth century, some reference to candles is necessary. Candles were employed in most households, in a proportion dictated by the preference and purse of the family, and for a time were considered to be more elegant than lamps. For example, the lighting devices and accessories at Mount Vernon as listed in an inventory taken early in 1800, shortly after the death of Washington, affords this information:

In the New Room.

4 Silver-plated lamps etc.	$60.00
2 Elegant Lustres [French candelabra]	$120.00

[There was a pair of bronze double-branch astral mantel lamps with crystals which stood on the Italian marble chimneypiece during the later days of Washington's life at Mount Vernon. These are not mentioned in the inventory.]

2 Candle Stands.	$40.00

[In the Little Parlor, the Dining Room, the Bed Room, in the Front Room on the second floor, in the Second Room, the Third Room, the Fourth Room, the Small Room, Mrs. Washington's Room, and in Mrs. Washington's Old Room: None.]

In the Study.

2 Brass Candle Sticks	$2.00
Among the Plated Ware	
(44 lbs., 15 Oz. @ $900.00)	
4 Pair High Candlesticks	$40.00
3 Pair Chamber Candlesticks	9.00
1 Snuffer Stand	1.00
2 Pair High Candlesticks	30.00
1 Pair Small Candlesticks	3.00
1 Lamp	10.00

[No mention is made of the square iron lantern with four glass sides, lit by a peg lamp for sperm oil, which hung in the passage at Mount Vernon for many years and was later removed to Arlington.]

Referring to her introduction to the White House, the second first lady, Mrs. John Adams, cites many shortcomings. She says in a letter written November 21, 1800:

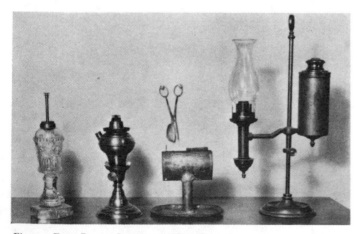

Fig. 2 — FOUR PATENT LAMPS, AND WICK SCISSORS
Left to right: Burner with wick similar to that used for whale oil; said to have been used with a patent fuel from Cleveland, Ohio. Brass, believed to be a solar lamp; no mechanism to raise and lower the wick; little wheel merely raises the small horizontal disc over the wick. Tin lard lamp stamped *D. Kinnears Patent Feb. 4, 1851.* Brass student lamp; patent date *1871*

Fig. 3 — PRIMITIVE TYPES WHOSE USE EXTENDED FAR INTO THE NINETEENTH CENTURY
First in the upper row is the familiar iron betty on a wooden stand; all others are tin. Fourth in upper row has a tubular wick support. This lamp still harbors some of the old whale oil. The first lamp in the lower row has an open top and two wick channels supported by a vertical centre wire

Lighting the apartments, from kitchen to parlors and chambers, is a tax indeed; and the fires we are obliged to keep to secure us from daily agues, is another very cheering comfort . . . where twelve fires are constantly required, and where, we are told, the roads will soon be so bad that it [wood] cannot be drawn. . . . I have no looking glasses, but dwarfs, for this house; nor a twentieth part lamps enough to light it. . . .

Gas lighting was introduced in the White House in 1848. Candles were still used in wall fixtures until 1891, when candles and gas were replaced with electrical equipment.

Fig. 4 — LAMPS SUITABLE IN ENTRY HALL AS LIGHTERS FOR CHAMBER LAMPS
A and b are pewter; c is of brass. B has a gallery around the camphene burner for a chimney, possibly of the type shown beside it. It has three vertical cylinders, which provide receptacles for wax tapers or folded paper spills. Marked *Dietz Brother and Co. N. Y.*

tons always clean and dry, as well as the stick to put them on. . . . When fresh cottons are put in let the oil down, so that they may get well soaked, after which put up that part that keeps the oil up. [I'd like to know what that means.] . . . Have a tin pot with a long spout to put the oil in with, to prevent spilling. . . . If the patent lamps be lighted up every evening, they should be emptied once a week. Do not put the oil that comes from them into the jar with the best oil, but keep it separate to burn in the common lamps. In the cold weather warm the oil by putting the lamps near the hall fire. . . . In frosty weather in particular, the glasses are very easily broken by sudden transition from cold to heat. . . .

Fig. 5 — CHAMBER LAMPS
Of tin, japanned tin, pewter, and brass. Fourth, upper row, has a small flat wick burner and was used for whale oil

Fig. 6 — CHAMBER LAMPS OF GLASS
For whale oil, camphene, and kerosene. Such lamps were "convenient for carrying up and down stairs"

On the basis of the evidence adduced it is safe to say that, by 1800, the lamp was already accepted by leading families for general illumination. Nevertheless, for many years thereafter the candle continued to reign in the dining room and over ceremonial occasions. It was not their expense but their untidiness that finally consigned candles to infrequent household use.

The second United States edition of *The House Servant's Directory*, Boston, 1828, which among other things gives "full instructions for cleaning Plate, Brass, Steel, Glass, Mahogany; and likewise all kinds of patent and common lamps," provides the succeeding quotation:

Lamps are now so much in use for drawing-rooms, dining-rooms, and entries, that it is a very important part of a servants work to keep them in perfect order, so as to show a good light. I have been in some houses where the rooms were almost filled with smoke and stench of the oil, and the glasses of the lamps clouded with dust and smoke, from the cottons being uneven, or up too high. . . . When you do this [clean the lamps] . . . take them all to pieces, observing where each particle belongs, that you may have no trouble in putting them together again. . . . When you have this done, wipe them dry and put them before the fire, or in the sun to dry: and when you have put them together, give them a good polish with a fine cloth or silk handkerchief.
When you are cleaning or trimming your lamps in the morning you should be very particular in emptying the dripper, or that part of the lamp that holds the droppings; for if this part is not kept clean to admit the air, the lamp will never burn well. . . . When you put on fresh cottons, you must be very careful to put them on the THIMBLE quite even. And likewise see that they fit exactly, or the cotton will slip from off the thimble when you go to raise it. You should never cut your cotton with scissors; it is much the best way to let down your oil, and light the cotton; when it burns a little so as to be even blow it out, and rub off the snuff with a piece of paper even with the burner or socket, which contains the wick. You should always use wax tapers for lighting lamps, as paper generally flies about and makes dirt. . . . Your lamps must be turned down, not blown out. Then push up the Keys of your lamps, that the oil may not flow over, to spoil the carpets.

From the fourth American edition of Mackenzie's *Five Thousand Receipts*, Philadelphia, 1829, comes the next selection:

There are generally two or three small holes in the common brass lamps, to admit the air; be particular to keep them open with a pin, or a piece of wire, as otherwise the lamp will smoke, and not give a good light. The patent lamps are more difficult to clean. . . . Be careful in cleaning the chimneys of the patent lamp; and also that part which receives the droppings of oil. . . . Keep the cot-

Use wax-tapers, or matches without brimstone for lighting them, but not paper. . . . The smoking of lamps is frequently disregarded in domestic life: but the fumes ascending from oil, especially if it be tainted or rancid, are highly pernicious when inhaled into the lungs of asthmatic persons. To prevent this, let a sponge, three or four inches in diameter, be moistened with pure water, and in that state be suspended by a string or wire, exactly over the flame of the lamp, at the distance of a few inches; this substance will absorb all smoke emitted during the evening or night.

The same book gives one of the most lucid descriptions that I have seen on the subject of rushlights. It appears under the heading *An Excellent Substitute for Candles:*

Procure meadow-rushes, such as they tie the hop shoots to the poles with. Cut them when they have obtained their full substance, but are still green. The rush, at this age, consists of a body of pith, with a green skin on it. Cut off both ends of the rush, and leave the prime part, which, on an average, may be about a foot and a half long. Then take off all the green skin except for about a fifth part of the way round the pith. Thus it is a piece of pith all but a little strip of skin in one part all the way up, which is necessary to hold the pith together.
The rushes being thus prepared, the grease is melted, and put in a melted state, into something that is as long as the rushes are. The rushes are put into the grease; soaked in it sufficiently; then taken out and laid in a bit of bark, taken from a young tree, so as not to be too large. This bark is fixed up against the wall by a couple of straps put round it; and there it hangs for the purpose of holding the rushes.
The rushes are carried about in the hand; but to sit by, to work by, or to go to bed by, they are fixed in stands made for the purpose, some of them are high, to stand on the ground, and some are low, to stand on a table [*Fig. 8*]. These stands have an iron part something like a pair of pliers to hold the rush in, and the rush is shifted forward from time to time, as it burns down to the thing that holds it.
These rushes give a better light than a common small dip candle; and they cost next to nothing, though the laborer may, with them, have as much light as he pleases. [Note that the date of this is the year 1829.]

The next passages are chosen from *Miss Leslie's Housebook*, Philadelphia, 1840, close to the period when various new fuels and burners for lamps were first offered. The discussion of lights is much too detailed to quote *in toto*. I hope I have extracted the more illuminating passages. Thus:

The best lamp oil is that which is clear and nearly colourless, like water. None but the winter-strained oil should be used in cold weather. Thick, dark-coloured oil burns badly (particularly if it is old) and there is no economy in trying to use it. Unless you require a great deal every night, it is well not to get more than two or three gallons at a time, as it spoils by keeping. Oil that has been kept several months will frequently not burn at all. . . . There are large oil-vessels with cocks, and keys belonging to them. . . .

In buying astral lamps [*Fig. 1*] for the table, choose the shades of plain ground glass, as they give the clearest and steadiest light, and are best for the eyes. . . . Lamp shades painted in bright colours are now considered in very bad taste. . . . The fashion of having shades decorated with flowers or other devises, cut on the glass and left transparent is also on the decline . . . though it may do well for mantel lamps and lustres. . . . To buy table astral lamps of inferior size, is by no means advisable [*Fig. 10*]. They only give light in proportion to their magnitude; and when they are small and low, the effort of seeing by them is so teazing to the optic nerve that the eyes seldom fail to become weak in consequence.

Management of Astral Lamps. Keep a distinct oil-can for the parlour lamp. Choose firm light-woven wicks, fine in texture, and with even edges. . . .

The lamp-scissors should be very sharp, or it will be impossible to trim the wick properly [*Fig. 2*]. . . . Clean out every morning the cup or candlestick part that catches the droppings. . . .

When you light it [the lamp], remove the shade and the chimney, and ignite the wick with a paper match, a supply of which should always be kept in some convenient place. . . . When you wish to extinguish the lamp entirely turn the screw to the left as far as it will go. . . . When all your lamps (Mantel etc.) have been in use for company they should next morning be emptied completely of oil and wick, and washed with luke-warm pearl-ash and water. . . . The oil that is removed from these lamps should be put into a can and saved for use in the kitchen. On the day of your next company, (and not till then) replenish them anew. Unless a lamp is used nightly, no oil and wick should be left in it, even for a single day. . . .

After the large entry lamp is extinguished on the family going to bed, a small brass lamp should be kept burning all night, on a table in the passage, or landing-place of the lower stairs [*Fig. 4*]. . . . When visitors are expected place a lamp on a shelf fixed for the purpose, in the fan-light over the front door. . . . Hall lamps of stained glass are very elegant, their colors throwing a beautiful tint on the walls and floors.

Lamp Rugs. These are small square rugs, to prevent the feet of the lamps from marking the table. . . . The handsomest lamp-rugs are worked on canvas with crewels of different colours [*Fig. 7*].

Chamber Lamps. Small japanned lamps are the most convenient for carrying up and down stairs, and for lighting to bed [*Figs. 5 and 6*]. . . . The wick should be about a quarter yard in length . . . it will not require renewing for three or four days. . . . The grocer sells it in balls.

Every evening before dusk, as many of these bed-lamps as may be wanted by the members of the family, should be arranged on a japanned waiter, with a brass lamp of a larger size burning in the middle, and a few paper matches placed on one side [*Fig. 4*]. The waiter of lamps should be kept on a small table (or on shelves connected by a frame) at the first landing-place of the stairs or in a recess or retired part of the hall or entry below. . . . The long or ball wick used for common lamps may be much improved by cutting it into pieces and steeping them in a cup of vinegar, then spreading them out to dry, and when quite dry winding them on a card.

Kitchen lamps. Should be of brass or block tin, with bottoms like chamber candlesticks. They also should be kept clean and replenished every day [*Fig. 9*].

Lanterns. Lanterns with glass sides are so easily cracked that we do not recommend them. They are much better when glazed with horn or perforated all over with small holes. . . . It is best to get a lantern with a socket at the bottom, so that either a lamp or a piece of candle can be

placed in it, as may be the most convenient. The small lamps used for placing in the sockets of lanterns are like those without bottoms or stands [peg lamps], that are made to place in broad kitchen candlesticks [*Fig. 11*].

Night lamps. There are a variety of lamps for burning all night in chambers; an excellent custom, which frequently prevents much inconvenience particularly in cases of sudden illness. In every house it is well to have a lamp burning the whole night, in at least one of the rooms. Many persons are unwilling to sleep in a lighted room, thinking that the sight of the objects all around will disturb them, and that none of the shaded lamps sufficiently obscure the light. To obviate this objection, we know of no better contrivance than a floating taper placed in a cup of oil, and shut up in a small dark lantern; such as may be purchased at a tin store for fifty or seventy five cents [*Fig. 8*].

Candles. Glass receivers [bobêches] for the droppings of candles are very convenient, as well as ornamental. Those that are of cut-glass are extremely elegant . . . in genteel families it is not customary to commence their evening with half-burnt candles.

In 1841 Harper and Brothers published a *Popular Technology*. It has something to say about lamp fuels:

The sperm oil, thus freed from spermaceti, is extensively used in lamps as a means of illumination; and, for many purposes, it is far more convenient than tallow. In the country, lard is frequently employed instead of oil, especially by the German population.

In 1847 Miss Catherine E. Beecher appeared as the author of a *Treatise on Domestic Economy.* Her discussion of lighting is very similar to Miss Leslie's. But the fact that by this time new illuminants had come on the market makes some of her remarks worth quoting.

Lamps are better than candles, as they give a steadier light, and do not scatter grease, like tallow candles. . . . Lard is a good substitute for oil, for astral and other large lamps. . . . It is cheaper, burns clearer, and has less disagreeable smell. It will not burn so well in small lamps, as in large ones. Melt it every morning in an old pitcher kept for the purpose. . . . Camphine is a kind of oil manufactured in New York, which does not smell disagreeably nor make grease spots, and gives a brighter light than the best oil. [Camphene seems to have first appeared about 1840. It was a mixture of turpentine and alcohol and dangerously explosive.]

The care of lamps requires so much attention and descretion, that many ladies choose to do this work themselves, rather than trust it to domestics. . . . If everything, after being used, is cleaned from oil and then kept neatly, it will not be so unpleasant a task, as it usually is, to take care of lamps.

Weak eyes should always be shaded from the lights. Small screens made for the purpose should be kept at hand. . . . Provide small, one-wicked lamps, to carry about: and broad-bottomed lamps for the kitchen, as those are not easily upset. . . . A good night-lamp is made with a small one-wicked lamp and a roll of tin to set over it [*Fig. 8*]. . . . Cheap lights are made by dipping rushes in tallow.

A catalogue of McKee and Brothers, Pittsburgh glassmakers, issued about 1859, shows "oil, fluid, and coal oil" lamps in the same illustration. Likewise a camphene chimney is illustrated along with globes for oil lamps and artificial gas. Here we have a visible meeting point of the old and the new and the start of a competition that resulted in the triumph of kerosene.

In a book called *Eighty Years of Progress*, published with data compiled about 1860, mention is made of the extent of the packing

Fig. 7 — Four "Common" Stand Lamps
Of a type "suitable for use in drawing-room, dining-room, or entry." Above, a lamp rug

Fig. 8 — Night Lamps and Rushlight Holder
A, dark lantern with whale-oil lamp. *B*, stenciled tin cylinder shield and night lamp, for whale oil

industry in Cincinnati and of between thirty and forty lard-oil factories. "11,000,000 lbs of lard were run into lard oil in one year which was sent to the Atlantic cities to be used as such, or in the adulteration of sperm oil. Much of it also was sent to France to be used in adulteration of olive oil." While this was going on, American whalemen were becoming despondent over the competition of "prairie whales," which provided the lard oil. The multitude of inventions of patent oils from coal and other substances was another source of discouragement.

Again in 1869 a book on domestic economy appeared with Catherine E. Beecher's name on the cover. Harriet Beecher Stowe was co-author. It was called *The American Woman's Home or, Principles of Domestic Science*. While this volume gives honorable mention to sperm oil, even in 1869, it is apparent that "coal oil or kerosene" is now in the ascendant. Lard oil is not mentioned. We must assume that, by this time, its use had been discontinued in the home. But I shall let the ladies tell the story in their own words:

Professor Phin, of the *Manufacturer and Builder*, has kindly given us some late information on this important topic [lights] which will be found valuable.

In choosing the source of our light, the great points to be considered are, first, the influence on the eyes, and secondly, economy. It is poor economy to use a bad light. Modern houses in cities, and even in large villages, are furnished with gas; where gas is not used, sperm-oil, kerosene or coal-oil, and candles are employed. Gas is the cheapest, (or ought to be;) and if properly used, is as good as any. Good sperm-oil burned in an Argand lamp — that is, a lamp with a circular wick, like the astral lamp and others — is perhaps the best; but it is *expensive* and attended with many inconveniences. Good kerosene oil gives a light which leaves little to be desired. Candles are used only on rare occasions, though many families prefer to manufacture into candles the waste grease that accumulates in the household. . . .

The effect produced by light on the eyes depends upon the following points: First, *Steadiness*. Nothing is more injurious to the eyes than a flickering, unsteady flame. Hence, all flames used for light-giving purposes ought to be surrounded with glass chimneys or small shades. No naked flame can ever be steady. Second, *Color*. This depends greatly upon the temperature of the flame. A hot flame gives a bright, white light; a flame which has not a high temperature gives a dull, yellow light, which is very injurious to the eyes. In the naked gas-jet a large portion of the flame burns at a low temperature, and the same is the case with the flame of the kerosene lamp when the height of the chimney is not properly proportioned to the amount of oil consumed; a high wick needs a high chimney. In the case of a well-trimmed Argand oil lamp, or an Argand burner for gas, the flame is in general most intensely hot, and the light is of a clear white character.

The third point which demands attention is the amount of heat transmitted from the flame to the eyes. It often happens that people, in order to economize light, bring the lamp quite close to the face. This is a very bad habit. The heat is more injurious than the light. Better burn a larger flame, and keep it at a greater distance.

It is also well that various sized lamps should be provided to serve the varying necessities of the household in regard to quantity of light. One of the very best forms of light is that known as the "student's reading lamp," which is, in the burner, an Argand. Provide small lamps with handles for carrying about, and broad-bottomed lamps for the kitchen, as these are not easily upset. Hand and kitchen lamps are best made of metal, unless they are to be used by very careful persons.

Sperm-oil, lard, tallow, etc., have been superseded to such an extent by kerosene that it is scarcely worth while to give any special directions in regard to them. . . .

In regard to shades, which are always well to use, on lamps or gas, those made of glass or porcelain are now so cheap that we can recommend them as the best

Fig. 9 — Tin Kitchen Lamps
Left to right: For whale oil, camphene, lard, lard oil, kerosene

Fig. 10 — Lithograph by E. B. and E. C. Kellogg (*1846*)
No doubt this young man is resting his eyes from the glare of the small astral lamp beside him

without any reservation. . . . Lamps should be lighted with a strip of folded or rolled paper, of which a quantity should be kept on the mantelpiece. . . . Fill the entry lamp every day, and cleanse and fill night lanterns twice a week, if used often. A good night-lamp is made with a small one-wicked lamp and a roll of tin to set over it. Have some holes made in the bottom of this cover, and it can be used to heat articles. Very cheap floating tapers can be bought to burn in a teacup of oil through the night. . . .

Cheap lights are made by dipping rushes in tallow; the rushes being first stripped of nearly the whole of the hard outer covering and the pith alone being retained with just enough of the tough bark to keep it stiff. [It does not follow that rushes were used at this late date. Evidently the authors, like most compilers, borrowed copiously from earlier writings.]

Now let us listen briefly to a voice from the 1880's, that of Clarence Cook, who wrote the first book intended to reclaim the public taste, following the worst of the Victorian and the late Eastlake fashions. This book is titled *The House Beautiful*. In it the author says:

Thanks to the good gift of petroleum oil, and thanks to the invention of the student lamp, there is no longer any excuse for one's hurting his eyes by reading at night; and thousands of people who a few years ago were lauding gas to the skies are now consigning it to its proper place, — in halls, and offices, and streets, — refusing to allow it in their parlors and bedrooms, and replacing the gas fixtures with lamps for burning kerosene. . . . However, I am well aware that there is a sufficient reason for our American wholesale adoption of mechanical contrivances in the miserably inefficient character of our servants. In nine cases out of ten, we use gas, furnaces, and plumbing instead of lamp or candles, open fires, and movable washing-apparatus, because it saves immensely in the labor and expense necessary to carry on a household.

We have now been conducted through that period of struggle for efficient and economical illumination which led to the solution of the problem as we accept it today, through the use of electricity and the Edison lamp (*Fig. 13*). This, it will be recalled, was demonstrated when the switch was thrown in the Pearl Street station, New York City, on September 4, 1882.

An evaluation of the preceding evidence still leaves much to conjecture. One of the most perplexing questions arises by virtue of the continued use of early forms side by side with successive improvements down to and including the beginning of the electrical era. It requires a considerable stretch of the imagination for dwellers in this age of novelty, rapid depreciation, and discard, to cast themselves backward to the American scene of post-colonial development, when thrift was a harsh necessity. The westward tide of empire carried primitive existence, much like that endured by the first settlers on the eastern coast, beyond the Alleghenies and finally to the Pacific. In some sections, log-cabin conditions prevailed until fairly recent times. The continuance of the primitive environment over a long period called for the continued use of primitive utensils.

The quoted extracts from domestic publications, then, can apply only to those localities where living conditions had risen above the primitive to the current standard. Thus in 1800 we are told that circular and flat wicks and glass chimneys were in use. We may also add that the small spur wheel which facilitated the adjustment of the wick was known. In 1828 patent and common lamps were much in use in drawing rooms, dining rooms, and entries. The patent lamps were probably of the astral or Carcel type. At this time no mention directly or indirectly is made of glass lamps, although ANTIQUES for March 1927 published an article by Rhea Mansfield Knittle which included this advertisement, dated 1828: "BAKEWELL, PAGE & BAKEWELL / Flint Glass Manufacturers /

Fig. 11 — SUNDRY LAMPS
Left to right: Petticoat lamp of tin with three wick tubes in line; peg lamp and wooden stand; peg lamp and glass stand; peg lamp in brass candlestick; petticoat lamp of japanned tin

Fig. 12 — SUNDRY LAMPS
Above: Blown top intended for a pressed base. *Below, left to right:* Time light for kerosene, domestic manufacture; glass oil container joined to brass base by a coil spring; kerosene night lamp dated *1911;* glass holder for peg lamp

Have for sale, an Assortment of / ASTRAL, OR SINUMBRAL LAMPS / On Pedestals and for Suspension. / Also, Tuscan, Vase, Mantel and / Chamber Lamps / Which, in addition to their usual stock of / Plain and Cut / FLINT GLASS / Patent Moulded, Plain / and Cut / Bureau Mountings (etc. etc.) / Will be disposed of on the lowest terms. / *Pittsburgh, November 20.*"

Up to and including 1869, wax tapers or tightly folded strips of paper are repeatedly recommended as the means for lighting lamps, although the friction match was invented in 1827. Rushlights are mentioned as an economical form of illuminant as late as 1869. Plate, gilt, or bronze for the "frame and stand" of astral lamps are the only materials anywhere specifically mentioned for such lamps. Special lamp scissors were to be had for trimming wicks. Lamp rugs were used to prevent the feet of lamps from marking the table. Small screens were advocated to protect weak eyes. Patterns for these screens were published as late as 1870 in the leading women's magazines.

Chamber lamps were of small japanned or other metal types convenient for carrying up and down stairs. Glass lamps were conditionally recommended for the purpose. A brass lamp (without chimney) was kept burning near the stairway to provide a light for the bevy of smaller chamber lamps, all nestled on a japanned waiter or tray. Kitchen lamps were of brass or block tin "with broad bottoms like chamber candlesticks." Most people who have written about the subject have indicated that brass lamps were too expensive for general kitchen use.

Lanterns glazed with horn or of pierced tin were recommended. This upsets the notion of the great antiquity of all lanterns glazed with horn. Peg lamps were used in lanterns as well as elsewhere. All-night-burning lamps were made from dark-lanterns or from a small one-wicked lamp with a roll of tin set over it.

It seems strange that, considering the number of glass and pewter lamps from the period under discussion in existence today, such brief reference is made to glass and none at all to pewter (unless, as some say, pewter was identical with "block tin").

The reference to lard is somewhat obscure. It seems that Miss Beecher's remarks should apply to lard oil. Lard as distinguished from lard oil, as I understand it, was used in grease lamps before the refining process was employed. Miss Beecher mentions nothing of the explosiveness of camphene, an attribute which seems finally to have ruled it out as a practical fuel for lamps.

Price was no doubt largely instrumental in winning a market for the new lamp fuels. Lard oil, which would remain liquid at 30° F. sold for a dollar a gallon when the medium grade of sperm oil was a dollar and a

Fig. 13 — SUNDRY LAMPS
Left to right: Kerosene lamp. Model of the first Edison electric lamp. Lamp with late Argand burner for kerosene; reservoir older than the burner

quarter. Camphene, I believe, was more expensive. Its use, however, was discouraged by insurance companies because of the risk of explosion. Kerosene was also of uncertain quality when first marketed, but it was cheaper than lard oil and became popular when the public could be educated to discriminate between the good and the bad.

Price must also have favored the wide distribution of the glass lamp. In 1859 McKee and Brothers were advertising turnip stand lamps (the ordinary type in use today) for coal oil at $8 per dozen, for fluid (camphene) at $4.50 per dozen, for oil (sperm) at $3.75 per dozen. The name "turnip" was evidently a descriptive term applying to the shape of the bowl. A glass lamp for lard oil has so far been too elusive for this hunter to catch. Neither the game nor the ammunition is plentiful in these times, though the zest is undiminished.

Note. Although the following quotations are from a London publication, *The Magazine of Domestic Economy,* they may prove of interest. From the Correspondence section, March 1841. "Among your remarks upon *cheap lights,* you have never noticed the recently invented solar lamps. . . . Is their management more troublesome for servants than the common Argand lamp? And are they more liable to get out of order? What, in short, is your opinion of these promising and attractive novelties?" The editor answered: "Our experience of the solar lamp does not justify us in recommending it. If a table lamp is preferred to candles it should be an Argand, and fed with the best sperm or vegetable oil."

In the April issue, one correspondent, having listed several "precautions in using the solar lamp," states: "A family burning two lamps, one in the parlour and one in the hall, will save about 10*l.* per annum by the use of the Solar, which I know must succeed if properly managed." Another writes: "I find a very great saving in the cost of the oil, and at the same time have a much more brilliant light. The Solar lamp in my opinion is also a much handsomer shape than the Argand." The editor, retracting, remarks: "We are now using one, and are making calculations." In January 1842 a correspondent declares: "I used one [solar lamp] during the whole of the last winter, and found it to be in every respect superior to any other light I ever tried."

Editor's Note. An excellent bibliography of books and magazine articles on the history of artificial lighting has just been prepared by L. L. Thwing of Belmont, Massachusetts, editor of the Rushlight Club bulletin. In an appendix to his careful compilation of reference Mr. Thwing makes some pertinent observations to which attention should be called. For example, he is doubtful that early American colonists burned rushlights, despite the fact that sundry American writers on lighting devices give directions for gathering and preparing rushes. Such directions, according to Mr. Thwing, were lifted more or less bodily from English books — a procedure not uncommon among compilers. Early inventories, in New England at any rate, make no mention of rushlight holders. Hence Mr. Thwing holds that such devices now on the market, if old, are importations either from abroad or certainly from communities outside New England. — H. E. K.

80

III Candleholders

The history of the candle is steeped in antiquity, immortalized in literature, poetry, and song. This simple lighting device has played an important part in nearly every religion, and its soft yellow light yields a romantic atmosphere to our homes today. Romantic as candlelight may be, it performed a serious and vital role in early American life. Unlike the lamp which needs care in the supply of fuel and adjustment of the wick, the candle is a self-contained lighting unit, clean and safe, and has required little or no attention from the user since 1825 when the introduction of the braided wick eliminated the need for snuffing.

The simple candle seems rather crude and primitive in this day of automation and computers. In 1860, however, the noted scientist Michael Faraday delivered a series of lectures on "The Chemical History of a Candle," in which he demonstrated how many physical principles combine to give an almost perfect source of light. When a candle is lit, the heat of the flame liquifies the solid fuel. The capillary attraction of the wick then acts to deliver the liquid fuel to the flame where the higher temperature converts the liquid to a gas which burns in a supply of air, constantly replenished by convection. In a properly made candle, combustion is complete, eliminating smoke, and the plaited wick is automatically consumed, obviating the need for snuffing. As Faraday noted, the candle is truly a remarkable chemical plant.

The candle, in common with the rushlight, has only two components, the fuel and the wick. Wicks were commonly of cotton yarn, originally loosely twisted and later braided. Other vegetable fibers were sometimes used, as well as rushes. The latter are still used in handmade candles in Japan. Vegetable waxes such as bayberry, animal fats including tallow, stearine, spermaceti, and beeswax, and the mineral paraffin wax have all been employed to make candles. The fuel was applied to the wick by repeated dippings, by casting in moulds, or by rolling on the wick when in a viscous state. Long thin coiled tapers were used in taper jacks in the nineteenth century for melting sealing wax. Short fat candles were made with rush wicks for Clarke's nursery and fairy lamps, as illustrated and described on p. 178. Early scientists adopted the "standard candle" as an international unit for light measurement, and it is still the basis of photometry.

The candle may be held by a spike or prong called a "pricket," or a spring clip, but most commonly is inserted into a close fitting socket. Since the socket leaves an unburned stub, thrifty housewives of the past often used a "saveall" designed to fit the candle socket. This was merely a small plate with three or four short upright wires which formed a cage to hold the short candle ends.

One drawback to use of the candle is the fact that, as it burns, the flame constantly changes position in pursuit of the fuel. This movement makes it impractical when used behind a lens for purposes of intensifying the light. To keep the flame position constant, many adjustable arrangements were devised, the most satisfactory of which was the springloaded candlestick in which the candle, enclosed in a cylinder, is gently pushed against a top cap or thimble.

The collector should have little difficulty in finding suitable candlesticks for his collection. These range from the rugged iron "hogscraper" to those of the graceful Queen Anne design in brass, and from the Sandwich dolphin pattern to Wedgwood jasperware. Wall sconces, however, present a challenge. Tin sconces, as pictured and described in "Amerian Tin Candle Sconces" (pp. 104-105), may still be found for a price, but do not expect to find many quillwork or Queen Anne mirror sconces. Equally rare are the iron and brass floor candleholders such as those made by Benjamin Gerrish, illustrated in the article by Richard H. Randall, Jr. (pp. 102-103), as well as country chandeliers of iron, wood, or tin.

Wrought iron sawtooth trammels, jointed extension candleholders, and miners' "sticking tommy" candlesticks add interest to any collection, as do many ancillary items such as candle boxes, snuffers, extinguishers, hurricane globes, etc.

For the reader interested in candlesticks, the articles by John Kirk Richardson, Benjamin Ginsberg, and G. Bernard Hughes present a chronology of early brass, silver, and glass candle holders, and contain a wealth of material written by authorities in this field of collecting. The two studies on chandeliers in early America by Charles Oman and Jane C. Giffen are noteworthy not only for their excellent coverage of the subject but also for their historical content. Of special interest in Oman's article is the illustration and the account of the two chandeliers in Boston's Christ Church (Old North).

BRASS CANDLESTICKS

By JOHN KIRK RICHARDSON

Part I

The subject of old brass candlesticks is one on which there has been a good deal of speculation, but not much substantial information. Even today there are many points on which it is impossible to make definite statements. This, by far the most comprehensive discussion of the subject we have presented, was prepared for us by a Richmond physician who has devoted to it a good deal of study. His special collecting interest has been Southern furniture, but of late years, he says, he has become more interested in English soft-paste porcelain and brass candlesticks. In the latter field he has made an important contribution, we feel, in clarifying and classifying available information.

THE USE OF CANDLESTICKS goes back to early Roman times, and even more remotely to the Egyptians and Hebrews. In Europe, tripod and pricket sticks were used from early times, but it is to Persia that we trace the form of the stick with nozzle holder in use today (*Fig. 1*). The Venetians are credited with the introduction to western Europe, sometime in the fourteenth century, of this type of brass or bronze candlestick. The brass of these early candlesticks was made of an alloy of copper with calamine, the impure zinc ore, which resulted in a porous vesicular metal quite different from modern brass.

The European prototype of the trumpet-base stick, as derived from Persia and transmitted through Venice, clearly shows its derivation (*Fig. 1c*). The base is not so tall, but the angle is about the same. An opening in the socket made it possible to remove the candle stub by inserting an instrument and prying it out. At first this was a vertical opening with round hole above of the Gothic-window type (*1c*), but later became a large horizontal opening (*1d*). The height of the base was increased, and the angle of the base with the grease pan became more acute, while the pan itself became deeper. Also, more lenticular moldings were added to the stem. We

may say in general that the fewer the lenticular moldings along the stem, the earlier the candlestick. An example with only one such molding appears in a triptych by Robert Campin dated 1430.

There is so much similarity among candlesticks of the fifteenth and sixteenth centuries, wherever they are found—in Scandinavian countries, eastern Europe, or the British Isles—that it has been suggested there must have been one common source for a large number of them. According to one theory, this may have been the city of Dinant on the Meuse, which in the fifteenth century numbered 8,000 workers in brass and copper among its population of 60,000.

During the last quarter of the sixteenth century and the first part of the seventeenth, the most noticeable feature in the evolution of candlesticks was the tendency to separate the wax pan from the foot (*Fig. 2, a and b*). This tendency increased until the pan was quite separate. A continuing upward trend at last resulted in the mid-drip stick, a form typical of English candlesticks in the mid-seventeenth century (*Fig. 2d*).

This same stick (*2d*) also illustrates another development which took place at the time, the replacement of the earlier rectangular opening in the socket by a round hole for the removal of the candle stub.

The placing of the pan at the center of the stick was by no means a universal arrangement. A stick which was made about 1675 has the grease pan placed just above the base (*Fig. 2f*). This position is usually associated with earlier examples, but the sophistication of workmanship in this particular candlestick places it at a later date. It is quite likely of Italian make, and may be seen at the Wythe House, Colonial Williamsburg.

It is impossible to lay down any hard and fast rules for

FIG. 1—FROM PERSIA TO VENICE TO ENGLAND. *Left to right, (a)* PERSIAN, trumpet-mouth base, bronze encrusted with silver *(thirteenth century); Brummer Collection. (b)* VENETIAN, with heraldic decoration, flat circular disc attached to base for grease pan *(probably fourteenth century); Victoria and Albert Museum. (c)* GOTHIC, stem with three lenticular moldings, vertical opening in socket with round hole above, producing "Gothic window" effect *(probably English, early 1400's); Victoria and Albert Museum. (d)* LATER GOTHIC, with higher base, four lenticular moldings on stem, one large horizontal opening in socket *(late 1400's); Metropolitan Museum of Art.*

dating candlesticks from the position of the grease pan. Another variation found about the same time is shown in Figure 2g. Here the pan is seen to be almost approaching the socket.

Another arrangement which is found off and on for a long period of time was the incorporation of the grease pan as part of the base (*Fig. 3*). Toward the end of the seventeenth century it was sometimes simply a decorative indentation in the base (*Fig. 3c*). Then at last the grease pan moved up to the socket and became a functioning lip, thus to remain to the present day.

The stems and sockets of candlesticks from the fifteenth to the early eighteenth centuries were cast solid in one piece and later finished on a lathe, the openings being filed out by hand. The stem was fastened to the base either by a threaded tang, or prong, or else by a plain tenon hammered out and riveted under the base. Sometimes the base underneath was left rough, showing the sand marks made in casting, but usually it was finished quite smoothly.

Since candlesticks are of no practical use without candles, it may be well to mention here the nature of the various candles which were used. In Europe the earliest candles were made from animal fat or tallow by repeatedly dipping a cotton wick into melted fat until the requisite size had been obtained. Wax candles, which stood up better in warm weather, were made in the same way from beeswax or from vegetable waxes like our bayberry. They were expensive, however, and were used only in churches or by the wealthy. Candles, too, were first imported by the Venetians from Persia.

The method of making candles in a mold was introduced in the fifteenth century by Bries of Paris, but wax did not lend itself easily to molding. As a matter of fact, in London there were two separate livery companies—one, the Tallow Chandlers and the other the Wax Chandlers Company.

The early candles employed a cotton wick, or in still more primitive forms the pith of a rush. It remained until quite modern times—1820, in fact—for another Frenchman, Cambaceres, to invent the plaited cotton wick. Because of the fact that it twisted while burning, the protruded end of this improved wick kept just outside the flame and was thus consumed to ash. Snuffing or trimming was thus no longer necessary.

FIG. 2—EVOLUTION OF THE MID-DRIP CANDLESTICK. *Left to right, above (a)* FLEMISH, with the pan becoming smaller and beginning to be separate from base *(c. 1600)*; *Ginsburg & Levy.* *(b)* SOMEWHAT LATER EXAMPLE *(c. 1620)*, *Millhiser Collection.* *(c)* SIMPLE TYPE OF MID-DRIP STICK *(c. 1650)*, found along Virginia seaboard; *Ahern Collection.* *(d)* TYPICAL ENGLISH MID-DRIP STICK *(c. 1650)*, with grease pan midway up turned baluster stem; *Victoria and Albert Museum. Right, (e)* FRENCH *(c. 1675)*, with gadrooning and beading around domed base; *Mount Vernon.* *(f)* PAN REVERTED TO FORMER POSITION, near base (probably Italian, *c. 1675*); *Colonial Williamsburg.* *(g)* PAN NEAR SOCKET, showing variations in contemporary sticks *(Italian or Spanish, c. 1675)*; *Ginsburg & Levy.*

Fig. 3—Some Examples with Base as Grease Pan. *Left to right, above (a)* Supported on ball feet *(second half of 1600's)*; *Victoria and Albert Museum.* *(b)* Square Base, with rim and paw feet *(late 1600's)*; *Joel Collection.* *(c)* Reduced to an indentation in the base *(c. 1690)*; *Ginsburg & Levy. Right (d)* Depression around base of stem *(early 1700's)*; *Millhiser Collection.* *(e)* Square Base with depression *(c. 1750)*; *Coons Collection.*

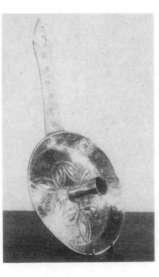

Fig. 4—Some Examples of the Chamber Stick. *Left to right, (a)* Usually referred to as the "frying-pan" type *(mid-1600's)*; *Joel Collection.* *(b)* With repoussé decoration *(c. 1710)*; *Ginsburg & Levy.* *(c)* French, with rimmed saucer base, hollow tubular stem, and the "frying-pan" handle of the previous century *(c. 1750)*; *Ginsburg & Levy.*

BRASS CANDLESTICKS

By JOHN KIRK RICHARDSON

Part II

In Part I, which appeared in September, Dr. Richardson traced the development of candlesticks from medieval times through the period of solid casting. He now continues the story to the nineteenth century.

ABOUT 1670 a very important change took place in the method of manufacture of brass candlesticks. Heretofore stem and socket had been cast solid in one piece, but at this time the process of hollow casting was introduced. Stem and socket were now cast in halves. The two halves were then brazed together, finished and polished on a lathe, and fastened to the base. This new method had two advantages: it produced a stick that was much lighter in weight, and it resulted in a considerable saving in brass. The same method was used on the Continent as well as in England, and for silver as well as brass.

The hollow stem made possible new arrangements for removing the candle stub (*Fig. 1*). The openings in the socket which had been used earlier now became obsolete. These apertures, starting with the "Gothic window" type (*Fig. 1a*), had become horizontal and finally round. Though the use of the small round hole in the socket persisted into the early years of the eighteenth century, it was discontinued soon after that, since it was no longer necessary.

In English candlesticks of the eighteenth century we often find a wire with a button at each end, fixed through the stem for the purpose of ejecting the stub (*Fig. 1b*). This type of wire ejector is not found on contemporary Continental candlesticks. Another arrangement was a slide for raising and removing the candle (*Fig. 1c, d*).

In examining candlesticks made after the introduction of the process of hollow casting, it is often possible to distinguish two lines along the length of the stem and socket where the brazing took place. When the quality of the brass and the workmanship are both excellent these lines are hard to find.

After 1700, types of candlesticks began to be more diverse. Before that, the forms had been more or less universal, but now national characteristics began to make their appearance. More thought and attention was devoted to design in candlesticks, both silver and brass.

After the bivalve process of casting was originated, brass candlesticks became the poor relation of silver, and the designs of the latter followed swiftly and closely the style changes as dictated by fashion and the silversmiths. Though we know from records that silver candlesticks were used much earlier in England, none have come down to us which can be dated before the time of Charles II. The surmise is that during the Civil War either the owners or Cromwell melted them all down. But once we do have silver examples for comparison, we can for the first time determine accurately the date of brass sticks, by comparing them with analogous silver examples that are hallmarked and dated.

One of the most persistent design details in candlesticks is the baluster stem, which first appeared in the sixteenth century and remained for several hundred years. The earliest type is derived from Renaissance stonework, being found also in Murano glass, and consists of two vase-shaped forms placed end to end with one lenticular molding between (*Fig. 2a*). This form provided the basis for the countless variations which developed subsequently.

The coming to England in 1689 of William and Mary brought a strong Dutch influence, seen in furniture and other household articles. Solidity was the salient feature. In candlesticks this was manifest in balusters that were square in shape and solid in feeling (*Fig. 2c*).

After Queen Anne's succession in 1702, though Flemish influence continued for some years, the baluster form gradually became lighter, simpler, and more slender (*Fig. 2d*).

FIG. 1—SOLVING THE PROBLEM OF THE CANDLE STUB. *Left to right,* (a) OPENING IN SOCKET of various shapes, in effect from the fifteenth to the end of the seventeenth centuries; "Gothic-window" type (*c. 1525-1550*); *Ginsburg & Levy.* (b) EJECTOR BUTTON for pushing out stub; underside of eighteenth-century candlestick; *F. Gordon Roe.* (c) SLOT AND BUTTON in hollow stem, used for raising the candle as it burns (*c. 1715*); *James Cogar.* (d) SLIDE for raising and removing candle (*c. 1725-1750*); *Mrs. Charles R. Beard.*

Later candlestick designs continue to follow silver examples. Under the Georges, the height of the stem was increased, and the vase-type baluster stem became more attenuated. It was often fluted, and the bosses were decorated with indented designs. In England, brass sticks were never as elaborate as their silver prototypes, but the French examples are often as finely made as any silver stick of the time (*Fig. 2e*). Incidentally, this French brass candlestick is almost identical in design with a pair of silver candlesticks by Jacob Hurd at the Metropolitan Museum of Art.

At this time the wide flange on the lip of the socket, which had been almost universally adopted, was no longer merely a functioning wax pan but a decorative addition. It was often ornamented with scallops or with lobes in shell and leaf design similar to those on the bases (*Fig. 3c*).

After the middle of the century, or about 1760-1765, neoclassicism began to be felt in matters of decoration, and the design of candlesticks followed the current vogue (*Figs. 2f, 3c*). Classical columns were used for the stem, both plain and fluted; capitals of various orders functioned as sockets; and the bases were designed to harmonize with the classical orders.

The varieties of baluster stems are so numerous that it would be almost impossible to catalogue them. The same is

true of bases. In general, from the end of the seventeenth century, candlestick bases were smoothly finished underneath, whereas previously many were left rough, showing the sand marks of casting.

Certain well-developed types of base design do emerge, however. The octagonal baluster stem with octagonal base is a form commonly associated with the early eighteenth century (*Fig. 4a*). Another very popular type in the Queen Anne period has a square base with indented or cut-out corners (*Fig. 4b*). Under the Georges, candlesticks of both silver and brass became more elaborate—not merely useful objects but something of distinct decorative value in home furnishings. Bases assumed many shapes—circular, circular with scalloped edges, or lobed. Some had four lobes with a shell or leaf design, and others, a trifle later, six lobes (*Fig. 4c*).

With the coming of neo-classicism, square bases became popular (*Figs. 2f, 3c*), sometimes flat, or again domed, the moldings often decorated with gadrooning. At the end of the century, a trend toward greater simplification was seen, both in stems (*Fig. 2g*) and in bases (*Fig. 4d*).

Sometime about the year 1780, another change in the technique of manufacturing brass candlesticks occurred. As we have seen, about 1670 solid casting had been discarded in

FIG. 2—SOME CANDLESTICK STEMS. *Left to right, (a)* EARLY BALUSTER STEM, two vase-shaped forms end to end with a molding between *(sixteenth century)*; *Curle Collection. (b)* ESSENTIALLY THE SAME FORM a century later, with the lower "vase" larger *(c. 1675)*; *Ginsburg & Levy. (c)* SQUARE BALUSTER STEM, reflecting Dutch influence *(c. 1690)*; *Author's Collection. (d)* ESSENTIALLY THE SAME FORM, rounded and refined under the influence of the Queen Anne style; *(early 1700's)*; *Victoria and Albert Museum. (e)* MORE ELABORATE vase-shaped baluster, with flutings and indented designs *(French, c. 1745)*; *Ginsburg & Levy. (f)* NEO-CLASSIC influence, with moldings and gadrooning *(c. 1770)*; *Ginsburg & Levy. (g)* CONTINUED SIMPLIFICATION, development of urn-shaped socket *(c. 1790-1800)*; *F. Gordon Roe.*

favor of hollow-stem casting, the two halves being then brazed together. Because of a gradual deterioration not only in the quality of brass used but also in the technique of the brass-workers, the ancient art of core casting was revived in the late eighteenth century. The whole stem and socket was again cast in one piece, which resulted in a saving of labor as well as a more finished piece of work. This is the technique used today when casting is done—a method going back to the Egyptians, and practiced to perfection in the fifteenth century at the famous brassworking center of Dinant on the Meuse, where so many fine candlesticks of the period are believed to have originated.

To sum up: the early brass candlesticks, up to 1670, were solid-cast, with stem and socket in one piece, and later finished on a lathe. From 1670 to about 1780 they were hollow-cast in halves and then brazed together and finished on a lathe. After 1780, or sometime close to that date, stem and socket were once more core-cast in one piece. These later candle-sticks, like the earliest ones, therefore show no lines of brazing.

In examining solid brass candlesticks, it is sometimes hard to tell whether they are early or late. For one thing, after the introduction of hollow casting, factory methods lagged behind the current style, so that we sometimes find candle-sticks made in the William and Mary and early Queen Anne period that still have solid cast stems with the round hole in the socket. On the other hand, later specimens may also be confusing. There is a candlestick at Colonial Williamsburg, for instance, which has such fine solid casting and beautiful baluster turnings that one would certainly say it had been made before the introduction of hollow casting. Nevertheless, it has been identified as a Russian candlestick made about 1800 or 1810.

Cases like this indicate that fine craft traditions did not altogether perish after 1780. In general, however, brass candlesticks made after the second adoption of core casting show a rapid deterioration in design.

FIG. 4—SOME CANDLESTICK BASES. *Left to right,* (a) OCTAGONAL, matching octagonal baluster (c. 1710); *Ginsburg & Levy.* (b) SQUARE BASE with cut-out corners (c. 1730); *Author's Collection.* (c) SIX-LOBED base (c. 1760); *Millhiser Collection.* (d) INCREASING simplification, plain circular or square bases (early 1800's); *Victoria and Albert Museum.*

Brass household candlesticks
of the Gothic period

BY JOHN KIRK RICHARDSON

1200-1300, Flemish or French. Made of latten, a granular, dull type of brass. Earliest type of skep, or beehive, base. Height 7⅞ inches. *Except as noted, illustrations are from the author's collection; photographs by Thomas L. Williams.*

1200-1300, French.
Early example of ring-type socket on a Romanesque tripod base. Unique. *Cluny Museum, Paris.*

GOTHIC BRASS CANDLESTICKS wherever we find them are usually Flemish or French in origin. The great center of metalwork on the Continent from the thirteenth century through the fifteenth was Dinant, situated on the Meuse in what is now Belgium, and its products in brass, copper, and bronze were sent all over Europe. Before the Tudor period brass was not made in England and had to be imported, either in the alloy or in the finished product. As it was relatively expensive, it was customarily reserved for church vessels, memorials, and more important things than household candlesticks. The French seemed to prefer the pricket type of stick while the English favored the socket variety, perhaps because they used tallow candles—which would split on a pricket.

The brass candlestick was cast solid in two parts, stem and base. The stem and socket were cast in one piece and later finished on a lathe, then the tang end of the stem was fitted into a hole in the base and held in place by hammering it out flat underneath. The socket was most often cylindrical, occasionally hexagonal or octagonal. A type of socket often used in early Gothic sticks, and especially on chandeliers of the period, was the so-called ring socket, which was somewhat elongated and hexagonal in shape, and rested on a ring that was attached to the base. In the earlier sticks the socket was perfectly plain, but in later examples it was often embellished by the addition of half-round moldings at top and base. One or two small apertures were cut in the socket with a cold chisel to facilitate removal of the candle stub. Usually these openings were square, or squarish, but occasionally they were oblong or roughly ogival, somewhat suggesting the shape of a Gothic window, with an additional small round hole above.

The stems of Gothic sticks were sometimes plain smooth columns, but usually they were encircled by one or several moldings, partly for ornament, no doubt, and probably also to give a sure grip. The commonest moldings are lenticular—thin and sharp-edged, like a double-convex lens—but rounder bead, ring, and even double-ogee moldings also occur at a fairly early date. In the late Gothic period baluster moldings appeared, combined with the lenticular or ring, showing the beginnings of Renaissance influence.

The earliest type of base is called the skep form because of its similarity to the shape of a beehive. Except in the very early candlesticks, the bases were almost all modifications of the broad, concave-sided form derived from Persia by way of Venice. They varied considerably in height, and incorporated drip pans of varying depths.

Figural sticks were sometimes made in Flanders, without base or stem, but in the form of a human figure supporting a typical ring socket; these were more likely to be in bronze than in brass. Occasionally fine candelabra with two or three arms supporting separate sockets are found, but they are very rare.

C. 1300, French.
Early type of double-arm candelabrum;
rudimentary drip pan in base.
Height 10 inches.

1300-1400, Flemish. Early ring socket
attached to modified Persian base.
Guildhall Museum, London.

1300-1400, French or Flemish.
An example of the pricket type
favored by the French.
Height 10 inches.

C. 1400, Flemish or French.
Fully developed Persian base.
Unusual lenticular moldings on stem.
Round and oblong apertures in socket.
Victoria and Albert Museum.

C. 1400, Flemish.
Fully developed single-socket stick
with four ring moldings on stem.
Typical but with exceptionally sharp
and clean-cut moldings. The finest.
Metropolitan Museum of Art.

C. 1400, Flemish. Typical brasswork of Dinant.
Two-arm stick with cast ornament
in the shape of a lion sejant on the stem.
Similar ornaments were used on
Flemish chandeliers of the time.
Kunstindustrimuseet, Oslo.

Left. C. 1400, English(?). So-called
altar stick of a type commonly found
in England, probably made in some
monastery workshop. Somewhat crude
in casting. The domed base seems to
be a late variant of the early skep
form.

Right. C. 1400, probably Dinant. An
unusual three-arm stick with crown
decoration below the arms. *Norsk
Folkemuseum, Oslo*.

C. 1450, Flemish. Late Gothic, with lipped socket, and window-type openings in it. Shallow base, reverting to earlier type. *Photograph by courtesy of Ginsburg & Levy.*

1450-1500, Flemish. Late Gothic stick, showing the Renaissance baluster introduced into stem along with lenticular moldings. Height 8⅝ inches.

C. 1500, Flemish or German. An oddity or sport in the late Gothic period. The base has reverted to a cone or trumpet shape, somewhat similar to that of the altar stick (facing page); and the mid-drip grease pan on the stem was not used again for a century. Height 8⅝ inches.

The Tax Collector, by Marinus van Roymerswaele (1497-after 1567). The candlestick on the cabinet has a lipped socket, strong ring moldings on stem, and a broad Persian base. *National Gallery, London.*

Dating English brass candlesticks

BY BENJAMIN GINSBURG

THE IDEA OF a stylistic sequence of shapes in English brass candlesticks which could be documented by dated examples in English silver came to me as long ago as 1951 from John Kirk Richardson. [Dr. Richardson's article *Brass household candlesticks of the Gothic period* appeared in ANTIQUES for December 1967, p. 818.] He had recently published two articles on brass candlesticks, and suggested that I begin a year-by-year record of styles up to 1800 to find the silver prototypes for brass. The assumption seemed reasonable that silver, being the more fashionable metal, had set the style for brass pieces.

For the past ten years my wife and I have been clipping illustrations of English candlesticks dated by the silver assay office. At least one form for every year from 1680 to 1800 was found, and some years yielded several, but on the whole there was less variety than one might have imagined. When we eliminated models that repeated earlier forms, gaps appeared in the chronology which we could not fill by new models. Some shapes continued for twenty-five years after their first appearance; we have chosen for our purpose the earliest instance found of any particular model. Since we sought only prototypes for brass, the possibilities narrowed to the main types. These are shown here in line drawings. Obviously in assembling this group of silver prototypes we have not covered all the forms made in brass that we could honestly consider English (avoiding Continental), because the brass founders altered shapes used by silversmiths and simplified or eliminated ornament to suit their harder material. We should also grant them a modicum of originality, and this is most notable in the periods before William III (r. 1689-1702) and after George II (r. 1727-1760).

The earliest English brass candlesticks derive from an older European tradition, particularly the Gothic. The mid-drip-pan style of Number 1 (1637) is scarcer in silver than in brass. Its tubular shaft with belt molding survives, however, in a brass stick with side ejectors, a type exported to the Americas in the late 1700's but unknown in silver. Also unknown in silver was the "economy hole" in the side of the socket for removing the candle end, found in so many brass sticks of the seventeenth century. Perhaps silver owners had no need to be economical about candle ends.

From 1690 to 1735 we find the greatest correspondence in *form* between silver and brass. From then to 1765 candlesticks in brass do not follow the tendency to greater elaboration in *decoration* that occurs in silver. The influence of the plainer styles of the Queen Anne period manifests itself in brass in simplifications of silver sticks made between 1760 and 1770. After 1765 there is a distinct break in the correspondence in form between silver and brass examples. Nearly all design in silver candlesticks of the late eighteenth century falls under Robert Adam's thrall. His neoclassic delicacy was more appropriate to silver and French ormolu, so actual brass counterparts are few. The common types of brass candlesticks of the last third of the century are coarser variants of earlier forms. The very few silver types of that period are of little help in dating brass. Another factor that probably accounts for the dearth of good late eighteenth-century brass candlesticks is the invention of Sheffield plate and other substitutes for solid silver, which lowered the cost so that the more elegant material was available at little more than the price of brass.

For clarity, I repeat that the choice of illustrations presented here has been made with two considerations in mind. First, only drawings of silver candlesticks that can help date brass examples are shown. Second, of the many models which continued to be popular for an extended period, the earliest dated example we could find has been used. Readers should keep in mind that this is not necessarily the earliest date at which a particular model was introduced—which is why the examples are not shown in strictly chronological order.

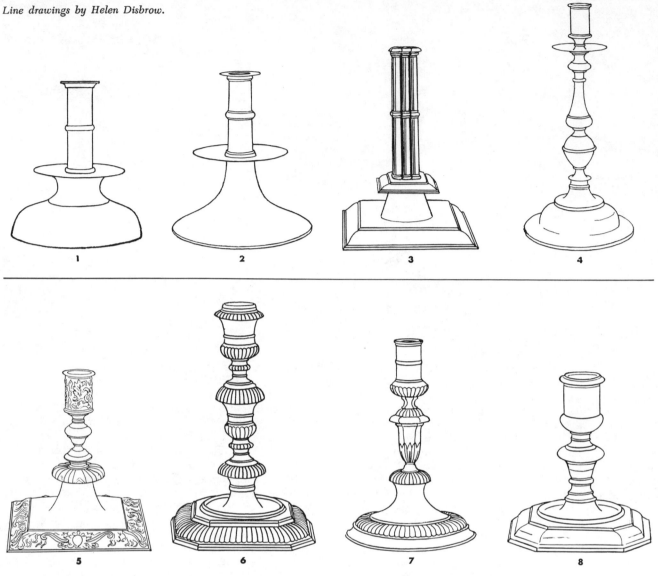

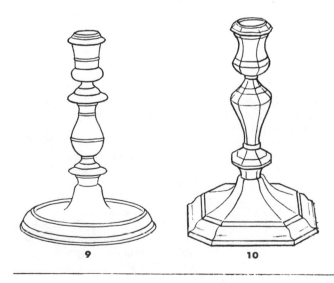

1. 1637   The earliest English form with mid-drip pan.
2. 1653   The type brought over on the *Mayflower*.
3. 1670   Cluster-column shaft such as Jeremiah Dummer made in Boston.
4. 1677   The drip pan raised to the socket.
5. 1684   The type used in silver for toilet sets but exceedingly rare in brass.
6. 1689   The earliest baluster stem.
7. 1693   Shape similar to that made by John Coney in Boston.
8. 1705   A favored shape in brass.
9. 1704   Form similar to that of candlesticks made by Nathaniel Morse in Boston c. 1720.
10. 1706   The socket is faceted like the stem and is waisted and the base has lost its saucer shape.

11. 1708 The tapered octagonal base is one
of the most elegant of the Queen Anne forms.

12. 1713 Base and socket are faceted octagons.

13. 1714 Circular base and socket;
in section, stem is square with rounded corners.

14. 1718 A provincial-city type simplified,
oblong base with cut corners: a true brass prototype.

15. 1720 A Huguenot maker brings French influence.

16. 1720 The incurved corner appears on the square base.

17. 1724 The earlier baluster shape grows taller,
with a distinct "shoulder" to the stem.

18. 1732 The base takes the flower-petal shape.

19. 1734 Base square, with rounded segments.

20. 1737 More complex base moldings with the first
appearance of the separate drip pan, or *bobèche*.

21. 1739   Shapes of base and stem become more complicated.

22. 1736   More detail on socket and stem,
and a shell motif at corners of base.

23. 1736   A well-known model.

24. 1747   Variant of the shell base.

25. 1745   Uncommon in English silver, but almost identical
to a pair made by Jacob Hurd in Boston,
now in the Metropolitan Museum of Art.

26. 1753   A model frequently found in paktong (a Chinese
alloy of nickel, zinc, and copper) as well as
in silver and brass.

27. 1750   Variant with less detail.

28. 1769   The same model with swirl in the lower part of the shaft.

29. 1757   A shell-base variant.

30. 1762   Molded-base variant.

31   32   33   34

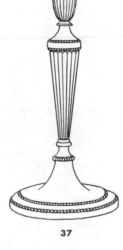

35   36   37   38

31.   1770   Another variant:
squared base has serpentine sides.

32.   1774   A touch of neoclassicism enters.

33.   1763   The classical influence in detail as well as shape.

34.   1766   The classical-column form returns,
here as a cluster column with lobed base.

35.   1760   Ionic capital on stop-fluted pillar.

36.   1786   Robert Adam's refined classic form.

37.   1782   This and No. 38 were popular in Sheffield, where
the same models were used for fused plate and solid silver.

38.   1785   A favorite in brass.
John Lynch in Baltimore used the shape in silver c. 1790.

39.   1791   The drip pan reappears
in the neoclassic development.

40.   1798   Heavier moldings foreshadow the nineteenth century.

39   40

A Chronology of English Candlesticks

Summary of Major Changes

By G. Bernard Hughes

EARLIEST glass candlesticks — made during the reign of Charles II (*1660–1685*) — represent the beginning of an independent evolution. Until 1715, stems tend to the turned baluster form, supporting a deep nozzle. From then on, balusters become more elaborate and complicated until about 1730.

From 1725 to 1745, the Silesian stem is popular. Tear drops in stems are common until 1740. Meanwhile, the first appearance of internal twisted decoration occurs about 1735; silver and mercury spirals, 1740–1760; cotton-white and colored twists, 1747–1780.

From 1755, stems begin to assume a pillarlike form. Cut stems are rare before 1740. They are frequent after 1760.

The shape of the nozzle is an indication of period. In the last quarter of the seventeenth century, nozzles are plain and deep. With the reign of Queen Anne (*1702–1714*), the plain nozzle with rolled rim appears. Early Georgian nozzles are plain, rolled, and have folded lip. Even before 1727, these nozzles begin to expand at the top into a saucerlike member. After 1770, flanges of nozzles are greatly widened and often support pendent lustre drops.

Feet of glass candlesticks are domical in form through the eighteenth century. Square pedestal bases appear about 1800; star-cut circular bases slightly later.

Note. Illustrations are, with the exceptions noted, from the collections of Miss Dora Mercer, Arthur Churchill, and the author. It has seemed best to print specific comment directly beneath the picture to which it applies.

Fig. 1 — BALUSTER TAPER STICK (small candlestick) (*c. 1715*)
Extremely simple in form with foot pressed into vertical ridges. The nozzle is long in proportion to the height of the stick, which, in common with other examples of the period, is somewhat chunky in aspect.

Fig. 2 — GEORGE I BALUSTER CANDLESTICK
Until the reign of George II, glass candlesticks followed contemporary types in metal, pottery, and wood. Those made before 1715 range from 7 to 9 inches in height, and have stems derived from the Venetian baluster design. Stems were relatively short and heavy. Bases were usually domed. The specimen pictured shows knop, air-beaded ball, and multiple collar.

Fig. 3 — GEORGE II BALUSTER TAPER STICK (*c. 1735*)
Here the features of the early type are repeated; domed, folded foot, multiple collar, and plain nozzle. The spreading flange is for the support of a tall glass shade, precursor of the all-enveloping "hurricane shade" of later years.

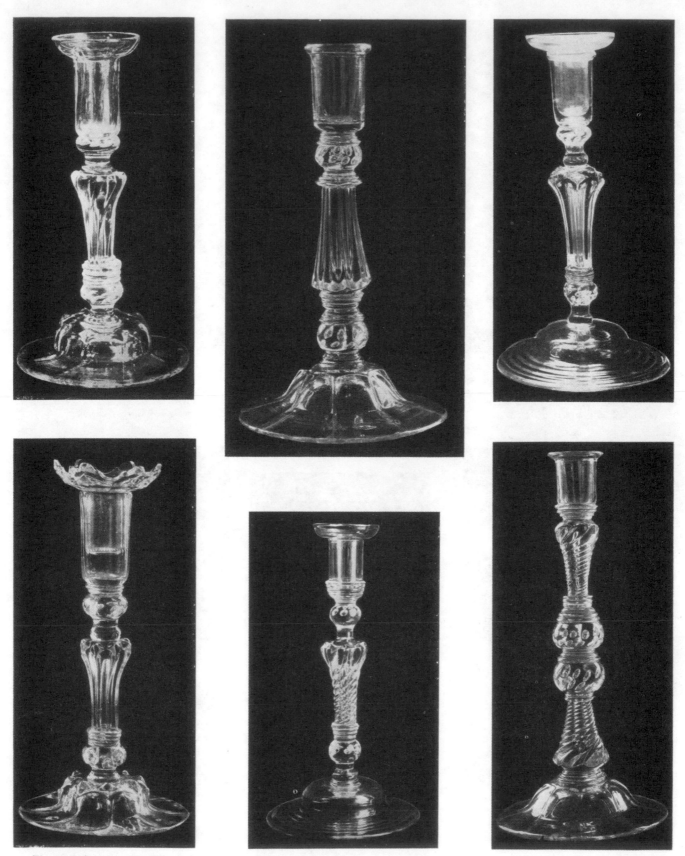

Figs. 4, 5, 6, 7, 8, and 9 — CANDLESTICKS WITH SILESIAN TYPE STEMS (*c. 1725-1745*)

The immigration of the Hanoverian dynasty brought German styles into vogue; hence the extensively used Silesian stem here illustrated. Its chief feature is a trumpet-shaped member, which may be plain, spiraled, or faceted. Knops — sometimes showing air beads — multiple collars, and sharply domed feet characterize these pieces. The candle cup of Figure 6 is removable. Figure 7 is an elaborate example with domed and ridged foot, and a removable cup, whose scalloped edge is an early manifestation of its kind. Figure 9 shows a doubled Silesian motive, two cone-shaped balusters strongly ribbed and twisted. But whatever the variations in this Silesian stem, the type is readily recognizable. Examples extend from about 1725 to 1745.

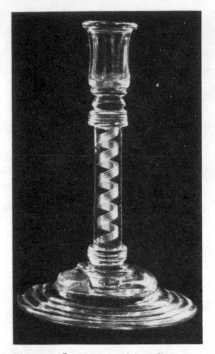

Fig. 10 — CANDLESTICK (*c. 1748*)
Spirals of cotton-white or colored enamel date from 1747 to 1780. But cotton white and colors were not mixed until after 1760.

Fig. 11 — BRISTOL GLASS CANDLE-STICK (*c. 1765*)
Produced in emulation of Battersea enamel with colored decoration of floral sprays.

Fig. 12 — CANDLESTICK (*c. 1750*)
Air-twist stem with beads, or tears, in the knops of the stem. The candle cup, with its saucerlike top, is removable for safe and easy cleaning.

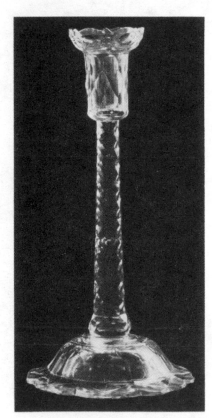

Fig. 13 — CANDLESTICK WITH COLUMNAR STEM (*c. 1770*)
The straight, slightly tapering, and severely plain stem may be a tribute to the Classical influence. The cutting is quite flat and, in the main, constitutes a diamond pattern.

Fig. 14 — CUT CANDLESTICK (*c. 1760*)
In this specimen the knops of the stem remain uncut, to the considerable advantage of the character of the piece as a whole. The scalloped rim of the candle cup follows the form of the foot.

Fig. 15 — CANDLESTICK (*c. 1780*)
In this item, the flange of the nozzle shows a slight contraction. The cutting, in general, is quite varied, and shows rectangular, sharply convex diamonds combined with passages of vertical fluting on the stem.

Fig. 16 (above) — Molded and Cut Girandoles (*early nineteenth century*)
The relative ages of these examples, from
earlier to late, are fairly well indicated by
their sequence in the illustration. The
delicately cut specimens, with square
molded plinths, in the upper row, somewhat antedate the more elaborate ones,
with circular flat feet, below. These
candlesticks clearly show how the earlier
scalloped flange of the nozzle became
greatly widened to support pendent
crystals, the latter flat, pear-shaped in
earlier forms, but afterward becoming
longer and more attenuated.
From the Delomosne collection

Fig. 17 — Glass Candlesticks
Obviously these are not arranged in
chronological order. In the upper row, the
set of four early Georgian specimens, with
wide inverted saucer-shaped foot supporting a stem with multiple collar, large air-
beaded knop and acorn, are perhaps the
most noteworthy. Except for the air-twist
knopped stem (*c. 1750*) in the centre, the
other pieces in this row are of the Silesian
type. In the second row, which shows cut
examples, the first and last somewhat
resemble the candlestick of Figure 15
(*c. 1780*). The central columnar, or "pillar," candlestick is a fine specimen of its
kind (*c. 1770*). In the third row, attention is called to the set of four superb
early Georgian specimens, with massive
baluster stems. The candlesticks of the
lower row date between 1725 and 1805.
From the J. Cecil Davis collection

101

Benjamin Gerrish, brazier

BY RICHARD H. RANDALL JR., *Assistant curator of decorative arts, Museum of Fine Arts, Boston*

THE HISTORY of iron and brass has always been the most difficult of all fields for the scholar and historian, due primarily to the dearth of signed and dated material, and also to the fact that it is usually impossible to determine where the signed material that does exist originated. It is also true that some marked pieces are of no artistic importance. When a single beautiful object in iron and brass is signed and dated, and its place of origin is known, it gives a tremendous insight into the many other examples that exist. Such is the case with the fine signed and dated candlestand illustrated in Figure 1.

When the stand came into the collections of the Museum of Fine Arts, Boston, in 1940, it was noted that it was signed in script on the base of the shaft B° GERRISH and dated on the opposite side *1736*. It is a fine tripod stand with double-curved legs, and a brass collar and plate at the base of the shaft. The shaft is square in section at the base, then twisted, and finally round for most of its length. The signature and date are engraved amid foliage, above and below the twist, and on a third side is engraved a small winged dragon. A turned brass ornament slides on the stem and rests where the squared section begins, hiding some of the engraving. The straight iron candle arm is fitted with the usual spring retainer, and screwed to its ends are two Queen Anne-style brass candle sockets whose wide drip pans have flaring rims. The finial has been renewed at some date.

A second candlestand signed by the same maker (Fig. 2) is in the Portsmouth, Rhode Island, room of the American Wing of the Metropolitan Museum. It was

bought in Boston in 1920. This example is nearly identical in form, but it lacks its finial, which originally fitted over the point of the shaft. This was probably also the case with the Boston example, which has since been threaded. The Metropolitan's stand is not so richly engraved on the shaft, and it bears only the name GERRISH in script and no date.

The name B. Gerrish is a perplexing one for the researcher, as it was relatively common in the mid-eighteenth century. Gerrishes can be found from Canada to New York, and many of them have B as their first initial. For example, a Benjamin Gerrish was a great merchant of Salem, the town treasurer, and his son bore the name also. Another was a Boston merchant who was collector of the port in 1702, and still another was a "joyner" of Newburyport. This type of candlestand has often been called "New York" because of its form, so it was suggested that its maker must have worked in that city. But a list of references to braziers in Boston archives made many years ago by Ledlie I. Laughlin when he was doing research on pewterers led to the rediscovery of this particular B. Gerrish.

Laughlin's note referred to a set of court records, where in an entry for 1746 from the Superior Court of Judicature of Suffolk County there appears a "Benjamin Gerrish of Boston afore'sd Brazier" (a judgment was rendered against him for £37.8.6 in favor of the Boston merchant, Thomas Greene). Through the mention of his wife, a series of other documents was identified as referring to the same Benjamin Gerrish and his life in part reconstructed.

He was born in Boston about 1686, the grandson of William Gerrish Jr. of Newbury. The earliest reference to him is a court entry of 1714 which calls him "Benj. Gerrish of Cambridge gunsmith and of Boston gunsmith." In 1716 he married Martha Foxcroft of Cambridge and with her appears again as "gunsmith" in litigation over land in Framingham. In two deeds of 1730 he is listed with his wife, once as gunsmith and once as shopkeeper, and the latter appellation is repeated on a deed of 1733. The candlestand of 1736 marks the next recorded date in his career. In that same year his wife died. He was remarried in 1738 to Abigail Bunker of Charlestown, whose name appears with his on a number of deeds, and in 1748 he is listed as an innholder in Charlestown. The inn, called the Ship Tavern, perhaps belonged to Abigail; it was sold in 1748. Abigail died in 1749, aged seventy, and Gerrish died on June 23, 1750, in his sixty-fourth year. There are a few Boston references, such as an entry in the records of the First Church, which may refer to the gunsmith-brazier or to another of the Boston Benjamin Gerrishes.

Like so many artisans of his period, Gerrish seems to have altered his profession from time to time as the occasion suited and as times demanded. The career of gunsmith, on which he first embarked, would account for his fine handling of both iron and brass as well as for his familiarity with engraving. What he did as a shopkeeper we have no way of knowing, but when the gun business was slow he apparently styled himself a brazier and made such objects as the candlestands. His final profession of innholder was probably the result of his marriage to Abigail Bunker. Unfortunately no estate inventory or will exists to tell us his success from his several endeavors.

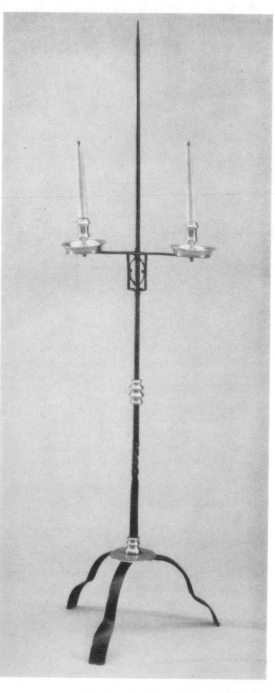

Fig. 2. Candlestand signed GERRISH.
Metropolitan Museum of Art,
Rogers fund.

American Tin Candle Sconces

Except as noted, illustrated from the collection of
Stephen Van Rensselaer

Fig. 1 (*left*) — EARLY FORMS OF AMERICAN TIN SCONCES
It will be observed that in most of these pieces the tradition of the bracket arm, such as we find in mirror sconces of the seventeenth and eighteenth centuries, is maintained. The sconce whose reflector is covered with tin leaves may have some association with the Liberty Tree lanterns of 1766 (see ANTIQUES for May 1934). The central sconce, 23 ½ inches in diameter, is said to hail from an old tavern in Massachusetts

Fig. 2 (*below*) — SCONCES OF INTERMEDIATE PERIOD
The first exhibits a punchwork design strongly suggestive of Pennsylvania workmanship. Two items are equipped with what appear to be pewter disc reflectors under glass. Two others exemplify mosaic mirror reflectors. The sconce with oval reflector and the two with concave corners suggest late eighteenth-century forms

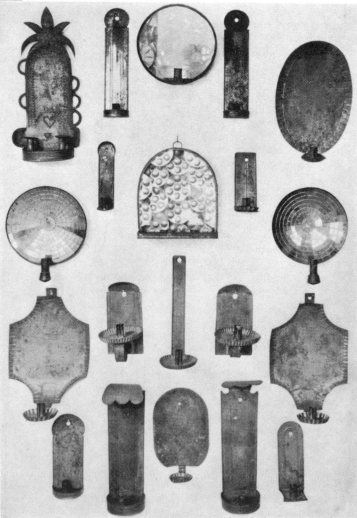

WHOSO would determine the age of the old-time American tin candle sconces that from time to time turn up in shops, or attics, or in those favorite places of storage, church belfries, may do his own guessing. Seldom will such a sconce reveal any stylistic feature indicative of specific period or a particular locality of manufacture. Here and there, some fanciful bit of elaboration may betray the hand of a Pennsylvania craftsman. Occasionally the delicate oval form of a reflector will suggest the medallion shapes popular during the Hepplewhite-Sheraton era. Again, to the probable period of the type most frequently encountered we find a clue in the handsome silver item, here pictured, one of a set of four recently sold at Sotheby's, London. The mark on these silver sconces proves that they were made in the year 1810. Since such items in silver would normally represent the latest vogue, it seems reasonable to assume that humble analogues in tin may be of no earlier date. If this reasoning is sound, we are justified in tentatively ascribing to the nineteenth century those tin sconces that exhibit a tall, rectangular reflector with rounded top, and, at the base, a projecting gallery serving as grease cup and socket support. Oval forms of reflector, as noted above, are likely to be of the last decade of the 1700's. Thus by a process of elimination we reach the conclusion that the one remaining major type of sconce, that equipped with circular reflectors, is the oldest of the three. The surmise finds further justification in the fact that the round reflectors, with their frequent elaboration of bosses and sunburst channelings, imply a greater expenditure of hand labor than is in evidence on sconces of either oval or rectangular form.

How old are the oldest of the surviving American tin sconces is beyond anyone's telling. The utilization of such devices was no doubt more usual in places of public assembly, such as churches, town halls, and ballrooms, where a diffused light was essential, than in domestic interiors, where illumination had to be concentrated for reading or sewing. When or whence came those elaborate sconces whose reflecting powers were intensified by mosaic mirrors or by faceted metal discs protected by a pane of glass, we know not. They were a luxury

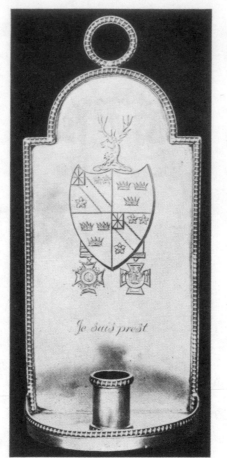

Fig. 3 (right) — SILVER SCONCE (*London, 1810*)
One of four recently sold in London. Exceptionally rare items and important as a clue to the style of the day.
By courtesy of Sotheby's, London

Fig. 4 (below) — SCONCES OF VARYING TYPES AND PERIODS
The three of the upper row constitute an exceptionally handsome and well-proportioned garniture. Note that the sconce with circular reflector is equipped with a bracket-arm candleholder. The next to the last example in the bottom row is supplied with a matchbox, indicative of relatively late date

item for fine establishments and today are reckoned among major rarities in the category of early lighting fixtures.

Though our knowledge of their source and date is necessarily limited and our basis for their classification must remain as vaguely general as that here outlined, tin sconces are eminently collectible. While rather closely restricted in general form, they rejoice the eye with an infinite variety of detail which, now and again, expands into quite delightful fantasy. ANTIQUES knows of no more comprehensive collection of these articles than that assembled over a long period of years by Stephen Van Rensselaer of Peterboro, New Hampshire. As pictured here, Mr. Van Rensselaer's specimens speak adequately for themselves. Where comment on individual items seems pertinent, it is associated directly with the illustrations.

Fig. 5 (below) — SCONCES APPARENTLY OF THIRD PERIOD
The middle item in the upper row is arranged for burning lard oil and is obviously of the nineteenth century. Except perhaps for the second sconce of the upper row, all the sconces in this illustration may well have been made in the 1800's. Two in the lower row are painted in colors on a black ground with a design suggesting the early nineteenth century. The remarkable seven-candle fixture between them is one of a pair said to have been fitted around the columns of a church interior

Eighteenth-Century Lighting Devices:
Wall Fittings and Candlesticks

By R. W. Symonds

IN MY two previous articles on room lighting in the seventeenth and eighteenth centuries, I discussed the chandelier and the lantern — fittings that were suspended from the ceiling. This article is concerned with fittings that were affixed to the wall, and with candlesticks and candelabra, the last named a form of candlestick with two or more branches.

Wall fittings may roughly be divided into two categories: sconces and wall lanterns. Sconces were made in silver, base metals, glass, and wood.

Silver sconces were fashionable from the reign of Charles II to that of George I; but since they were naturally costly their use was confined to the royal palaces and the houses of the wealthy. They are mentioned in inventories as far back as Tudor times, but unfortunately no example of that early period has survived. During the civil war of 1642–1646 many were melted, particularly those made in the reigns of James I and Charles I. Unfortunately the same fate must have overtaken a large proportion of those belonging to later periods.

Only this can account for the scarcity of silver sconces today, as there is plenty of contemporary evidence that, in the eighteenth century, numbers of them belonged to the royal household and the families of the nobility. For instance, it is recorded

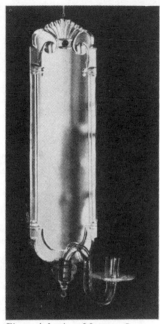

Fig. 1 (above) — MIRROR SCONCE (*early eighteenth century*)
The design is cut in the glass itself.
From the collection of Percival D. Griffiths

Fig. 2 (right) — MIRROR SCONCE (*Queen Anne*)
Exceptionally tall; mirror lightly framed in metal. Intended for the corner of a room

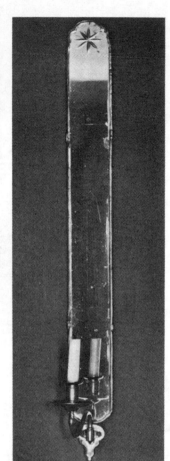

that, in 1795, no fewer than seventy-nine sconces were sent from Saint James' Palace to the court goldsmiths for repairs. Again, in 1755, ten sconces were sent from Kensington Palace to one Fox, a goldsmith, to be melted. The present-day rarity of the silver sconce is therefore due, not to the fact that few were made, but to the habit of melting old plate in order to make silver of new design in accordance with the prevailing fashion. Had it not been for this practice, which continued to the reign of Queen Victoria, we should today possess many beautiful seventeenth- and eighteenth-century examples of both silver and silver gilt.

Sconces of brass and tin, such as were used by the less well-to-do classes, have survived, but in still fewer numbers. Because they were considered of no intrinsic value, they were thrown away when rendered useless by the introduction of gas in the nineteenth century.

Glass sconces with mirror backs were in vogue in the late seventeenth and early eighteenth centuries. They had shaped backs often decorated with an engraved or cut design, with branches, sometimes of glass and sometimes of metal (*Figs. 1 and 2*).

The following newspaper advertisement concerning mirror sconces appeared in the *General Remark on Trade* in the year 1707.

Christopher Thornton, living in Peter Street in the Mint, Southwark, at the sign of the Looking Glass, hath several sorts of goods now by him, to dispose of at Reasonable Rates, Viz Looking Glasses, Sconces, Chimney

Fig. 3 — MIRROR SCONCES (*early eighteenth century*)
Frames of walnut veneer surmounted by hoods. Many of this type have survived.
From the collection of Percival D. Griffiths

Fig. 4 — NEEDLEWORK SCONCE (c. 1720)
A very rare example whose veneered walnut frame encloses a needlework panel

Fig. 5 — NEEDLEWORK SCONCES (1720–1730)
Gilt gesso frames with needlework panels. Rare.
Figures 4 and 5 from the collection of Percival D. Griffiths

Pieces and Pannel Glasses for New ones and Glasses for Coaches and Chariots are wrought by him.

Lustre sconces with festoons of cut-glass drops also were made in the eighteenth century to match the glass chandeliers (ANTIQUES for August 1932). Unfortunately few specimens now exist.

The earliest type of wooden sconce, which dates from the reign of Charles II, would appear to be that with a walnut veneered frame surrounding a mirror (*Fig. 3*). Rarer examples had needlework pictures substituted for the mirror (*Fig. 4*).

A few sconces with gilt gesso frames also surrounding needlework, similar to the rare pair illustrated (*Fig. 5*), have survived from the early eighteenth century. Sconces of carved wood and gilt of a type similiar to that shown in Figures 6 and 8 were most probably made in considerable numbers; but few genuine examples, especially of English provenance, are in existence. To judge from the popularity of lacquer in the first half of the eighteenth century, considerable numbers of sconces in Japan lac must have been made, as, indeed, is shown by the following advertisement from *The Weekly Journal*, March 26, 1714. But none, so far as I know, has survived.

On Thursday the 31st of this instant March 1714. At the Sign of the Angel the Corner of Poppins

Fig. 6 — CARVED AND GILDED SCONCE (*early eighteenth century*)
Coronet and escutcheon with crest of the Earl of Radnor

Fig. 7 — CARVED AND GILDED GIRANDOLE (*c. 1750*)
One of a pair. Suggesting inspiration from the delightful Chinese fantasies of Pillement.
From the collection of Francis P. Garvan

Fig. 8 — CARVED AND GILDED SCONCE (*c. 1700*)
Surmounted by a crane, probably the crest of the family for whom the work was executed

Fig. 9 — FOUR METAL SCONCES (*c. 1750*)   *From the Pennsylvania Museum*

Alley, in Fleet Street; will be Sold by Auction, the Goods of James Bradford, Japanner, he going to leave off Shop-keeping: consisting of Cabinets, Desks, and Bookcases, Chests-of-Drawers, Union Suits, Tables, Peer-Glasses, Sconces, Screen-Frames, Glasses, Dressing Glasses, with all sorts of Japanned Goods; the Goods to be viewed Monday.

In the mid-eighteenth century, wall lights known as girandoles came into fashion. They were of rococo design in the French style, often combining Chinese motives such as mandarins and temples. Many of these girandoles are shown in contemporary books by such designers as Chippendale, Ince and Mayhew, and Lock and Copeland. Girandoles were of carved wood gilt (*Fig. 7*), and were used in rooms with walls that were either papered or hung with damask — treatments that, by the mid-eighteenth century, had superseded the wooden wainscot, which, in the first half of the century, was almost universally employed in the better class of houses. Wall lights of this type continued in fashion up to the end of the century. The design of these later examples followed the simple classical style that belonged to this period; the ornament, however, on those of inferior quality was often in composition and not in wood. Girandoles are rare today, especially those of the earlier type—a fact not surprising when their fragile construction is considered.

Sconces of lacquered brass were also popular in this period; these were usually in the French rococo style similar to those of Figure 9.

The only kind of eighteenth-century sconce that appears to have survived in any quantity is that framed in walnut with mirror back, similar to the examples illustrated (*Fig. 3*). In the first forty years of the century this design of sconce — and perhaps also examples with Japan lac frames — must have been largely used in the unpretentious houses of the less well-to-do classes. Glass sconces must also have been used in considerable numbers; that so few have survived may be attributed to the brittle nature of the material of which they were made.

In the first half of the eighteenth century, mirrors both large and small nearly always had a pair of metal candle branches affixed to them (*Fig. 10*). In the majority of cases these branches are now missing, but that they

Fig. 10 (above) — MIRROR WITH CANDLE BRACKETS (*c. 1730*)
A noble walnut and gilt frame. The lacquered brass candle branches are original.
From the collection of Percival D. Griffiths

Fig. 11 (left) — WALNUT AND GILT SIDE LANTERN (*c. 1725*)
Front and sides of clear glass. Mirror back

Fig. 12 (right) — MAHOGANY SIDE LANTERN (*c. 1750*)
A noteworthy example, of graceful design and outstanding quality of workmanship

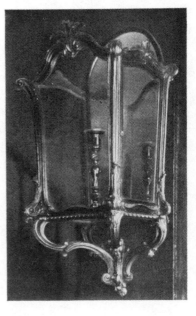

Metal candlesticks, in the late seventeenth and the eighteenth centuries, were low; but after about 1750 they increased in height and became more massive in design. This is particularly true of those of silver and Sheffield plate.

The difference between the use of the chandelier and the wall sconce and that of the candlestick is that the two first named were used for the general illumination of a room, whereas the candlestick was employed for various definite purposes, because it could be moved. Furniture was designed with contrivances for candlesticks. The bureau-bookcase had slides that pulled out from beneath the doors of the bookcase; card tables were designed with a space at each corner; and reading stands had movable brackets that pulled out from below the book rest. In the late seventeenth and early eighteenth centuries, the dressing table was flanked by a pair of tall candle stands (*Fig. 13*).

Many newspaper advertisements of this period mention tables and stands for sale. These candle stands and their attendant candlesticks were of walnut, mahogany, and gilt wood; many must also have been of Japan lac. Chippendale illustrated a number of candle stands in his *Gentleman's Director*. Some of his designs are, however, so overornamented that it is difficult to believe they could have been satisfactorily executed in wood. A fine pair of stands of this school of design is shown (*Fig. 14*).

Candelabra dating prior to 1735 are exceedingly rare, but they became decidedly popular in the last quarter of the eighteenth century. They were made in silver and in Sheffield plate. Only a few examples have survived in base metal, presumably because this kind of candle fitting, which burned more than one candle, was too extravagant for the poorer classes.

The invention of the Argand lamp, in 1784, which was referred to in my first article, caused the candlestick and candelabrum gradually to go out of use. By the nineteenth century, when gas had become universally employed in the towns, the candle was relegated to the use of houses in the country districts where gas illumination was not obtainable. By this time oil lamps also had vastly improved and were thus a contributing factor to the cessation of the use of candlesticks and candelabra.

once existed is clearly shown by the design of the frame, which provides spaces for the back plates to hold the branches. The prevalence of this custom of making a mirror — primarily intended to be used as a looking-glass — into a sconce by fitting metal candle branches to its frame shows unquestionably that wall lighting was a most usual method of illuminating a room in the first half of the eighteenth century. A proof of this is the survival of many thousands of mirrors that originally had candle branches attached to them.

If mirrors were so largely employed in this fashion, how much more common must the use of the actual sconces have been. That they were undoubtedly made in tens of thousands is proved by the innumerable advertisements inserted in contemporary newspapers; but today only a fraction remains. The destruction of the mirror has naturally been much less, because, when it ceased to be used as a sconce, it still retained its decorative value and its usefulness as a looking-glass.

Wall lanterns, or "side Lanthorns," as they once used to be termed, were employed to light halls, passages, and staircases. Figure 11 illustrates a type of which many have survived, and dates from the period 1725–1735. A very fine mahogany example of elaborate design is illustrated in Figure 12. A wall lantern of as elaborate a design as this, however, is today of the greatest rarity. Presumably, therefore, but few were made. Lanterns of tin, painted or japanned, must have been in common use; but, unfortunately, they have practically disappeared.

Candlesticks were used in ever-increasing numbers from the reign of Charles II to the end of the eighteenth century. Examples of Elizabethan and Jacobean date are of such rarity that they can be counted on the fingers of one hand. Candlesticks were made in silver and base metals such as brass and pewter. They were also made in wood and glass, in pottery such as delft, and, later in the eighteenth century, in porcelain such as Chelsea.

English brass chandelier installed in St. Michael's Church,
Marblehead, Massachusetts, in 1732.
Photograph by Richard Merrill.

English brass chandeliers in American churches

BY CHARLES OMAN

THE BRASS CHANDELIERS which date from the colonial period and still adorn a few of the older American churches have never been treated as a group, though they are mentioned proudly in church guides and histories; and many of the legends which have grown up about them have remained unchecked. When I visited the United States in 1963 I found myself able to add a footnote to the study of the colonial background since I had published a pioneering study on English brass chandeliers in 1937 (*Archaeological Journal*, Vol. XCIII, pp. 263-283). Valuable additional material has since been collected by other English students, particularly Robert Sherlock, but it has not been necessary to alter substantially the opinions I expressed thirty years ago.

I should make it clear that I am dealing here only with those chandeliers of English origin which reached America soon after they were made. I shall not include

examples in such institutions as Colonial Williamsburg or the Winterthur Museum; these have all been imported within recent years. I shall also exclude examples which are not of English origin, such as the magnificent Dutch one in the Touro Synagogue at Newport, Rhode Island.

During the Middle Ages, England did not produce the ingredients necessary for making brass, but a brass industry grew up that depended on imported metal and scrap. The main center was London, though brass founding must have been carried on in most of the larger cities. In the reign of Elizabeth I the base-metal resources of England began to be explored with the aid of German experts. Many of the early enterprises failed but in 1702 the Bristol Brass Wire Company began the manufacture of brass at the Baptist Mills, Bristol. Calamine was available from mines in the Mendip Hills a few miles away and copper could be brought without much difficulty from Cornwall. Nearby collieries provided fuel for smelting and there was plenty of water power. Though Bristol became the main center in the West Country for the

Fig. 1. Christ (or Old North) Church, Boston; one of a pair; probably made by John Bailey, Bridgwater, Somersetshire (attribution based on similarity of candle sockets to those of Fig. 2); acquired 1724, installed 1725. *Photograph by Richard Merrill.*

Fig. 2. Stogursey, Somerset, England; made by John Bailey, Bridgwater; dated 1732.

Fig. 3. St. Michael's Church, Marblehead; probably made by Francis Billo (d. 1754), St. Stephen's Parish, Bristol (attribution based on similarity of branches to those of Fig. 4); installed 1732. See the frontispiece for a detail view. *Photograph by Richard Merrill.*

Fig. 4. Dunster (near Bristol), Somerset, England; made by Francis Billo; dated 1740.

brass industry, Bridgwater was only slightly less favored by nature, and Exeter should also be noted.

That the chandeliers surviving in America are predominantly of West Country origin is a reminder of the importance of the trade between the Bristol Channel ports and the Colonies. The main center for the manufacture of chandeliers was London, where it was much easier to tap the market for luxury goods. Chandeliers were always costly and they were never made in England on as extensive a scale as in Holland. During the eighteenth century important town churches got them but they were rare in country ones. They were to be found in major public buildings but only in the very largest of private houses.

The two chandeliers in Christ Church, Salem Street, Boston, are the earliest surviving ones in America (Fig. 1). Mary Kent Davey Babcock in her interesting history, *Christ Church, Salem Street, Boston: The Old North Church of Paul Revere Fame* (1947), killed a legend that they had been captured from a French ship in 1758 by a Captain Grushea. She showed that the chandeliers (called both "branches" and "sconces") had appeared in the list of "utencils" handed over by the wardens to their successors in 1735 and that the accounts prove they had arrived in the summer of 1724, though they were not hung until January 6, 1725.

Since they are not inscribed, any attribution must be based on comparison with others whose makers are known. Every chandelier was made up of a series of castings from models of wood or metal. If some of the parts of two chandeliers are cast from the same models they can generally be attributed to the same foundry. The chandeliers need not be identical in every respect since founders kept a stock of models which they did not invariably combine in the same manner. I have not been able to identify conclusively the maker of the Boston chandeliers but the candle sockets look very like those used by John Bailey of Bridgwater on the chandelier, dated 1732, at Stogursey in Somerset (Fig. 2). He had a good business and a considerable stock of models.

Though other Boston churches must once have had chandeliers, the nearest surviving one of this period is now a few miles up the coast at Marblehead, in St. Michael's Church (Fig. 3). Installed in 1732, it was the gift of John Eldridge, collector of the Port of Bristol, who had acquired it from Francis Billo of Bristol. Billo was the maker of the chandelier (Fig. 4), dated 1740, at Dunster, about fifty miles west of Bristol, and the branches of the Dunster and Marblehead chandeliers were clearly cast from the same models. While the records show that the examples at Christ Church, Boston, were originally hung from ropes, that at Marblehead has a very handsome wrought-iron suspension rod. It is closely similar to the one supporting the Stogursey chandelier and both may be the work of William Edney, the leading Bristol smith at the time.

Turning southward, the next examples to be found are in Trinity Church, Newport. There are three but only one

(Fig. 5) bears an inscription—*Thomas Drew, Exon, 1728.* Their design is much less sophisticated than that of those already discussed and it is suggested that Drew used a set of secondhand models. (He was undoubtedly the Thomas Drew, bell founder, who is recorded as having paid one penny in the Exeter Poor Rate in 1732.) The general effect is that of London-made chandeliers of the end of the seventeenth century.

The two remaining chandeliers represent the new pattern introduced in London shortly after 1740, in which the central stem is vase shape instead of being composed of a series of globes. (The old design continued to be used in the West Country for another thirty years.)

The chandelier at Christ Church, Philadelphia (Fig. 6), is an early example of the new design as it was brought from London in 1740 by a Captain Seymour from whom the church bought it for £56. Though the West Country founders signed much of their work, the Londoners rarely did. I have not succeeded in identifying the maker of the Philadelphia example.

The chandelier of St. Michael's Church, Charleston, South Carolina (Fig. 7), was obtained in 1804 from G. Penton of London for £102/18/10. As I have been unable to trace a brass founder of this name it is likely that Penton was merely an intermediary. While the high price suggests that the chandelier was not secondhand, it must have been cast from models which had been long in stock, perhaps as long as half a century. By the end of the eighteenth century brass chandeliers had become less fashionable in England so that manufacturers were less willing to incur the expense of making fresh models for new designs.

The brass chandelier was the ideal solution for lighting the sort of church which followed the architectural tradition of Sir Christopher Wren, and many colonial churches must have had examples. Now that the subject has been opened, I hope that others may be found, even if they survive only in illustrations or in church records.

I should like to record my thanks to the following persons who have afforded me generous help in providing photographs: Mrs. Y. H. Buhler and the Reverend Howard Kellett of Boston, Beatrice Ravenel of Charleston, the Reverend David W. Norton Jr. of Marblehead, and the Reverend Lockett Ford Ballard of Newport.

Fig. 5.   Trinity Church, Newport; one of three, of which this one is inscribed *Thomas Drew, Exon, 1728.*

Fig. 6.   Christ Church, Philadelphia; probably made by a London brass founder; imported in 1740. *Photograph by Jules Schick.*

Fig. 7.   St. Michael's Church, Charleston, South Carolina; probably made by a London brass founder; bought from G. Penton of London in 1804. *Photograph by Louis Schwartz.*

Chandeliers in Federal New England

BY JANE C. GIFFEN, *Curator of ceramics and textiles, Old Sturbridge Village*

THE REVEREND William Bentley of Salem commented, in 1801, on visiting the church at Exeter, New Hampshire: "I observed a Chandelier in this old building which is a very rare thing in our Churches." Reading in Bentley's diary, one is struck by the way he changed the time of his afternoon services from two o'clock in the winter to a later hour in the summer and then back to an early hour in the wintertime in order to take advantage of the natural length of daylight. In 1792, he described preaching at Newbury and staying to the last prayer of the service: "The first time I ever spoke in a Meeting House by Candlelight." From this and other sources, it seems clear that the majority of the early New England churches were not fitted with any sort of lighting devices at the end of the eighteenth century and that a special effort was made to conduct services during the hours of daylight.

Even so, at exactly this time the use of chandeliers in churches and other public buildings was increasing. The number of surviving chandeliers from New England churches which were presented during the early Federal period is remarkable. Three well-known and well-published brass chandeliers had been given to New England churches earlier in the eighteenth century: those in Trinity Church at Newport, Old North in Boston, and St. Michael's in

Fig. 1. Waterford-type glass chandelier given to the First Baptist Meeting House in memory of Nicholas Brown by his daughter Hope and lighted for the first time on the occasion of her marriage to Thomas Poynton Ives in 1792. *First Baptist Church in America, Providence, Rhode Island; photograph by Paul Darling.*

Fig. 2. First Baptist Meeting House, Providence. Undated stereograph, presumably fourth quarter of the nineteenth century, showing the Hope Brown chandelier in use with at least three additional chandeliers as well as sconces and pulpit lights. During the 1957-1958 restoration of the meetinghouse, the hurricane shades were not thought to be original to the Hope Brown chandelier and were removed. *Society for the Preservation of New England Antiquities.*

Fig. 3. This elaborate glass chandelier has been reassembled from two that were presented during the 1790's by Lady Selina Huntington to the Prospect Street Church in Newburyport, Massachusetts. Of non-lead glass, the two are thought to have been made in Bohemia. *Henry Francis du Pont Winterthur Museum.*

Marblehead (ANTIQUES, August 1966, p. 192). A survey of the early nineteenth-century examples shows a change of preference from brass to glass and the installation of chandeliers primarily in large churches in growing urban centers.

In 1792, Hope Brown presented to the First Baptist Meeting House at Providence a handsome Waterford-type glass chandelier (Figs. 1, 2), in memory of her father, Nicholas Brown. It was first lighted on the occasion of her wedding to Thomas Poynton Ives in 1792. A pair of similarly spectacular chandeliers was presented about the same time to the Prospect Street Church in Newburyport by the wealthy English patroness Lady Selina Huntington (Fig. 3). It was she who had contributed to the education of the Reverend Charles W. Milton. Born in London in 1767, he preached at Newburyport in the First Presbyterian Church in 1791 and the following year organized a religious society. On May 30, 1793, he organized a new church, known then as the Independent Calvinistic Church of Newburyport, which was incorporated on February 22, 1794, as the fourth religious society in Newburyport. On March 9, 1796, land and a meetinghouse on Prospect Street were conveyed to the proprietors of the society, and

Fig. 4. Central chandelier in the United Church on the Green in New Haven, Connecticut. When the church was completed in 1815, two slightly smaller but very similar chandeliers were also installed. They were subsequently removed and in 1867 sold: one to the Episcopal Church in Durham, the other to the Episcopal Church in Woodbury. The large chandelier was lighted by gas from c.1850 until 1957, when it was electrified. *Photograph by Jack Stock Studio.*

Fig. 5. Purchased in New York in 1826 by a committee of ten members, this chandelier was given by them to the First Parish Church in Portland, Maine, where it remains. *Photograph by Mason Philip Smith.*

it seems likely that Lady Huntington's gift was made shortly thereafter.

Another elaborate glass chandelier was given in 1802 by Mrs. Catherine Sweetster at the wish of her husband, John, to the Old South Church in Boston. It had three tiers with hurricane shades, swags and drops in great variety, and a handsome glass pineapple above. It was described by William Bentley in 1803: "While in Boston . . . the rich chandelier of the Old South, lately given to them by Mrs. Switcher, is the best I have ever seen. It cost 800 dollars. I saw it then for the first time." Although the chandelier survived the great Boston fire of 1872, it fell on December 23, 1887. Fragments and early photographs showing it in place are still displayed in the Old South Church.

Numerous newspaper advertisements of the last decade of the eighteenth century and the first quarter of the nine- teenth indicate that glass chandeliers were available to those who could afford them. For example, on November 16, 1799, the *Columbian Centinel and Massachusetts Federalist* in Boston carried this notice:

Richard Salter, Jr./No. 4 Court Street/Has just received per the Minerva & Merchant, from London . . . direct from the Manufactories . . . Glass China Composition and Frosted Wares . . . viz . . . Chandeliers, with 6, 12, and 14 lights, elegantly adorned with rich paste drops; Girandols with two and 3 lights.

Besides those mentioned, enough examples still exist in other New England churches dedicated during the early nineteenth century to indicate that glass chandeliers were popular (Figs. 4, 5) and that at least one glass-and-brass example was used (Fig. 6). A much smaller number of tin or wood-and-tin chandeliers have survived in country churches. Those with well-documented New England his- tories are few indeed. The examples illustrated here are

Fig. 6. Brass-and-glass chandelier presented to the Princeton, Massachusetts, Church in 1832 by John Lane Boylston, and believed to have been used earlier in the Maverick Church in East Boston. This chandelier has been considerably restored. *Courtesy of the Princeton Congregational Church; photograph by Alan Brzys.*

undated and thus far undocumented as to maker, yet they are among the few known to have been in use in specific churches apparently since they were built (Figs. 7, 8, 9, 10).

During the same period, chandeliers were used almost as a matter of course in theaters. A letter to Charles Bulfinch from Josiah Taylor in August 1793 states that the Assembly Room of the Boston Theatre on Federal Street would be lighted by three glass chandeliers, four large girandoles with four arms each, ten single girandoles, and twenty tin hanging candlesticks. The girandoles had been made especially for the new theater by Robert Cribb, a carver and gilder in London. On one occasion, lighting the theater for the entire evening cost $31.00 and surviving bills show that there were consumed twenty-three pounds of spermaceti candles, thirty-three pounds of tallow candles, and fifteen pounds of hog lard. Both chandeliers and

girandoles were lost in the disastrous fire suffered by the theater in 1798, and no illustrations of them are known.

The use of chandeliers in public buildings is only slightly documented. In January 1783, Judge William Pyncheon of Salem noted in his *Diary*: "The glass chandelier for the Assembly Room comes from Boston." Fifteen years later, William Bentley visited the Assembly Room at Amherst and commented on illumination "by Chandeliers." The bills and papers for the 1824 Lincoln County Courthouse in Wiscasset, Maine, include sketches for a chandelier, presumably of wood and metal with glass candle sockets, apparently manufactured or sold by Proctor & Palmer of Boston. It was described in a letter of 1824:

I enclose you a sketch of a chandelier . . . it is very handsome. The price, thirty-nine dollars, is the lowest it can be bot for. Our courthouse is lighted with candles. Park Street meetinghouse has lamps suspended on the sides of the gallery

117

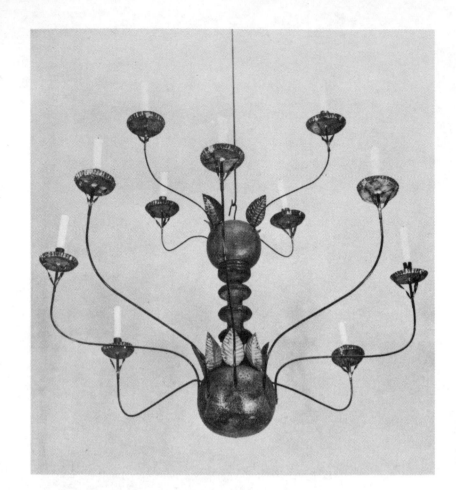

Fig. 7. Tin-and-wood chandelier from the Bunganuck Baptist Church, Brunswick, Maine. An airy design supporting ten lights with faceted metal leaves to increase the amount of reflected light. *Old Sturbridge Village.*

Fig. 8. One of a pair of very simple four-light tin chandeliers used in the church in Mason, New Hampshire. Basically a cone to which four wire arms and four reflectors are soldered, these are nearly identical to a slightly smaller pair presumably by the same maker in the Baptist Church that was built in 1827 in the part of Mason originally known as Mason Village and in 1872 set off as Greenville.

Fig. 9. A simple tin chandelier, possibly of local origin, found recently in the Hancock, New Hampshire, Congregational Church. Made of easily formed elements with minimal decoration, the chandelier supports six candles. *Privately owned; photograph by Bill Finney.*

Fig. 10. An elaboration of the fairly common design exemplified in Fig. 9 —cylindrical shaft, flat arms, and ridged cups—this three-tiered chandelier has been greatly embellished by the addition of numerous coils of crimped metal. This attempt to multiply reflecting surfaces provides a highly decorative quality even when the candles are not lighted. The chandelier originally hung in St. Matthew's Episcopal Church in East Plymouth, Connecticut, built in 1792. It now hangs in the Representatives Chamber of the Hartford State House. *Photograph by courtesy of the Connecticut Historical Society.*

Fig. 11. Tin chandelier of a very common type thought to have been used, with two others, in a Keene, New Hampshire, tavern during the early nineteenth century. *Smithsonian Institution.*

Fig. 12. This brilliantly faceted glass chandelier is one of two presented to the East India Marine Society by Captain Benjamin Carpenter in 1804. *Peabody Museum of Salem.*

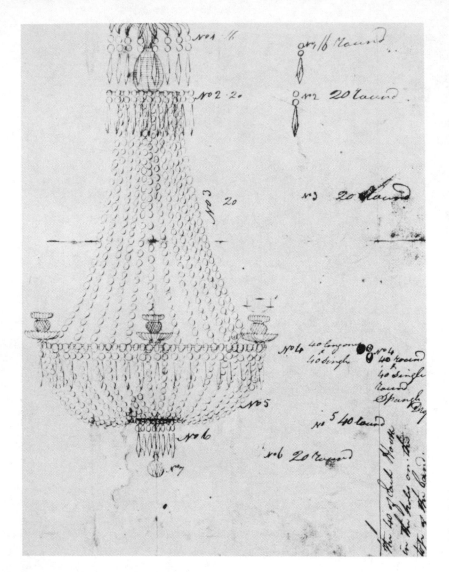

Fig. 13. Design for a four-socket glass chandelier which was made for the parlor of the Sullivan Dorr House, 109 Benefit Street, Providence, Rhode Island, c. 1810. The chandelier was modified for gas illumination by 1877 and removed from the room by 1884.

which furnish, I think, a better light than the old style chandelier. I have not been able to find any low priced chandeliers after making very particular inquiries. . . .

An important comment, this underlines the fact that chandeliers were, even at the end of the first quarter of the nineteenth century, an expensive luxury, as were the lights they bore.

Many early New England museums and special exhibitions were open in the evening and their advertisements make it clear that the large public rooms were quite brilliantly lighted on these occasions. The Portsmouth Museum assembled on Demerara Street by Nicholas Rousselet in January 1800 was graced by a "pair of Crystal Chandeliers" which had cost sixty dollars. The East India Marine Society in Salem received two crystal chandeliers from Captain Benjamin Carpenter in 1804 and they still hang in the same place in which they were hung for the dedication of the New Marine Hall in 1825 (Fig. 12).

At the same time, some New Englanders were certainly purchasing chandeliers and other elaborate lighting devices for their homes. These were included more and more frequently in inventory listings in the years after 1800. For example, the Little Harbor, New Hampshire, estate of Martha Wentworth (widow of the governor Benning

Wentworth) and of Michael Wentworth (Martha's second husband) included in 1806 "one glass chandelier," and a glass chandelier graced the mansion house of John Brown in Providence in the 1790's. Similarly, when Sullivan Dorr began the construction of his house at 109 Benefit Street in Providence in 1809, he included in the original designs for the parlor a handsome four-light glass chandelier (Fig. 13). Even the saloon of *Cleopatra's Barge,* the Crowninshield family yacht, furnished in Salem in the early nineteenth century, had a chandelier, which was described in the *Salem Gazette* of March 4, 1817, as having cost one hundred and fifty dollars.

Further documentation of the introduction of fashionable chandeliers into New England interiors in the early nineteenth century can occasionally be found in contemporary paintings. *The Dinner Party* (c. 1821) by Henry Sargent in the Museum of Fine Arts, Boston, is an excellent example. The Boston newspaper *Columbian Centinel* for February 16, 1814, describes an auction sale at the house on Beacon Street next west of William Stevenson, Esq., at which Paris-made furniture was offered, including: "one elegant Grecian Chandelier." Certainly such lighting devices were a vehicle for stylish design as well as for added light in the household.

120

IV Other Lighting Devices

Attribution of lighting devices all too often must depend upon guesswork or hearsay evidence. Rarely is one so fortunate as to find the kind of documentation described by Harrold E. Gillingham in "An Historic Lamp" (pp. 124-125). More often, one must be satisfied with building a representative collection that is fairly well identified as to types.

Few lighting collectors, however, can long resist the urge to broaden their interest by expanding their collection to include the many accessories required for lamp and candle "management," or, to narrow their interest by concentrating on some specific specialty. Arthur Hayward found that patented devices offer a fascinating specialty as do lard and lard oil lamps. Candlemolds and snuffers described in this section are also appropriate subjects for specialized collections.

Few accessories offer more variety and interest than early firemaking devices. Prior to the electric light, every light source required a flame, often available from the fireplace or another lamp or candle. Lack of a flame, or at least glowing embers, was a serious problem. It was sometimes easier to borrow a flame from a neighbor than to create one, in which case a covered ember scoop might be used. Inside the home, the sparking lamp, and outdoors, the pierced tin lantern, were as useful for carrying a flame as for illumination. Spills and splints were used to transfer a flame from one lamp to another. Total loss of a flame was not so serious on a sunny day when a burning-glass could quickly provide a spark, but on a cloudy day or at night, a patient bout with the tinderbox was required. For those who could afford one, the tinder pistol, fashioned after a flintlock mechanism, simplified the process. There is at least one record of a family using an unloaded musket with tinder and a touch of gunpowder to strike a light. After 1827, as Lura Woodside Watkins tells us in "Early Firemaking Devices" (pp. 133-135), chemical sources, culminating in the friction match, gradually replaced the old-fashioned flint and steel.

The Dobereiner lighter, explained by William F. Noe in "Platinum Lighters of the Nineteenth Century" (pp. 135-136), is a remarkable device, extremely rare and not generally understood. Like the "chemistry of a candle," it is a marvel of chemistry and automation. Sitting quietly until needed, it instantly produces a flame, as if by magic, at the touch of a button.

We think of candles as simple and carefree in operation, but their manufacture required a great deal of time and labor. Candle-dipping sticks—the kind that nimble and quick "Jack" jumped over in the nursery rhyme—and drying racks speeded the monotonous process of repeated dippings, and the multiple candlemold further simplified the work. Old dipping devices are relatively rare, but candlemolds, especially in tin, are fairly common.

Although the braided candle wick made scissors-like snuffers obsolete, there continued to be a need for conical extinguishers. Snuffers were *never* used to extinguish a candle, but rather to keep it alive and burning properly.

Until the introduction of kerosene, the light from lamps was so feeble and fuel costs so high that few people could enjoy the amount of light required for close visual tasks. To make the most of what little light was available, reflectors of many forms and materials were utilized. Glass lenses were sometimes applied directly to pewter or tin whale oil lamps, and water refractors illustrated in Frank L. Horton's article "New Thoughts on Eighteenth-Century Lighting" (pp. 141-142) were made to use singly or in multiple with separate adjustable candlesticks or lamps.

Many of these devices may be seen in the outstanding collections of Old Sturbridge Village in Sturbridge, Massachusetts, and The Henry Ford Museum in Dearborn, Michigan. At Old Sturbridge Village one finds not only a well-organized lighting exhibit open to the public, but a large additional study collection available to researchers by arrangement with the Curatorial Department. There is also a continuous demonstration in the summer months of candlemaking, rush dipping, and various lighting devices, including the water lens. All of the Village buildings are properly furnished with period lighting devices. The Henry Ford Museum has an equally fine lighting exhibit, and an outstanding collection of early electric light bulbs. An "extra" for the light bulb historian is the original Edison laboratory and workshop, moved from Menlo Park, New Jersey, to the Henry Ford Museum.

So-Called Paul Revere Lantern
Such products of the local tinsmith
required no glass, yet were reasonably
windproof, and gave some light

Paul Revere's Lantern
Said to be one of the lanterns hung in Christ Church tower
to signal the departure of the British troops for Lexington
and Concord, April 18, 1775

So-Called Paul Revere Lantern
The feeble gleam from such a source
could hardly have carried from Boston
to Charlestown, where Revere waited

Paul Revere's Lantern

ON THE night of April 18, 1775, some eight hundred of the British troops then occupying the city of Boston were secretly withdrawn from their barracks, and sent, under cover of darkness, on a march through Lexington and Concord. Their purpose may have been to apprehend John Hancock and Samuel Adams, who had retired to Lexington in order to escape arrest; again, it may have been to seize the military stores that the Colonials were reported to have gathered at Concord.

The secret invasion, however, quickly lost its secrecy. No sooner had the British shown signs of activity, than William Dawes was dispatched to Lexington to warn Hancock and Adams of their new danger. Meanwhile, Paul Revere arranged with a friend to hang a signal high in the Christ Church tower should the British soldiers begin moving from the city, and then crossed by boat from Boston to Charlestown. The agreement was fulfilled. Watching from the Charlestown shore, Revere presently descried lights winking from the Boston belfry. A moment later he was on horseback and hurrying along the proposed British line of march to inform the inhabitants of an unwelcome visitation. So Paul Revere and his lanterns became famous.

Among trusting souls it appears to be a matter of common belief that the lanterns that admonished the alert Revere to be up and galloping were cylindrical affairs of tin with conical tops, pierced above and round about with tiny apertures, and in general more closely resembling cheese graters than sources of illumination. Indeed, contraptions of this kind are almost always called "Paul Revere lanterns," although no one of them yields more than enough light to guide a farmer from his house to the barn and back again on a moonless night.

Under such circumstances, ANTIQUES feels rather specially privileged to reproduce the portrait of what is reputed to be an actual Paul Revere lantern — lately exhibited in a glass-covered niche in the new building of the Concord Antiquarian Society at Concord, Massachusetts. How this important trophy was acquired, or on what evidence its authenticity is accepted, ANTIQUES does not know. It is, nevertheless, an obviously efficient utensil, quite capable of serving as a beacon. Furthermore, it is gratifyingly good to look upon, with its tooled edges, its pierced two-storied chimney, its turned finials on the four corner posts, its remaining vestiges of lacquer. So dignified and handsome a piece of tinware may well have played an heroic rôle.

In picturing this historic object, ANTIQUES places beside it two of the familiar pretenders to the same family name. Both are owned by the Archæological and Historical Society of Ohio. No other device for illuminating casts such alluring patterns of light and shadow.

An Historic Lamp

Originally Owned by Thomas Jefferson

By Harrold E. Gillingham

"**B**ETWEEN the dark and the daylight, when the night is beginning to lower," how convenient it is to push a wall switch, turn on the electric current, and have "the swift winged arrows of the light" shoot through the room. How little thought do we, who enjoy the brilliantly illuminated houses of the present, give nowadays to the light of former times.

Some readers of ANTIQUES may remember the argand gas reading lamps of the Victorian era, generally used on the library table, with a long rubber tube for the gas dangling from a ceiling fixture above. We read that "Argand, between 1780 and 1783, perfected his cylindrical wick lamp, which provides a central current of air through the burner, thus allowing the more perfect combustion of gas issuing from the wick."* The lamp shown here, evidently made after the invention of Aimé Argand, the Swiss chemist and philosopher (1755–1803), whose name it bears, is of Sheffield plate, of graceful Adam design, and is seven inches high and three and three quarters inches in diameter. It is similar to that illustrated by Frederick Bradbury in his *History of Old Sheffield Plate* (p. 395), but more ornate; though, unfortunately, the chimney frame is missing.

At the top may be seen a small acorn-shaped lever for raising and lowering the wick. The piercings around the upper part of the oil reservoir, as well as those at the base, communicate with the chimney to allow circulation of air inside and outside of the flame. These perforations were part of the Argand patent. In the centre are two concentric tubes or cylinders, between which passes the tubular wick. Originally a wire frame extended above the present top to hold a ring which supported a glass chimney; but, through the ravages of time, and possibly the many cleanings of the past one hundred years, both

Fig. 1 — EARLY ARGAND LAMP (c. 1784)
A gift from Thomas Jefferson to Charles Thomson.
Owned by the author.

ring and chimney have been lost or broken (*Fig. 4*). The wick raising device is similar to that illustrated by Bradbury. The writer knows of other Argand lamps of Sheffield plate, with a button turning device—evidently the later patent of 1803 of George Penton.

In the *Annals of Philadelphia* by John Fanning Watson, under the chapter of *Furniture and Equipage*, one reads, "They had then no Argand or other Lamps in Parlours, but dipt candles in Brass or Copper Candlesticks were usually good enough for common use." (*Fig. 2*.) In a footnote, Watson adds, "The first which ever came to this country is in my possession, originally a present from Thos. Jefferson to Chs. Thomson." It had been secured by Mr. Watson from Charles Thomson, the first Secretary of the Continental Congress, who died August 16, 1824, in the ninety-fifth year of his age.

A few years ago, my wife, on entering a smelter's shop, recognized a direct descendant of John F. Watson leaving the place. Within, she found the lamp here illustrated, for the Watson descendant had just sold it to the smelter. Needless to say, to a collector's heart this was a veritable find; and it has been one of our cherished possessions ever since. Attached to the lamp was a small paper tag, bearing, in Watson's own handwriting, the inscription, *The first Argand lamp, a present from Thos. Jefferson to Chas. Thomson* (*Fig. 3*).

A careful comparison of the handwriting on the label has been made with many manuscripts in the possession of the Historical Society of Pennsylvania (to whom acknowledgment is given for the illustration of Watson's manuscript here reproduced) and the label is, without doubt, that of Watson himself.

May not this fine Sheffield specimen be the identical lamp referred to by Mrs. Fiske Kimball, in her article on

*Encyclopaedia Britannica, 13th edition, Vol. 16, p. 640.

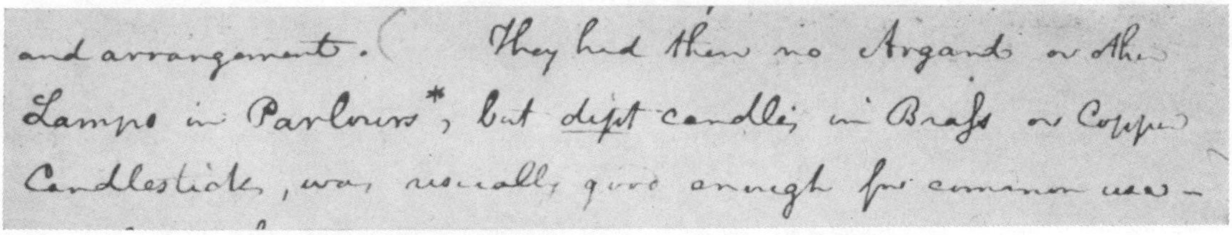

Fig. 2 — FACSIMILE FROM WATSON'S *Annals* OF PHILADELPHIA

*The Furnishings of Monti- cello,** purchased by Thomas Jefferson in 1784 and recorded in his account book "Feb. 27, pd for plated reading lamp 31/6".? Evidently "31/6" indi- cated the English method of denoting shillings and pence, which sum was not an excessive price, even in those days, to pay for such a graceful and use- ful piece of furnishing.

Mention is also made of Jefferson's corre- spondence with Mr. Boulton regarding other pieces "plated in the best manner, with a plain bead."† Inasmuch as Bradbury illus- trates a similar lamp, made by Messrs. M. Boulton & Co. of Birmingham, Soho

Fig. 3 (left) — MEMORANDUM ATTACHED TO THE JEFFERSON LAMP
The handwriting is clearly the same as that of the *Annals.*

Works, it is reasonable to assume that Jefferson also purchased this identical lamp from Messrs. Boulton, and had it sent to Philadelphia in one of the "eighty-four packing cases" when he returned to this country in 1789.

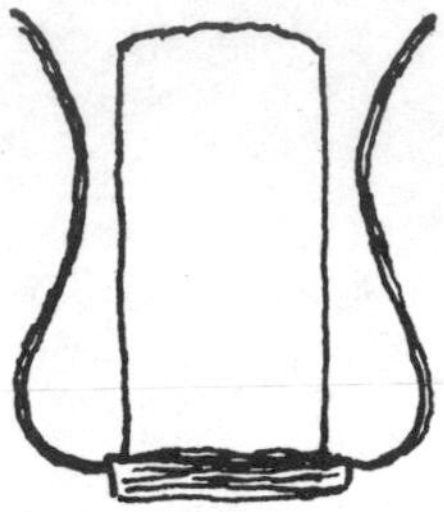

Can you imagine a more appropriate piece for an old secretary desk or a tea table? Surely John Fanning Watson, noted antiquarian that he was, would be grateful to know that this lamp which he so fondly cherished is today as carefully preserved and appreciated as when it was in his own possession.

Fig. 4 — WIRE FRAME AND RING FOR HOLD- ING GLASS CHIMNEY
Four inches high. Illustrated by Frederick Bradbury in his *History of Old Sheffield Plate,* p. 395.

*Antiques, Vol. XII, p. 382.
†Ibid.

Jefferson's Reading Table

An Editorial Note

OMITTED, because of lack of space, from its proper place in Mrs. Marie Kimball's articles on the furnishings of Monticello, Thomas Jefferson's reading table here receives honorable recom- pense by being given consideration by itself. Far from notable because of any distinction or grace of style, heavy in its apron, and with its un- beaded drawer overweighted with un- suitable brasses, the piece yet possesses considerable interest. The legs, which terminate in brass shoes with castor attachments, are decorated with round- headed tapering panels, similar in form to the inlaid designs common to much of Hepplewhite's work, but carved in relief instead of conforming to usual practice. The chief feature of this table, however, is its ingeniously devised top, which may be raised, tilted forward, and held in place by a rack, thus enabl- ing writer or draftsman to adjust it to any required angle. Brass sockets on either side appear to have been intended to hold lamps.

Whether or not Jefferson obtained the idea for this piece of furniture from the contemplation of similar examples encountered abroad may not be sur- mised. If so, he doubtless made his

drawings from memory, and probably supervised their fulfilment by a local cabinetmaker.

The outcome is more creditable to his inventiveness than to his sense of the exquisite. Indeed, that this sense was highly developed in the sage of Monti- cello may be questioned. His vast erudition and his untiring creative industry appear to have been accepted by his own and by a later generation as evidence of the concurrent possession of a discriminating taste. Yet contempor- ary descriptions of Monticello leave an impression less of classic orderliness than of cluttered heterogeneity, while the Jefferson touch in furniture design seems invariably to achieve clumsiness. When it was laid upon architecture, as Thomas E. Tallmadge aptly remarks, "We look in vain for any originality or subtlety, any architectural grace such as we find, for instance, in the New York Hall and the White House in Washington . . . If his work is great it is because its author was great."*

*Thomas E. Tallmadge, *The Story of Architecture in America,* New York, 1927, p. 83.

Patented Lamps of the Last Century

By ARTHUR H. HAYWARD

JUST as the nineteenth century was nearing the halfway mark it seemed to dawn upon a number of persons in widely scattered parts of the country that the lighting appliances then in use were lagging behind the general march of progress, and were far from capable of furnishing adequate illumination.

The principal sources of light, and in fact the only sources, were candles and oil-burning lamps. Candles, of course, had been in use for many years and were reasonably satisfactory; but, if used in the quantity necessary to extensive lighting, they were costly, and for this reason prohibitive to many. Lamps burning sperm oil were in general use, and the improved methods of refining their fuel afforded a fluid that was free from the greasy smoke and disagreeable odors common to earlier oils and greases.

There were other illuminants on the market. Lard oil, which was burned in lamps provided with wide, flat wicks, was used to some extent, and there had more recently been introduced a new illuminant called "camphene," which, in so far as burning qualities went, was a great advance over rival products. It was made by distilling oil of turpentine over quicklime, a process that achieved a limpid, colorless fluid burning freely with a bright, clear flame and with virtually no smoke or odor. Its one disadvantage was its explosiveness. Great care had to be exercised lest the gases from it (for it was very volatile) should come in contact with flame, with resultant disaster. But camphene was so great an improvement over oil that it was quite generally adopted, and various devices were employed to minimize its dangers. The first consisted in reducing in diameter the tubes carrying the closely-woven, round wicks, and in lengthening them so that the flame might be kept as far as possible from the oil font. Extinguishers to cap the tubes were also used when the light was no longer needed.

One of the few successful patents for the safety of camphene was that issued to J. Newell, October 4, 1853. The principal feature of this invention was a very finely meshed wire cylinder, which went down into the oil reservoir, completely surrounding the wick. In some way the fine wire cylinder was supposed to lessen the dangers of an explosion. I have been fortunate enough to find two lamps equipped with this arrangement. One is a double-wick pewter lamp, marked with name and date on the rim of the cover carrying the long camphene wick-tubes. The other, a small glass reservoir resting in a tin base, has a single

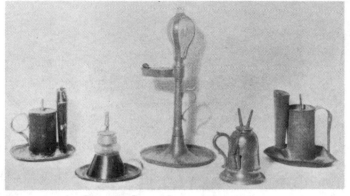

Fig. 1 — a and e: CYLINDER GREASE LAMPS
b and d: Camphene hand lamps. c: European pewter time lamp. For full descriptions, consult the text.
Illustrations from the author's collection

Fig. 2 — PAIR OF EARLY AMERICAN GUEST-ROOM LAMPS, ONE FITTED WITH TRAY FOR BURNING SPICES
Centre: Brass lard-oil lamp

tube, and the cover is simply marked *J. Newell's Patent 1853.* Both, however, have the same fine wire cylinder arrangement within (*Fig. 1 b and d*).

Many of the lamp patents that were issued during the twenty years or so preceding the discovery and introduction of coal oil, or "kerosene," as we know it today, were utterly impractical and probably were never put into actual use. In consequence, marked patented lamps of this period are seldom found.

One of the most interesting lamps in my collection, while not a patented article, undoubtedly would have been thus protected had patents been granted in the sixteenth or seventeenth centuries. It is the tall pewter object shown in the centre of Figure 1. Known to collectors today as a "time lamp," it registered approximate hours by the dwindling fluid in its glass reservoir. On the sides of the glass oil container are three strips of pewter marked at regular intervals with the hours. One begins at the top with nine, and the other two with eight. This timekeeper was anything but accurate, as oils of different density and wicks of varying size would greatly alter the rate of burning.

Two other unpatented lamps, original in conception, are pictured in Figure 2. They are of tin with cylindrical reservoirs and are sometimes called "pig lamps" for reasons visible to the discerning eye. They are really early American guest-room lamps, and their three large wicks would yield a considerable volume of light. A novel attachment is the little tin shelf suspended directly over the burner at the end of one of the lamps. On this were scattered powdered spices or incense that would smoulder when the lamp was lighted, and help to counteract any disagreeable odor from burning oil or other smelly sources.

Another interesting lamp is shown in Figure 1. I was so fortunate as to find two of these, identical in principle, though not quite alike in shape (*Fig. 1 a and e*). Only one is marked. This bears, on the side, the inscription *Tilton & Sleeper, Fremont, New Hampshire. Pat. Aug. 1854.* The large upright cylinder is equipped with a closely fitting screw plunger. When a key (almost any old clock key will do) turns the top, the plunger head is forced down and the grease or other heavy burning fluid which fills the cylinder is squeezed through a small opening into the smaller cylinder at the side, where a broad, flat wick can pick it up to burn.

There were various other devices for burning heavy fluids. Some had a clocklike arrangement within the cylinder; others used double cylinders, one floating inside the other, to keep the wick evenly submerged. Such a one is shown in Figure 3 c; but I think some parts are missing, as the method of operation is not clear.

One of the difficulties of collecting unusual patented lamps is that of finding examples intact. Often some part has disappeared, and, except for the improbable event of finding another to match, one has to take his prize in a more or less mutilated condition, or not at all.

Z. Swope (whoever he was) devised an ingenious lamp that he patented in 18— (half the date is illegible) (*Fig. 3 a*). It was for burning lard oil, a medium whose habit of solidifying in cold weather proved most annoying. The body of Swope's lamp was of tin, but the tube that terminates in a bell just over the flame is of copper. The idea was that the copper, a good conductor of heat, would carry a current of warm air from the flame down into the oil cylinder, and thus keep the lard oil in a fluid condition. This lamp is marked *Z. Swope's Self Heating Lamp, Pat. March 18 — Made by Leitersburg Lamp and Tin Ware Manufacturing Co., Leitersburg, Maryland.*

A quite decorative pair of tin wall lamps is shown in Figure 4. Here the oil is held in the removable square containers at the back. When they are filled, the oil runs down into the frontal cylinder, which is equipped with a round wick. Little openings at the bottom allow air to pass up through the centre of the wick, thus supporting combustion. The holders suspended from the top of the wick tubes are evidently intended for glass chimneys. Both of these lamps lack their burners. They are marked *Manufactured by W. Carlton, Boston,* but without a date.

Fig. 3 — *a*: Z. Swope's Self-Heating Lamp
b: Kinnear's patent lamp. *c*: Double-cylinder grease lamp

Fig. 4 — Tin Wall Lamps

Fig. 5 — *a*: Tumbler Lamp
b and *e*: Lard-oil lamps with tipping fonts (one reflector missing). *c*: Astral lamp, with original chimney. *d* and *f*: Two similar; one marked *London Lamp,* the other *The New York Safety Lamp*

the heated air down and maintain the fluidity of the oil. Its purpose is similar to that of Swope's invention pictured at the left in the same group.

The tall brass lamp shown in Figure 2 is another of the considerable number of patented lamps for burning lard oil. While my specimen is unmarked, a brother collector has a very similar one that is stamped on the bottom of the saucer *Patented by Samuel Davis, May 6 1856.* This helps to prove my contention that many of the lamps of this period, though patented, were not marked, the patentees evidently placing so little value on their ideas that it made no difference to them whether their lamps were marked or not. This lamp, by the way, is particularly sturdy and well made. The wick tube, which comes up in the centre of the reservoir, is round, although it is planned for two flat wicks, each curved to form a half circle as it enters the tube. The main shaft is hollow, and air is fed to the centre of the wicks by means of the large opening just above the saucer base. Slits in the top of the wick tube allow the insertion of a pick to force up the wick as it is burned: a device common to almost all the older oil lamps and not superseded until the cogwheel came into use. Several lard-oil lamps in my collection, both for wall and for table, have one peculiar feature in common: their fonts are arranged on hinges and held by a spring, so that, when the oil is low, the font can be tilted forward to allow the wick more easily to absorb the remaining oil (*Fig. 5 b and e*).

To me one of the most interesting of the patented lamps, although it is a late one, is the little tumbler lamp of Figure 5. Here, again, a lamp complete with tumbler, tin top,

Another lamp of particular interest to collectors from Boston and its vicinity is illustrated in Figure 3 *b*. While such pieces are not so hard to find as some previously mentioned, a specimen like this — complete even to the original tin shade, which is held over the lamp by two wires fitting into slots at the ends — is worth hunting for. On the side of the flattened oil container appears a plate bearing the words *S. N. & H. C. Ufford, 117 Court Street, Boston, Kinnear's Patent, Feby 4 1851.* The unusually broad, flat wick is evidently for lard oil. On one side is the capped filling hole, and, on the other, an open tube to conduct

wire handle, and inside lamp is considered a lucky find. An ordinary pressed-glass tumbler is fitted with a tin top supporting a curious boxlike arrangement, apparently designed to hold the vessel in which milk or other liquid is to be heated. Through a small hole in the cover extends a wire handle by which the small single tube lamp can be lifted. Just how sufficient air flows into the tumbler to keep the lamp burning, I do not understand. On the cover is stamped *Star Tumbler Pat, Jan 13, 1874.*

Mica windows for lamps and lanterns were something of an innovation. I have two small, single-wick, whale-oil lamps, each with protective chimney of tin to steady the tiny flame (*Fig. 6 a and d*). In the chimney front appears a small, translucent window of mica. These two lamps, found at different times and places, are alike in principle, but vary slightly in shape and in the size of the hinged tops. Mica windows were also adopted by the makers of lanterns. I have a good-size tin lantern with a small, square, whale-oil lamp (*Fig. 6 c*). Windows on three sides are made of single sheets of mica; the fourth side shows a tin sliding door. A small tin pocket lantern, which, by an ingenious arrangement, may be folded flat and slipped into one's pocket, has mica windows on two sides (*Fig. 6 e*). I judge this to be a patented device, although it has no name or inscription of any kind.

Lanterns offer a fruitful field for the collector who is searching for unusual lighting utensils. They are infinitely varied in design, shape, and material, and are sufficiently hard to find to give zest to the hunt for them. I have two or three wooden lanterns, one triangular, which is particularly odd. Then there are the tin and iron examples, some of the very early specimens having windows of thinly scraped cow's horn.

Among later specimens, the metal candle lantern of Figure 7 *a* is of interest. The candle holder pulls down; the front and top open up; and the piece is transformed into quite an effective lighting appliance (*Fig. 8 f*). I have also two lanterns which I think were undoubtedly used in the early days of the bicycle. The tin one pictured closed in Figure 7 *e* and open in Figure 8 *e* is marked *Stevens Patent Sept 7 1875*, and contains a small, square lamp with a kerosene burner. It was made so that it could be attached in front of the handlebars of the old-fashioned tall-wheel bicycle. The second one (*Fig. 7 d*) is beautifully fashioned of brass with a threaded opening at one side for fastening to a bicycle of a more modern type. This last is stamped on the bottom *Walker, Cornhill, Boston*. It has a bull's-eye front and is lighted by a snugly fitting, tiny, half-moon lamp, which fills the lower half of the case (*Fig. 8 b*). Beside the handlebar fastening, it has folding handles and a suspension hook on top.

Dark lanterns offer a wide diversity to the discriminating collector. The earlier ones are square with tin shutters. Then there came the more familiar round, bull's-eye type, many of which had a convenient sliding tin door. Several va-

rieties of both types of lantern are shown in Figures 7 and 8.

Relics of the early days of railroading constitute yet another class of collectibles. Some of the early whale-oil, and the later kerosene, lanterns carried by train conductors would make a fascinating shelfful.

The latest addition to my patent-lamp collection I acquired but recently. Of a kind that I have never before seen, it is pictured in the centre of Figure 5. This tall table lamp with a glass chimney represents one of the later patents, issued just before the general introduction of kerosene, which sent most of the earlier burners to ash barrel and scrap heap. Around the rim is inscribed *Sargent's Patent, March 4, 1856*. A double tin cylinder encloses the round wick and extends completely through the oil chamber. Air is carried to the centre of the flame through this tube from perforations at the bottom of the reservoir. An interesting feature is the original glass chimney, such as was then in use on many table lamps. The wick was adjusted by turning the little knob near the air intake. While its molded-glass base is without any artistic merit, this lamp is chiefly interesting as representing one of the many experiments for better and more efficient lighting. Doubtless it burned one of the fluids used in astral lamps.

The fact that the general adoption of kerosene relegated this and other similar lighting devices to the discard would probably account for their scarcity today. It is, however, an addition to the comparatively small number of patented lamps with which this article deals, and which may be found today only after diligent search by one whose enthusiasm on this particular subject will sustain his interest to a successful conclusion.

In these notes I have merely skirted the fringe of the story of the early curiosities among patented lamps and lanterns. Probably another collector could show an entirely different group, and one equally interesting. If one wished to delve more deeply into this subject, the records of the patent office for the years, say, from 1840 to 1870 would supply absorbing reading and would furnish material for a good-size book.

This subject of pre-kerosene patented lamps is a most fascinating one, and merits further study and research. It is to be hoped that lamp collectors will bring more data to light.

Fig. 6 — Centre: TIN LANTERN WITH MICA WINDOWS ON THREE SIDES, SQUARE WHALE-OIL LAMP
a and d: Small, hand, whale-oil lamps with hinged mica windows. *b:* Brass candlestick with concealed spring to keep candle at top, marked *Palmer & Co, London. e:* Tin pocket lantern, for small candle

Fig. 7 — a: EXTENSION CANDLE LANTERN (*see lantern open, Fig. 8f*)
b and c: Tin dark lanterns. *d:* Early brass bicycle lantern. *e:* Early sport lantern for oil (shown open, *Fig. 8e*)

Fig. 8 — a: EARLY SQUARE DARK LANTERN FOR WHALE OIL
Tin sliding shutters conceal the light. *b:* Brass bicycle lantern open (shown closed in *Fig. 7d*). *c:* Tin whale-oil lamp for heating liquids. *d:* Railroad conductor's whale-oil lantern marked *B C & M R R* (Boston, Concord, & Montreal Rail Road). *e:* Tin bicycle lantern open (shown closed in *Fig. 7e*). *f:* Candle lantern (*Fig. 7a*) open. *g:* Early candle holder on wood base. Holder slides on the upright iron rods

LARD-OIL LAMPS

By ARTHUR H. HAYWARD

Illustrations from the author's collection

FIG. 1 — THE INVENTION OF ZURIEL SWOPE, LANCASTER, PENNSYLVANIA

Patent granted March 13, 1860. Swope's special claim for his device was the arrangement of a copper funnel directly above the broad wick, and a connecting tube, also of copper, to collect heat generated by the flame and conduct it down into the oil reservoir. A rectangular lid covers the opening for filling. A small hole at the end opposite the heat tube is probably for a pilot light. This lamp now shows no patent, though it may have borne a stencil when new. Finding one of these lamps whole and in good condition may necessitate for the collector a long hunt

TO THE collector of lighting appliances who wishes to specialize in some particular department of his favorite field, I should suggest consideration of lamps made to burn lard oil, and more particularly the patented examples.

Lard oil was a heavy, yellowish fluid, a by-product of the process of lardmaking. In the fall, when fattened hogs were killed to furnish the farmer's winter supply of smoked, corned, and otherwise processed meat, rural housewives were busily occupied with "trying out" the fat from the pigs to form lard for the year's cooking. Slabs of clear, pinkish fat were first cut into cubes, then melted in huge iron kettles. After the liquid had been strained into pails or earthen crocks to solidify into lard, there always remained a persistently liquid residue.

Someone discovered that this fluid would burn well in a lamp equipped with a broad, somewhat loosely woven wick. Thenceforth the use of lard-oil lamps in country districts became not uncommon. Lard oil, as it was called, burned with a steady and fairly bright flame. Its chief drawbacks were its tendency to thicken in cold weather to an extent that prevented its absorption by the wick; and its heaviness, even when warm, of such a degree that the capillary attraction of the wick was strong enough to lift the fluid only a short distance. Hence it was necessary to keep the distance between flame and oil as brief as possible.

These faults in an otherwise satisfactory burning fluid, which had the appeal of inexpensiveness, prompted many fertile minds to invent corrective devices of a mechanical kind. In consequence, some fifty patents for lard-oil lamps were granted between 1833 and 1863. In the latter year, coal oil or kerosene, as it was later called, came into general use. It rapidly supplanted the porcine by-product.

Like other patented lamps of the first half of the nineteenth century, many if not most of these contrivances proved to be of little practical use and were cast into the discard. Hunting for patented lard-oil lamps, therefore, becomes quite a sporting proposition. Furthermore, the asset of value of patents seems for such lamps to have been lightly regarded, and many ingenious

FIG. 2 — A MORE POPULAR TYPE OF PATENT LARD-OIL LAMP

Patented February 4, 1851, by Delamar Kinnear of Circleville, Ohio. The two with tin shades are marked; the other two, with saucer bases, are unmarked, but evidently represent the same patent. While the inventor hailed from Ohio, brass plates on the two marked items proclaim the maker as *S. N. & H. C. Ufford, 113 Court St., Boston.* The only marked Kinnear lamps that I have seen all bear this Boston label. I surmise that the Uffords were the only firm licensed

to manufacture such lamps in New England. Kinnear's application claims a patent only for "the angular chamber for the fluid and the dovetailed slide (covering the filling hole) and the angular channels or grooves above the reservoir." Singularly, neither of the Ufford lamps has

a sliding cover, one of the patented features; but the two unmarked examples have this device. Again, both the Ufford lamps exhibit a small round tube (a pilot light) in the top at the far end from the filling hole. All four lamps are similar in having an "angular" reservoir, apparently the inventor's chief pride. Wick tubes are unusually wide (one measuring two inches), and the slots for inserting the wickpicks are very prominent. Original tin shades, supported by wires at the ends of the reservoir, are now seldom found with lamps. I was fortunate to find two complete examples, shades and all. Not one of this lamp group is precisely like another in every detail. Note that even the design for the cast-iron bases differs. Infinite variety helps to account for the fascination that lard-oil lamps have for the collector of lighting devices

FIG. 3 — ANOTHER GROUP OF LARD-OIL LAMPS

The patent for this type was issued to Ira Smith and John Stonesifer of Boonsborough, Maryland, August 8, 1854. On the top of the plunger within the cylinders of the pair of plain tin lamps is imprinted in bold type, *I. Smith Pat. Aug. 8 1854*. The single japanned example above is faintly stenciled on one side, *Patented Aug 8th 1854*, and on the opposite side, *Tilton & Sleeper, Freemont, New Hampshire*. It is as ingenious as any of the lard-oil lamps. The large cylinder that holds the oil encloses a plunger with a tightly fitting head. The plunger bar, protruding from the top, reaches down the full length of the cylinder. By turning the top, the plunger is forced down, thus squeezing the oil through a small opening at the bottom into a connecting tube, whose broad wick is thus consistently fed. This invention must have been fairly successful; for I have seen in shops a number of these lamps, most of them bearing the scars of steady use. Why a small New Hampshire town should have produced a lamp invented in Maryland is a mystery

FIG. 4 — A FOURTH VARIETY OF LARD-OIL LAMPS

While doubtless patented, none is so marked. In all three items the principle is the same, though designs vary. The reservoirs for the burning fluid are kept in any desired position by a strip of brass. As the oil is consumed, the reservoir may be tilted forward, thus maintaining a fixed distance between flame and fuel. When the fuel is almost gone, the position of the reservoir will be that shown at the lower right of the illustration. One of the lamps in this group retains its original reflector. The other two have been less fortunate (see ANTIQUES for August 1936, *p. 58*)

forms are found quite innocent of protective designation. The descriptions filed with patent applications make interesting reading; but it is a bit pathetic to note how often the inventor's faith in his supposed marvel of ingenuity was doomed to suffer disappointment.

The accompanying illustrations picture a number of lard-oil lamps, some of the ordinary kind, others carrying a patent mark. The four types presented by no means exhaust the variety discoverable by the zealous collector.

The entire subject

of early lighting is fascinating. As lighting devices, outmoded by improved mechanisms, were usually discarded, it becomes increasingly difficult to find examples sufficient to form an adequate picture of the development of illumination. Collectors and museums should not delay until it is too late.

FIG. 5 — ORDINARY LARD-OIL LAMPS

This group indicates something of the size and variety to be found. The tallest example is probably a patent lamp but carries no marks. Except for the glass item, all members of the group are made of tin

130

The Canting Lamp

By H. M. CORDELL

IN COLLECTIONS of early American lighting devices the student often finds certain curious tin lamps, which, while exhibiting slight diversities in form, all possess one feature in common. Such lamps are variously known as "canting," "tipping," or "tilting" lamps. The period of their chief vogue was the two decades from 1840 until 1860. Quite evidently they were widely used.

Although the manner of operating these interesting little lights is obvious, their actual *raison d'être* seems not always to be clearly understood. It is frequently believed that their tilting device was to permit consumption of the last vestiges of fuel in the reservoir. This, however, was not the sole purpose of their peculiar construction. The more scientific intent was to maintain the distance between fuel and flame at a constant interval, so as to ensure a steady light of full efficiency. Accordingly, a merit of the tipping or tilting lamp, and one dwelt upon by its sundry inventors, was the fact that, upon being extinguished, the lamp remained in such a position that it could be as readily relighted as an ordinary candle, while the material within was rendered immediately fluid by the action of its own flame.

Dr. Norton, in an early article in the *Connecticut Magazine*, describes a patented "lard oil" lamp of 1818, known as the "canting fount lamp." A search of American patent records reveals no such patent. Furthermore, lard oil was not discovered until 1841–1842. Although the majority of American "canting" lamps appeared coincidentally with M. Chevreuil's discovery of the process of obtaining lard oil, it is evident from the construction of their various wick tubes that they were virtually all intended to burn lard or some other heavy oil which, in cold weather, had a tendency to become frozen or chilled. So many persons have failed to distinguish between lard and lard oil in discussing old-style lamps that a word concerning the lard-oil process may prove enlightening.

Lard oil is the limpid and nearly colorless oil obtained by subjecting lard to pressure. The more solid portions of the fat that remain after the process constitute what is known as lard stearin. The ratio between the oil expressed and the stearin residue depends largely on the temperature at which the pressure is applied. Furthermore, the quality of lard oil depends not only on its purity, but also on the part of the animal from which it is derived.

The idea of the tipping lamp was by no means new. For centuries various ingenious arrangements for maintaining a constant oil level had been pondered. The earliest inventions of the kind on record are those of Hero, of Alexandria, about 200 B.C. In one of these the raising of the oil was effected by the pressure of a liquid of greater specific gravity. In another, Hero attempted to counteract the depression of the oil level by means of a float, actuated by a rack and pinion gearing, providing an automatic control of the wick. The form of the lamp used was exactly that of the betty lamp of our earlier days.

The oldest form with which Americans are familiar is the ancient Scotch *crusie*, so often, and mysteriously, termed the Phoebe lamp. This is pictured in Figure 1, and the manner in which the oil container may be canted as the oil is consumed is plainly observable. But of course the readjustment of the upper saucer had to be accomplished by hand. No automatic gadget did the work.

The "automaton," invented by Porter in 1804, consisted of a plain rectangular reservoir so weighted and balanced that, as the oil was consumed, the reservoir gradually assumed the position shown in Figure 2. Here we have the true self-tilting lamp. Several years later Bordier Marcet, brother-in-law of Aimé Argand, utilized the annular reservoir of the "astral" lamp for the dual purpose of minimizing alteration in the oil level, and of eliminating the objectionable shadow thrown by reservoirs of other kinds.

One of the earliest records we have of the canting lamp is that of Woodward's *tallow tip lamp*, invented in 1841. The patent description indicates that this is on the order of the other lamps illustrated in this article. The reservoir is held in a supporting yoke, the arms of the yoke furnishing the spring tension necessary to keep the reservoir at the desired angle.

The six canting lamps illustrated opposite in Figures 3 to 8 constitute an unusually interesting group. All are of japanned tin; several have stenciled decorations. The first (*Fig. 3*) is an early non-automatic form (in fact, automatic tilt lamps are few and far between). It has the old-time saucer base, and the standard has the vertical slot and key valve formerly used to regulate candle height. A slip of brass, hinged to the bottom of the reservoir, forms a part of the valve within the cylindrical standard. Thus the reservoir may be canted at the proper angle by means of the slot and key. A variation of this lamp lacks the slot and key but employs the same valve construction.

The holding tension in the lamp of Figure 4 is supplied by a short, springy, curved piece to be seen just below the drum-shaped reservoir. This lamp is equipped with an adjustable reflector. An exactly similar lamp, one of a pair used by Noah Webster while compiling his dictionary, was obtained from Webster's old home at Amherst, Massachusetts, in 1852. It is now, I believe, among the treasures of the National Museum.

The example in Figure 5 retains the old form of saucer and shaft, but the tension is furnished by an unusual device. At the top of the standard is soldered a small cup, within which rests a short length of coil spring, whose pressure against the oil drum suffices to hold the latter at any point to which it may be inclined. A different device appears on the lamp of Figure 6. Here a strip of metal rises from the ring handle to join another strip fastened to the standard. These strips constitute a spring, which presses against the reservoir.

Probably the last of the canting lamps offered to the public was that invented by Dexter Chamberlain, in 1854 (*Fig. 8*). Nevertheless, though he was last on the scene, Mr. Chamberlain quite evidently reverted to the idea incorporated half a century previously in the Porter lamp of 1804 (*Fig. 2*). He produced a truly automatic feeder.

The discovery of petroleum gradually banished these ingenious little lamps and many others, equally fascinating because of their curious yet futile devices for obtaining that desideratum of the ages — adequate illumination. Those of the type here described are of great interest in a collection of early American contrivances, for they are distinctively of the lard and lard-oil era.

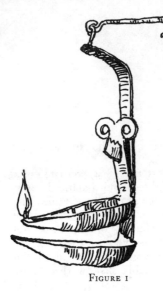

FIGURE 1

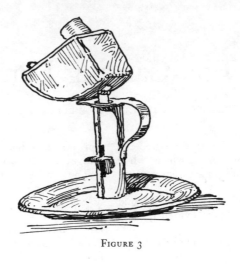

FIGURE 3

FIGURE 2

FIGURE 4

Fig. 1 — The "Crusie," Colonial Form of Canting Lamp

Fig. 2 — Porter's "Automaton" (*1804*)

Figs. 3, 4, and 5 — Japanned Tin Canting Lamps
Figure 3, tipped and held in position by a hinged rod operating in a socket; Figures 4 and 5, maintained at the desired angle by spring friction

Figs. 6, 7, and 8 — Japanned Tin Canting Lamps
Figure 8 tips automatically as the fluid in the reservoir is consumed

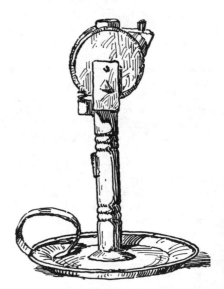

FIGURE 5

FIGURE 6

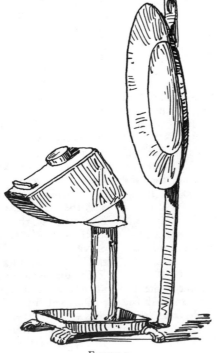

FIGURE 7

FIGURE 8

Early Firemaking Devices

I. *From Flint to Matches*

By Lura Woodside Watkins

IN modern times the process of obtaining a light or fire is such a simple one that it is performed automatically and rarely presents a problem. A turn of an electric light switch, or the passing of a match across a roughened surface, and there is our light or the flame for obtaining it. How hard it is to realize that, until the nineteenth century, our ancestors were almost as dependent upon primitive means of firemaking as were the savages in the forest. To lose the fire in the household was a domestic calamity indeed. With luck and patience a new flame might be fanned into life, but to accomplish this required considerable skill. Alice Morse Earle, in her *Home Life in Colonial Days*, says that, although she has repeatedly experimented with a tinder box, she has never succeeded in striking a light by such means.

All primitive methods of producing a spark depended on one of two principles — friction or percussion. Savage races have always known how to apply these principles by rubbing two sticks together or by striking two stones one

Fig. 1 — Complete Tinder-Box Outfit
Box with inner lid for keeping the tinder within bounds; curved piece of steel, worn with much sparking; flint; lid with candle socket.
From the collection of Charles L. Woodside

upon another, and nourishing the resultant flame.

Variations of the friction method have been observed among primitive peoples in all parts of the world. The fire-drill — a sharp stick whirled rapidly in a hole bored in another piece of wood — produces fire in a few minutes; but great skill in selecting the proper woods and in manipulating the apparatus is necessary. It would probably be impossible for the uninitiated to obtain results. But so fundamental is the principle involved in this operation that the ability to obtain fire by rubbing sticks together is still considered a necessary part of woodcraft.

The devices used in Colonial times were elaborations of the two ideas of friction and percussion. The flint and steel is perhaps the most familiar. A fragment of flint — one of the hardest substances known — was struck against a piece of steel until sparks flew into a mass of charred linen, known as tinder. The needful implements were usually kept in a round tin box — the tinder box (*Fig. 1*). An entire outfit included a horseshoe-shaped piece of steel,

Fig. 2 — Lighting Devices
(*From left to right*) — Flintlock lighter; sulphur tipped matches; pocket tinder box of brass; wheel-and-flint lighter.
From the collection of Charles L. Woodside

a flint, a tin disk to cover the loose bits of tinder in the bottom of the box, and some splints of wood dipped in sulphur to catch the flame, once the tinder had ignited. In actual practice the curved steel was looped well over the fingers of the left hand, while the flint was struck against it. In many cases a surviving steel will be found worn away at the point where the blows of the stone have repeatedly fallen upon it.

A more complicated and perhaps more successful device produced sparks from the rapid whirling of a little wheel against a piece of flint (*Fig. 2*). The turning was accomplished by pulling a string that was wound about the wheel. The resultant sparks popped into a bit of tinder in the box which formed part of the apparatus.

Another arrangement used in the homes of the well-to-do was contrived on the plan of a flintlock pistol, which, when fired, sparked against the steel (*Fig. 2*). This apparatus much resembled a small pistol of its day, but it was supported on legs, and a metal socket on the side held a tiny candle to capture the flame from the burning tinder in the forepart of the machine. The tinder box flew open at the instant of percussion, exposing a scrap of tinder to the spark.

Ordinarily the use of such tedious devices was avoided. In winter the fireplace fires were always burning, and, even in hot weather, each home maintained an open fire for cooking. A box of spills — twisted bits of paper — or of splinters of wood, was kept in a convenient place, ready to convey a light to candle or pipe. Various kinds of iron tongs for picking up lumps of burning wood were also kept hanging by the fireplace (*Fig. 3*). Some of these tongs were hinged in such a way as to extend into the fire when the handles were closed. These extension tongs often showed delicate craftsmanship in the making, and their owners felt a pardonable pride as they manipulated them to light their pipes.

The earliest matches, or "spunks," were used only in connection with tinder devices. They were dipped in sulphur to make them ignite readily, but they could not be fired by striking. The idea of lighting matches by friction originated as early as 1680, just after a means of preparing phosphorus had been discovered by Robert Boyle. Godfrey Haukwitz, working under Boyle's direction, found that minute portions of this phosphorus,

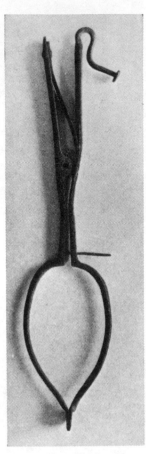

Fig. 3 — PIPE TONGS
For extracting a hot coal from the fireplace. The bent handle may be for pressing the coal down on the tobacco, or for other tamping purposes.
From the collection of F. F. Sherman

Fig. 4 — INSTANTANEOUS LIGHT BOX
Containing matches which take fire on being inserted in the accompanying vial of chemical.
From the collection of Luther Hill

when rubbed between folds of brown paper, would take fire and ignite a sulphur match. But the discovery was not put to use for over a century, principally on account of the excessive cost of phosphorus.

Several chemical devices for producing combustion were employed during the early nineteenth century. One was a small bottle in which a piece of phosphorus had been stirred with a hot wire, thus coating the interior with oxide of phosphorus. This bottle was kept tightly corked except at the moment of using, when a sulphur-dipped match could be ignited merely by being thrust into the bottle.

In 1805 a Frenchman named Chancel, assistant to Professor L. J. Thenard of Paris, invented an instantaneous light box — a small tin box containing a bottle filled with fibrous asbestos soaked in sulphuric acid (oil of vitriol) and a supply of specially prepared matches (*Fig. 4*). These matches were splints of wood dipped first into melted sulphur and then into a paste composed of chlorate of potash, powdered loaf sugar, and gum arabic, with vermilion for coloring. They were known as oxymuriate matches. When dipped into the acid, they ignited instantly. This apparatus, however, was dangerous, on account of the destructive qualities of the sulphuric acid, which, moreover, when exposed to the air, absorbed moisture and soon became useless.

The first true friction matches were made in England, in 1827, by a druggist, John Walker of Stockton-on-Tees, Durham, and were known as "lucifers." They were tipped with a mixture of sulphide of antimony, chlorate of potash, and gum, and were ignited by being drawn between folds of "glass" paper or sandpaper. These matches were made in a strip of a dozen or so, like a comb, and they retailed at a shilling for a box of eighty-five, paper included.

When first introduced into America, the lucifers were called "locofocos," a term derived from the Latin *loco foci*, in place of fire, apparently with the idea that the word meant self-lighting. Locofoco became the nickname of the Democratic party in 1835. A political meeting had been called in Tammany Hall, New York, and the extremists of the gathering, in order to gain possession of the hall, blew out all the candles, thus obliging their opponents to leave the building. Once in possession, the radicals proceeded to relight the candles with the new-style matches. Thus they earned for themselves the name "Locofoco," which stuck for thirty years.

The following advertisement appeared in the *Evening Gazette*, a Boston weekly, on June 18, 1836:

Loco Foco

Matches by which fire can be produced in an instant, by rubbing them upon a broad stone, or even the coat sleeve — in tin boxes — some on pasteboard, prepared with nitre, and very compact, being particularly designed for lighting cigars — at Preston's Medecine Store
Corner of Federal and Williams Sts.

The term "locofoco" was also applied to a self-lighting cigar with a match composition at the end, invented, in 1834, by John Marck of New York. Ingenious device!

The lucifers were imitated and manufactured by several competitors in England. In 1830 Samuel Jones of London patented his "prometheans." These were short rolls of paper dipped in chlorate of potash and sugar, with a tiny glass globule of sulphuric acid attached at the point. Pressure on the end broke the globule, freeing the acid and causing combustion. Such early matches were styled "congreves," after Sir William Congreve, who invented the Congreve rocket, and were so called because they exploded with much noise. They sometimes behaved like a rocket, too, as the pressure exerted on the tips occasionally caused the flaming ends to fly on the carpet or on people's clothes.

Phosphorus friction matches were first introduced commercially in 1833, and were made simultaneously in several places in Austria and Germany, where their manufacture on a large scale continued for many years. Matches of this type would, of course, strike anywhere, although the names "congreve" and "lucifer" were still applied to them. The poisonous yellow phosphorus first used has, in later years, been supplanted by phosphorus sulphide.

True friction matches were advertised in the *Evening Gazette* on October 20, 1836:

Superior Patent
Friction Matches

For the immediate production of a light caused by the rubbing the match quick and lightly against any hard substance. These matches, for quickness, sureness, and safety, surpass any yet ever in America. Warranted not to be in the least affected by damp atmosphere, or impaired by long keeping.

For sale by Levins & Co., 118 State Street, the only authorized agents for the city of Boston. Be particular to call as above, as a spurious article is circulated.

The first improved friction matches to be made in the United States were manufactured by Alonzo Phillips of Springfield, Massachusetts. A list of the manufacturers doing business between 1864 and 1883 may be found in Scott's Postage Stamp Catalogue under "United States revenue stamps."

In 1855 a safety match was invented by J. E. Lungström of Jönköping, Sweden. This differed from the ordinary match in that the phosphorus required for ignition was contained in the striking surface, instead of in the match end. This prevented the match from taking fire when struck on any other surface. This invention brings us to the modern era. Except for speed and quantity production, the method of manufacture remains today practically as it was in the 1850's. Until the pocket mechanical lighter becomes an affair of certainty rather than a sporting proposition, we shall probably continue to use matches by the million.

II. *Platinum Lighters of the Nineteenth Century*

By William F. Noé

MORE than a hundred years have passed since, in 1823, Professor Johann Wolfgang Doebereiner of Jena invented the platinum lighter, which was extensively used about the middle of the nineteenth century, before matches were perfected. Very unlike the present-day vest-pocket cigarette lighter, the *Doebereiner Platin-Feuerzeug* consisted of a specially constructed jar, from eight to twelve inches high, within which a piece of zinc, suspended on a wire, hung in a dilute solution of sulphuric acid. The action of this lighter was based on the remarkable property of spongy platinum, which, when a current of hydrogen gas is allowed to flow against it, becomes sufficiently heated to ignite the gas.

As shown in the sketch of Figure 1, the jar is constructed so that the inflammable hydrogen is produced only as needed. *A* is a glass tube, opening like a bell at the bottom, but tightly sealed to the brass lid of the jar. Inside

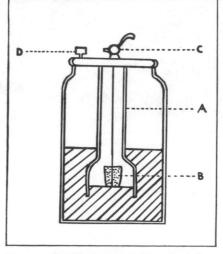

Fig. 1 — The Doebereiner Lighter (*1823-1847*)
For description see text.

this glass tube hangs the zinc, *B*. The jar is filled with enough dilute sulphuric acid to submerge the zinc completely. But the chemical action of the acid on the zinc produces hydrogen gas, which fills the tube, *A*, and forces the sulphuric acid down and out into the surrounding space of the jar.

As soon as the surface of the acid falls below the zinc, the production of hydrogen automatically ceases, and the lighter is ready for use. In the centre of the lid stands a brass stopcock, *C*. When this is opened, hydrogen is liberated through a fine aperture which points toward the spongy platinum located in the cup-shaped holder, *D*. This spongy platinum, as stated before, now becomes heated and ignites the jet of hydrogen.

As the hydrogen in the tube is consumed, the acid rises to occupy its place and again acts on the suspended zinc. Within a short time, the tube is once more filled with hydrogen; the

Fig. 2 (*left*) — DOEBER-
EINER LIGHTER
The jar is of red glass.

Fig. 3 (*right*) — DOEBER-
EINER LIGHTER
Clear glass jar with en-
graved bands. The inner
tube with its bell mouth is
clearly shown.

Fig. 4 (*below*) — SIR HUM-
PHREY DAVY'S LIGHTER
The removable hat of
Pierrot is attached to the
lighting apparatus.

acid has subsided; and the lighter is again ready to perform its function.

Subject to the necessity for pure chemical materials and for the occasional replacement of neutralized acid, these lighters gave good satisfaction; but they had to be kept in daily use. Surviving specimens, which are found in considerable variety, qualify today as antiques. Those with jars of colored glass are the rarest. Figure 2 shows a Doebereiner lighter with a dark red glass jar, while Figure 3 illustrates an unusual type whose jar bears an engraved decoration.

Another type of platinum lighter was that invented by the English natural philosopher Sir Humphrey Davy. The Davy lighter consists of a bottle, to whose stopper is attached a metal rod, which, at its lower end, carries a small sponge partly encased in metal. A little alcohol is placed in the bottle. When light is wanted, the bottle is shaken so as to moisten the sponge with alcohol. The stopper, with its attached sponge, is now removed and a pinch of platinum black,* carried in another bottle, is applied to

the alcohol-moistened sponge. Genial contact with alcohol causes the platinum black to glow with sufficient warmth to ignite a sulphur-tipped splint of wood called "spunk."

Davy's method of striking a light was even more complicated than the rites and incantations performed by a dry-fly fisherman. The great scientist's device, as we may well imagine, never came into general use, and specimens of the type are, in consequence, very hard to find. The one illustrated in Figure 4 is in the form of a kneeling Pierrot with a removable hat, to which is attached the metal rod which carries the sponge. This quite delightful bit of white porcelain, with its green base and blue-trimmed costume may well cause collectors to grieve over the non-success of Davy's invention.

The platinum lighter was, at best, an interim device. By 1847 it was losing ground to other methods of obtaining fire, chiefly to matches. Yet, throughout the nineteenth century, some specimens remained in use among conservative old people who had become so used to them that they preferred them to matches. Indeed, I remember lighters that were performing regular service as recently as ten years ago.

* Platinum black is finely divided platinum, resembling lampblack. It absorbs eight hundred times its volume of oxygen from the air.

136

Sundry Candle Molds

Based on notes and illustrations supplied by ELYSE S. RUSHFORD *and* STEPHEN VAN RENSSELAER

CANDLES were probably evolved from such more primitive lighting devices as resin-soaked tow, grease-impregnated rush or fibre, or masses of fat or wax hand molded about soft wood cores. In early colonial days, and still earlier abroad, candles were made by the process known as *dipping*. This implied first the twisting of wicks, several of which were then successively looped over a tapering stick and dipped in melted tallow. It was over such a stick or rod that the nimble Jack of the Mother Goose rhyme did his jumping.

With the first dipping a thin layer of tallow adhered to the wicks, which, still dangling from their stick, were set aside to cool, while another batch was being immersed. By that time the first lot was perhaps cool enough to be subjected to a second torrid bath, to acquire a second coating of grease, and again to be set aside to harden. So the process continued until the original slender wicks had taken on a sufficient covering of tallow to enable them when dry to stand upright in a candle holder and sustain a fair flame in the wick.

Just when this slow and painstaking method was superseded by the employment of candle molds is a debatable question. Probably the date coincides with the advent of the tinsmith, for the great majority of surviving molds are of tin. Now and then one may run across a pewter mold apparently of American make, while late molds of red earthenware supported in a heavy wooden frame are by no means uncommon. In Europe candle molds of glass appear to have been occasionally employed, but they must have been dangerously fragile.

While it may seem strange that purely utilitarian articles such as candle molds should exhibit any great diversity of design, the fact remains that they do. Apparently every tinsmith had his own notions as to how the individual tubes should be shaped, how they should be grouped, and at what angle they should be set to ensure best results.

The molding of candles presented no very serious difficulties. Each tube of the mold was perforated at the lower end. Through this a flax or cotton wick was threaded until it projected slightly from the tube, effectually sealing the small terminal aperture. The upper end of the wick was looped about a piece of wire laid across the cup framing the large opening of the tubes. Into this cup melted tallow was poured until it had filled the attached tube, or tubes, and completely encased each inserted wick. After the tallow had cooled and hardened, sometimes for twenty-four hours, the mold was plunged into hot water to loosen the tallow. The completed candles were then withdrawn from the mold and hung out-of-doors to season.

Some skill and care were, however, requisite to the success of this labor-saving method. Wicks had to be exactly centred in their tubes, and drawn taut enough to obviate kinks. The tallow,

Fig. 1 — VARIOUS CANDLE MOLDS
   Third in second row and first in lower row have pewter tubes. Large mold centred in lower row has sixteen earthenware tubes (see ANTIQUES, December 1926, *p. 460*). Smaller molds are for running tapers and lantern candles.
From the collection of Stephen Van Rensselaer

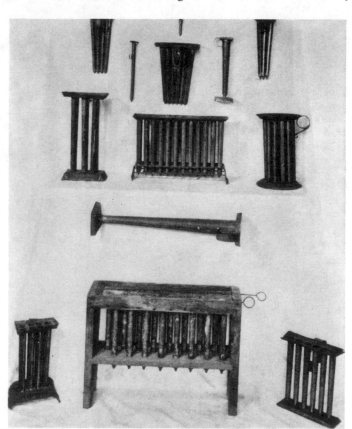

Fig. 2 — VARIOUS CANDLE MOLDS
   The single trumpet-shaped tubes are said to have been made for church candles. Note the wires for supporting wicks in the large mold with twenty-four earthenware tubes, shown centred in the lower row.
From the collection of Stephen Van Rensselaer

137

rendered from deer suet, bear's grease, and the leftover fats from domestic butchering, had to be of just the right consistency and purity. Sometimes it was supplanted by beeswax, which, however, could not be used in molds. Bayberry wax, which in burning yields a faintly spicy odor, was also occasionally employed. In large communities the making of both candles and soap was carried on commercially at a fairly early period — witness Gilbert Ash's advertisements in the New York papers of 1759 (ANTIQUES for March 1932, *p. 123*). On farms, however, and among families who were obliged to exercise rigid economy, these allied arts continued to be domestic occupations until well into the 1800's. In remote regions of the United States they may be practiced even today.

The accompanying illustrations from the collections of Stephen Van

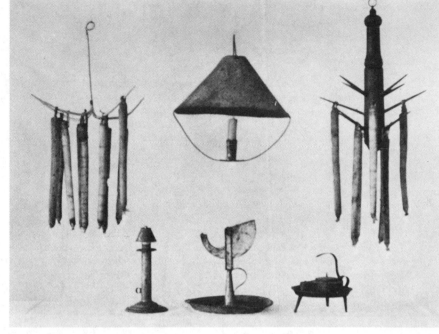

Fig. 3 — CANDLE DRIERS
The wrought-iron hook at the left might also have served in place of a stick to hold the wicks in making candles by the dipping method.
From the collection of Stephen Van Rensselaer

Rensselaer and Elyse S. Rushford portray virtually every known type of American candle mold, from miniature examples, in which Christmas lights and small tapers were cast, to huge affairs whose equipment of tubes permitted the running of a dozen or two plump candles at a single pouring.

The age of these sundry examples is probably beyond guessing. Nevertheless, in view of human conservatism even in the adoption of improved methods, it is reasonable to surmise that molds exhibiting tapered tubes are earlier than those whose tubes are vertical cylinders. The dipped candle was, of necessity, slightly conical in form; but it inevitably established a conception of candle propriety that was not immediately overcome when new methods of manufacture were introduced — an event that is impossible to date.

Fig. 4 (above) — SINGLE AND DOUBLE TIN CANDLE MOLDS
From the collection of Elyse S. Rushford

··❦◉❦··

Fig. 5 (left and right) — TWO CAPACIOUS TIN MOLDS
That at the left has a capacity of twenty-four candles; that at the right, thirty candles.
From the collection of Elyse S. Rushford

Fig. 1 — A SNUFFER SEQUENCE

a, Early wrought iron type; *b, c, d*, cast types with greater or less elaboration of treatment. Of these, *d* — perhaps the latest — has a shutter in the container, presumably for better preventing the dropping of bits of greasy wick. The very simple type shown in *e* may have been used for lamp wicks.

Old-Time Iron Snuffers

By FREDERIC FAIRCHILD SHERMAN

Illustrations from the author's collection

HAVING become interested in the variety of decorative designs in the handles of old-time American iron candle snuffers, I began, sometime ago, to collect such snuffers with the idea of determining how many variations I might discover and how many motifs constituting the basis of design common to them. For a time it seemed that I scarcely ever found duplicates; and even now, with over thirty designs in my modest collection, I run across a "new" one every now and then.

The collecting of snuffers is a fascinating pursuit, and, as these little household objects may usually be purchased for a really trifling sum, one can indulge himself without any of that feeling of extravagance which often follows the acquisition of a really expensive object of antiquity. Of course snuffers do not make so brave a show or so decided a hit with one's friends as fine old clocks; nor are they so useful as gateleg, or Dutch-foot tables, or Windsor chairs; but a number of them hanging along a fireplace, beneath a mantel, are quite as successful a decoration as a similar number of framed samplers or silhouettes hung about the house.

As soon as one has secured a number of snuffers, it is wise, in collecting, to have each specimen photographed or to make tracings of the handles (wherein they vary most) so as not to duplicate forms already acquired. It must be remembered, of course, that some which have identical handles vary in the form or decoration of the boxlike wick container. These containers have flat, oval, or other shaped tops, which are often decorated.

The earliest form of snuffer was probably a pair of plain hand-wrought scissors. The next, perhaps, was like that illustrated herewith in Figure 1 *a*, still hand-wrought but with a boxlike container added to catch the cut off portion of the wick. Following this came *b*, in all respects similar to the foregoing except that it is "cast." Next we have the addition of feet supporting the snuffers, as in *c*; and, following that, *d*, a patented form, and perhaps the latest, which has in the box container an automatic slide — lifted and released by opening the snuffer — which effectually prevents the cut off portion of the wick from dropping out before the snuffers have been closed. Figure 1 *e*, the last of those illustrated, is included in the belief that it is a snuffer evolved for use with old-time whale oil lamps. It is put together with screws and has sharpened scissorlike blades, evidently constructed to cut a thick wick. The lower blade bears a simple tray, for catching burnt fragments.

This pair of snuffers, which chances to be dated, bears the legend *J. Phares, Patd. Sept. 12, 1854.*

The candle snuffer continued to be used long after the introduction of oil — and even of gas — for lighting purposes. The cast metal specimens of the early nineteenth

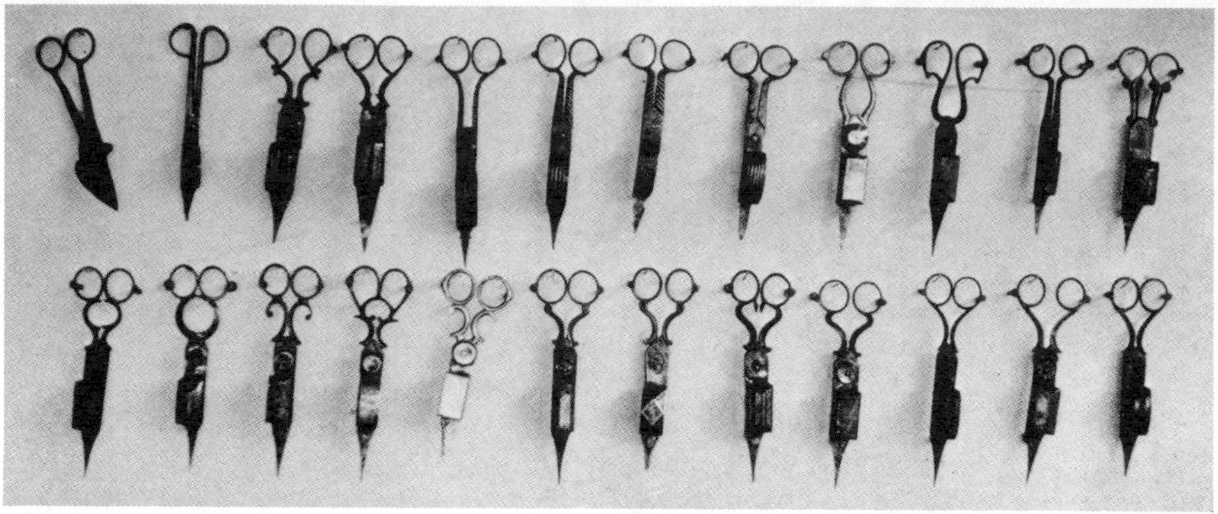

Fig. 2 — SNUFFERS, VARIOUS AND SUNDRY

century were turned out in great quantities. In earlier days, snuffers were hand wrought by the village blacksmith, and show finger holds which are simply bent to the desired form, while the container is cut out of the upper piece and turned over against the flat bottom in a half circular form. As soon as they were made by casting, snuffers began to be decorative, even before they acquired feet.

With the advent of this decorative treatment of handles and containers, there came a seemingly endless variety of patterns. It is this fact which makes the collecting of snuffers a happy and exciting pastime. Snuffers are found oftener than not with the simple iron or painted tin trays that originally ac-

companied them. By scouring the rust from the snuffers themselves and by furbishing up the trays, these venerable utensils may be made to serve very well today in a country house where candles are used — particularly if the old type of iron candlesticks can be secured to use with them.

For brass candlesticks one should have brass snuffers, and for silver, snuffers either of silver or of Sheffield plate. However, as a large proportion of old houses which are now used for summer homes or dwellings are lighted throughout by electricity, the arrangement of snuffers above the fireplace, as in the accompanying illustration, is suggested as an effective method of displaying a collection.

Fig 3—SNUFFERS BY THE MANTEL'S RIM
At Cedar Cottage, Westport, Connecticut, a row of snuffers makes pleasing tracery against white woodwork.

140

BY FRANK L. HORTON

New thoughts on eighteenth-century lighting

SOME THREE YEARS AGO I WAS INTRODUCED to the glass ball illustrated here by Mrs. Lucy Leinbach Wenhold, a direct descendant of John Leinbach, who had been a shoemaker in the old town of Salem, North Carolina. Carefully unwrapping this strange object, Mrs. Wenhold told me the family tradition that it was used, when filled with water, to concentrate the light of a candle on the shoemaker's work.

About a year later I came across a second bit of information which, like a jigsaw puzzle, locked with this interesting tradition. My routine research for material relating to the building of the Moravian town of Salem (now a part of Winston-Salem) had led me to the German rec-

Shoemaker's ball as it was used to concentrate the light of the candle. *Photograph by Ed T. Simons.*

ords of the various business boards of Wachovia, the tract of land purchased by the Moravians from the Earl of Granville for their settlements in North Carolina. Bethabara was the first of these settlements and it was in the minutes of the town's Elders' Conference for January 1771 that the second link was found: "It was held desirable that for this spring we should order white [clear] fish-oil and white [clear] glass lamps for illuminating our sleeping halls. The latter could be ordered from Br. Becker in Litiz, at least 3 dozen. Also we must order several balls for the shoemakers."

A check in the ledger of the Bethabara books revealed an account headed *Johann Becker in Litiz* which was credited with the following item on September 30, 1771: "Salem, Glass Lamps and Balls, 1 Roasting Oven . . . £ 15:2:5."

I am indebted to Miss Mary A. Huebener of Lititz, Pennsylvania, for the information that John Becker, from whom the lamps and balls were ordered, was the *Vorsteher* or business manager of the Brothers' House in Lititz at the time. In this capacity he sold items belonging to the Single Brothers' Choir.

A group of inventories of the various trades conducted in the Single Brothers' Choir at Salem contained additional information. Five inventories of the shoemaker's trade, from 1773 through 1777, list under the head *Equipment* the two items: "4 Glass Balls . . . 14 [s] . . . 1 Candlestick . . . 2 [s] 6 [d]." All the other inventories of this choir were examined, especially those of the saddler and tailor, since their crafts were similar, but none contained these items.

Raymond Townsend of Colonial Williamsburg supplied me with two inventories of shoemaker's equipment. One, dated 1759, of a shoemaker in Baltimore, does not list such equipment. The other, an inventory of George Wells, a shoemaker of Williamsburg, probated in 1754, lists "1 shoe makers window, 1 table . . . 3 [s] 9 [d]."

Two devices equipped with glass balls similar to the one found in Salem suggest to us how they must have been used. The simple wooden stand from Old Sturbridge Village has three of the four original globes suspended by leather straps attached to the crosspiece. The straps are adjustable and provide for raising or lowering the globes for better light. The wooden candle-board is more elaborate and has adjustable wooden nozzles to hold the glass balls. Each of these devices intensified and directed the light of a single candle sufficiently to enable three or four people to work by it.

Similar candle-boards were known as lacemaker's lamps and widely used in Switzerland and Germany during the nineteenth century. Some were designed with a central globe to hold oil and a floating wick. A simpler form was a glass ball mounted on a wooden base and then set in front of the candle.

The plates illustrating the eighteenth-century work-

shops and equipment of the jeweler and silversmith in Diderot's encyclopedia show a variation of the globe on a footed wooden base. In both engravings the globes are shown on a shelf in the window of the shop. Perhaps they were used to concentrate the sunlight as well as the light of a candle. No mention is made of the device in the section on shoemakers, however.

The two nineteenth-century prints illustrated show that glass globes were known and used well into the century. The lithograph, *The Shoemaker*, printed in Berlin in 1840, shows two globes hanging against the wall while not in use. The engraving of the *Pillow-lace Maker* appeared in 1871 as an illustration for a magazine article about the highly specialized art which flourished in Saxony at that time. The picture shows the globe actually being used to concentrate the light of the candle on the painstaking lace work.

The same entry in the Moravian records which introduces us to the shoemaker's ball offers fresh evidence of early use of *glass oil* lamps. The 1771 minutes quoted imply that the fish oil mentioned was to be used in the glass lamps. An inventory of church property in Salem, entitled *Gemeinhaus* and dated 1776, adds a specific notation: "In the Saal, Vestibule and otherwise belonging to the Gemeinhaus: . . . 2 brass chandeliers . . . 7 metal wall Sconces, of which 2 large ones at the table, 4 glass Oil Lamps in the Vestibule in iron brackets . . ." Though I have found no other mention of the use of glass oil lamps until the first quarter of the nineteenth century, these seem clear indications of their existence in the 1770's.

Stand using the same principle as the candle-board and hanging globe. This stand probably originally had four globes, since there is a mortise for a leather strap cut through the center of the cross piece on each of the four sides. *Courtesy of Old Sturbridge Village; photograph by Dick Hanley.*

Wooden candle-board with four adjustable wooden nozzles holding glass balls for water to concentrate the light and so enable four people to work by the light of a single candle. *Collection of Mrs. Charles P. Gorely.*

The Pillow-lace Maker, an engraving from *Every Saturday* magazine published in 1871. *Bettman Archive.*

The Shoemaker, colored lithograph published by A. Felcher in Berlin, c. 1840. Prominently displayed on the wall beside the window are two glass globes for concentrating light. Perhaps the stand on the shoemaker's table was intended to hold the globes around a candle? *Collection of Kennedy Galleries, Inc.*

Food warmers and their lamps

BY LURA WOODSIDE WATKINS

IN THE EIGHTEENTH CENTURY lamps of various kinds were used to provide heat for food warmers. Their similarities to lighting devices of the same period, and sometimes their peculiarities, have aroused curiosity. It is well known that John Miles of Birmingham, England, patented in 1787 a lamp with an upright burner tightly wedged into it in such a way that it could be carried about or overturned without spilling the oil. But what of similar lamps that appear in heaters before his time? Were they intended to burn alcohol, whale oil, or some other fuel? The search for an answer to these questions led to the discovery of a variety of warmers, heated in different ways and made of different materials.

Food warmers, toddy warmers, and teakettle heaters all had lamps. Toddy warmers and teakettle heaters were used for quick heating; this brief discussion is limited to food warmers, which were intended to keep a food or liquid warm all night.

Several types of food or pap warmers were made in England and on the Continent during the 1700's and well into the nineteenth century. All were intended primarily for the needs of an invalid or for the nursery. (In England, pap was a drink made of milk in which a little oatmeal had been boiled and which was afterwards strained, then beaten with egg yolks and butter, and flavored with orange-flower water and ambergris. Nearer home my grandmother made a drink—she called it gruel—which was similar, although it contained no eggs and was certainly not flavored or perfumed!) English potters began to make pap warmers long before 1750; they appear in many types of ware, beginning with delft and salt glaze and continuing through the era of Whieldon, and they were made by Wedgwood for many years. In the late eighteenth century and early nineteenth they appear in Leeds creamware and in Staffordshire earthenwares. For about a century they held their own with little change of form, though the heating equipment did change over the years.

A delftware food warmer (Fig. 1), made at Bristol, England, is among the earliest of these contrivances. Delft warmers have certain characteristic features. They consist of a cylinder or pedestal with an opening for inserting the lamp; a pan with handles, for the food, resting on a flange directly over the flame; a cover with a candleholder; and a lamp in the form of a little porringer with ear, or handle. Directly over the lamp opening is a mask. This had a function exactly like that of the projections on later tin nursery lamps (Fig. 9): it was open underneath to provide a draft for the heater.

In this delftware example the heater was a float lamp with a separate wick supported on a small cork-and-tin device that rested on the surface of the fluid. It burned whale or fish oil, since lamps burning other oils had been forbidden in English houses since 1709. Whale oil tended to impart an undesirable flavor to pap, as well as giving off a disagreeable odor. This difficulty was obviated by placing a wet sponge within the pedestal. As in night lights, the float wicks insured long burning without snuffing. Since a float-wick lamp, especially when enclosed in a device of this kind, gave out little light, a candle was probably lighted from the burner and placed in the holder on the cover as a light for an invalid's tray or bedside stand.

Delftware warmers and possibly other early types all have functional masks for ventilation, sometimes in front and back, and sometimes on the sides. It was not long, however, before the idea of making scattered perforations in the pedestal for the purpose was tried as an improvement, while the mask was retained as a decorative adjunct. The Whieldon example (Fig. 2) has such a mask; two holes giving the effect of a moustache were punched under the nose, while additional holes in the pedestal increase the draft. This piece is glazed with gray, green, and yellow flowed together on a cream ground, as on Whieldon plates, and it is equipped with free-standing vertical handles, such as were generally provided after the earliest period. Unfortunately, the lamp for this specimen is missing. We may assume that it was of a type that gave out light as well as heat, for the cover has a knob instead of a candleholder.

A rare Continental food warmer (Fig. 3) of French (Niderviller) porcelain dates from about 1770. This has dog, or lion, masks, each of which covers an air hole approximately three quarters of an inch in diameter.

Another early warmer of creamware (Fig. 4) has its original porringer-shape float lamp. Masks on the sides of the pedestal are mere ornaments; vents are provided by six large holes in the stand. This piece is peculiar in having no handles other than small projections below the masks.

These four early specimens have one feature in common: the interiors of their bases are perfectly plain, without the rim or ring that often appears on later examples.

While various types of lamps are found in pap warmers, candles were also used, but without much success at first. The principal difficulty with a candle was that it required frequent snuffing during the night to prevent it from

Fig. 1. Bristol delft food warmer with painted decoration attributed to Joseph Flower; c. 1750. The porringer held oil with a float wick. The mask conceals an air vent. *Victoria and Albert Museum; crown copyright.*

Fig. 2. Whieldon-type food warmer with scattered perforations to admit air; c. 1760. The mask with its two small holes is primarily a decoration. The missing lamp was undoubtedly a porringer. *Nelson Gallery and Atkins Museum.*

Fig. 3. Food warmer of Niderviller porcelain; France, c. 1770. The masks on this piece are functional, as on Fig. 1. *Victoria and Albert Museum; crown copyright.*

Fig. 4. English creamware heater with original float-wick lamp; c. 1785. Masks are merely decorative; air holes provide ventilation. *Old Sturbridge Village.*

1

2

3

4

smoking or going out. Not until 1799, when a method of compressing wax and tallow was discovered by William Bolts, did the candle become practicable. Spermaceti wax made into thick candles known as mortars furnished a light that would burn evenly all night. Mortars had wicks made of flax rather than cotton for better combustion and were sometimes pressed from sweet-smelling beeswax.

With the use of burners that gave out more intense heat, a warmer of five parts became necessary. Few of these have survived in their entirety. One fine and nearly complete example from the Wellcome Museum of Medical Science in London is illustrated by G. Bernard Hughes in *Country Life*, October 31, 1957. It has a pedestal with outstanding handles and a simple perforated pattern of air holes. Within the stand, and resting upon it, is a cylindrical water container under the food pan. The food container has two prominent loop handles placed vertically and a pouring lip. The cover, which is missing, was probably shaped to fit over the lip. The important part of this device is intact—a whale-oil lamp unlike anything familiar. A low cylindrical box in form, it has a loose cover set within its rim, as in a sugar bowl. A wick

Fig. 5. Remarkable food warmer of pierced creamware; c. 1800. Brass lamp with upright wick tube has a screw top, following John Miles' patent of 1787; a ring on its base fits into the ring in the heater. *Collection of Grace Lyman Stammers.*

Fig. 6. Illustration of a teakettle heater from Wedgwood's 1774 catalogue of creamware; an example of this type is in the collection of Nina Fletcher Little. Spirit lamp with drop burner gave quick heat for teakettle. A closely similar device, even to the air holes, has been found in silver, made by an unknown English smith in 1807. *Smithsonian Institution.*

Fig. 7. Illustrations from Wedgwood's 1817 catalogue showing food warmer disassembled, and assembled with burner in use. The lamp is an oil cup in which the small wick holder at the right was placed. The principal parts of the heater were the covered food container and water pan. *Smithsonian Institution.*

Fig. 8. Food warmer in blue-printed Staffordshire ware; c. 1825-1830. This was the type of whale-oil lamp known before Miles' invention of 1787. *Collection of Nina Fletcher Little.*

5

6

projects upwards through the knob, while three round holes in the lid insure proper combustion. There is a small handle at one side.

A food warmer of pierced creamware based on the same principle has a brass lamp with a screw-in whale-oil burner (Fig. 5). The fact that the lamp has a flange on its base that fits into the rim inside the stand shows that this was the original device. The screw-thread burner points to a date after the Miles patent of 1787 referred to above, while the candle-socket cover indicates that it is an early application of the patent—probably about 1800.

Wedgwood specialized in these food warmers, which he advertised in his 1774 creamware catalogue as "Night Lamps, to keep any liquid warm all night." His invoices also list them as "nursery" lamps. They may have been the same as the "lamps of the newest patterns, very useful for sick persons" advertised in New York in 1770 (Esther Singleton, *The Furniture of Our Forefathers,* p. 311).

Wedgwood made similar contrivances for heating a teapot. The essential difference between the two types of heater is shown in the illustration of a teakettle and stand from the 1774 catalogue (Fig. 6). The lamp inside it is a spirit lamp, apparently made of creamware, with a cover in the center of which is a small metal burner. This has a tiny handle and seems to be the familiar Continental drop burner. The use of alcohol as a fuel was practicable enough for the brief process of heating water for tea, but not, of course, for the all-night needs of a food warmer. The lamps under early eighteenth-century tea urns were also designed to burn alcohol.

Excellent illustrations of Wedgwood's food warmers appear in his creamware catalogue of 1817. His regular nursery lamp at this period was made up of six parts (Fig. 7). First there was the food container with a lip and double strap handles; this was rounded on the bottom to fit well into the water pan and had a cover, with an

145

acorn knob, shaped to extend over the pouring lip. The receptacle for water had straight, tapering sides, a flat bottom, and a heavy flanged lip that rested on the rim of the pedestal. The cylindrical pedestal had two vertical loop handles, an opening of convenient shape for inserting the lamp, and openings for air vents. The oil container was exactly like a little cup. These features are seen in other heaters, but the little holder for the wick is something new. Apparently made of creamware too, it is a little tripod with a wick tube, probably of metal, in the center, and a long handle. It was inserted into the cup of oil and lighted. A picture of the food warmer assembled (Fig. 7), on the same page of the catalogue, shows the little wick arrangement burning inside the stand.

Food warmers were also made in the familiar blue-printed Staffordshire. One example is remarkable in having its matching lamp which appears to be unique; it has a loosely fitted cover, with two wicks rising through it (Fig. 8).

As far as we know, ceramic food warmers were not made in America. Tin nursery lamps, however, were advertised by William Howe of Boston soon after he had patented such an appliance on December 31, 1812. His advertisement, headed "Improved Nurse Lamp," was published in the Boston *Columbian Centinel* for January 16, 1813, and illustrated an example that corresponded to a specimen owned by the late Mrs. S. C. H. Brand of Rumford, Rhode Island (see *The Rushlight*, Vol. I, p. 8, July 1935).

The body of this combination lighting device and heater had an outer casing and an inner lining, called the eclipser, which was equipped with an isinglass window that could be turned about as in a dark lantern to give illumination or to shut it off. The lamp itself was the familiar whale-oil type with a solid burner. When the appliance was to be used for heating, the eclipser was removed and the food was placed in a covered container. Made of many parts, this rather complicated device provided also a hollow handle for the insertion of a candle and a false base in which a tinder box with flint and steel was concealed. The tinware was japanned in a chocolate brown hue, and an oval brass plate on the eclipser was marked WM HOWES PATENT BOSTON.

As a consequence of Howe's invention many other tin lamps by different makers came on the market. Most examples seem to belong to the period between 1830 and 1850. Their original lamps are small straight-sided affairs with screw-thread whale-oil burners (Fig. 9), lacquered to match the ground color of the heater. Tin nursery lamps invariably have a section for water under the food container; in effect they are double boilers. Triangular vents on each side are reminiscent of the mask openings on the very earliest warmers.

A peculiar device which could never have had any very successful application was made probably around 1850 and fitted with a fluid lamp (Fig. 10). Its entire body was perforated in a fine mesh in order to release any accumulation of explosive gases, and its lamp, resting on a tin support, could be adjusted to any heat level by pushing a knob up or down in a slot. Although the top section has a spout like a teakettle, this appliance, like the whale-oil nursery lamps, is actually a double boiler. The water pan is an indication that it was intended primarily for keeping a liquid warm for an extended period.

The last device to be made on the principle of the

146

Fig. 9. Typical American tin nursery lamp of the early 1800's with a whale-oil lamp. Air vents performed the same function as in early delft examples. These heaters are always provided with a water pan, or double-boiler, arrangement. *Author's collection.*

Fig. 10. A food warmer of doubtful practicality, because designed for use with a fluid lamp; c. 1850. Painted red, it is constructed of fine meshed tin for release of explosive gases. The knob at the side raises or lowers the level of the lamp. *Author's collection.*

Fig. 11. Inexpensive nursery lamp made by Samuel Clarke and heated by one of his night lights; made as early as 1867. The lower section is provided with a glass globe like those of Clarke's fairy lamps. The food container is of porcelain; water pan and stand are of tin. *Author's collection.*

9

10

11

old ceramic heaters was Samuel Clarke's Patent Pyramid Nursery Lamp Food Warmer, which was in use before 1867. It was heated in the same manner as were Clarke's more familiar fairy lamps. The example shown here (Fig. 11) has a base and water pan made of tin, while the food container and cover are of porcelain—hence breakable. This specimen has its pyramid candle with the suggestive label "*The Burglar's Horror,*" and the original glass dome over it. An advertisement, said to be from an old *Whittaker's Almanac,* offers such candles at eight shillings per box; the number in a box is not stated (*The Rushlight,* Vol. VI, No. 2, p. 7, May 1940). The inventor says, "The Pyramid Night Lights have a patent prepared rush wick, are made much larger than any other Night Light, and give double the light; they are, therefore, very suitable for Nursery Lamps, lighting Passages, Lobbies, &c., and adaptable to many purposes for which the common Night Lamps are useless."

Clarke says of these warmers that "by their peculiar construction—the glass chimney conducting and concentrating heat to the bottom of the water vessel—a larger amount of light and heat is obtained than can be in any other lamp of the same class." And he adds, "*Without smoke or smell.*" His directions for using the food warmer and light read: "The food which is required to be kept hot to be placed in the porcelain panakin, and water in the tin vessel—just sufficient to admit of the porcelain panakin being placed therein. Care should be taken in lighting the Night Lights not to injure the top, which is a protection for the wick, but simply apply a lighted match or taper, and allow the material to melt away." Clarke's patent food warmers were made in three sizes, to hold one-half pint, three-quarters of a pint, or one pint, and were priced from three shillings, sixpence, to six shillings each; they were on sale "by all respectable dealers throughout the kingdom."

147

BY C. MALCOLM WATKINS

Associate Curator, Division of Ethnology, Smithsonian Institution

The collections: lighting devices

UNTIL 1800 THE LIGHTING OF THE New England small town was little different from what it had been when the Colonies were founded. Candles, now and then an open lamp or a pine splint, rarely a rush soaked in tallow—these constituted the traditional means for combatting darkness.

To them were added, around the turn of the century, the first fruits of the era of invention and expansion. Into Nantucket and New Bedford came supplies of whale oil; from Europe, inventions that made its use feasible and convenient. In 1784 Ami Argand, having applied scientific principles to lamp design, had invented the first successful lamp with air drafts and glass chimneys for increased combustion; and in 1787 the simple enclosed lamp, with burners screwed tightly into the top of the reservoir, had been patented by John Miles. By 1800 these improvements on candles were available in New England, where craftsmen made a variety of lighting devices, typically simple and practical.

Chandeliers, toggle arms, adjustable reading stands. well-proportioned lamps and candleholders—all these and many more are in the Old Sturbridge Village collection, which is one of the most important of its kind in the world. Beyond showing in detail the progress of artificial illumination in New England, it richly demonstrates European prototypes and comparative developments elsewhere. We can see the greater conservatism of the Pennsylvania German in his lamp forms, while we are soberly discouraged from inflating the New Englander's superiority in matters of ingenuity as we look at the work of his contemporaries. We can trace the course of inventions that were adopted in New England but originated elsewhere, and find lavish illustration of the backgrounds of form and design against which New England lighting devices should be considered. Thus, in presenting the entire sweep of the history of artificial illumination among western European peoples, the collection shows the early lighting of rural New England in proper perspective.

We may turn first to a charming variety of rushlights, those graceful wrought-iron contraptions with pincerlike jaws for grasping fat-soaked rushes. These examples were virtually all purchased in England by A. B. Wells, but it is likely that their counterparts were occasionally used here. One in the Woodside collection was found in the chimney of an eighteenth-century house in Haverhill, Massachusetts, and there are a few indications of their use elsewhere in the Colonies.

It may well be that they served as splintholders, for there are several early allusions to pine splints as lighting sources. Higginson, Wood, and Winthrop all refer to them. According to the last, splints were burned in the "corner" (probably the chimney corner, or fireplace) on a flat stone or iron, except when a stick was taken in the hand to go about the house. Sylvester Judd's *History of Hadley* has much to say about the use of pine splints,

or "candlewood," in the interior Massachusetts towns. The Reverend Nathan Perkins of Hartford, in his account of a tour through Vermont in 1789, wrote complainingly of a lodging in Jericho which "had no comfortable refreshment . . . was almost starved because I could not eat ye coarse fare provided for me . . . no candles pine splinters used in lieu of them . . . bed poor and full of flees." There are numerous holders specifically designed to hold splints, of which the majority are known to be European, but it is clear that in New England splints were used in any manner that was convenient.

At best, splints served only as inexpensive and inferior supplements to the tallow candle, whose evener light was the staple illuminant in New England farmhouses. The history of candlemaking devices is depicted in a fascinating adjunct to the lighting collection at Sturbridge. What is probably the earliest dated candle mold in any collection is a Swiss specimen of walnut, inlaid with a cross and *1578*. It divides in two lateral sections, as did many Continental ones. There are pewter and pottery molds, mostly Pennsylvanian in origin, and a wide diversity of the tin molds which were used in every farmhouse. Most typical of New England are the bundles of "candle sticks" or "broaches"—long whittled rods of wood from which wicks were suspended and dipped in the hot tallow to make candles. "Turnstiles" or dipping machines are also represented, but these are usually associated with commercial manufactories. One such device, characteristically chaste in design, is of New England Shaker origin. Hanging from the ends of its revolving spokes are square panels with holes bored through them for suspending the wicks. It is supported on three slender legs and painted red.

To what extent spermaceti candles found their way to the interior of New England is not known. Probably the owner of the Village's mansion house and others who, like him, bought their furniture in Boston allowed themselves the occasional elegancy of a spermaceti candle. There was sufficient demand by 1761 to justify the existence of the United Company of Spermaceti Candlers in and around Boston. The sign of one of its members, Joseph Palmer, now hangs in the Village, a spouting whale proclaiming the nature of his business.

New England excelled in making handsome devices for holding candles. The turn-of-the-century chandeliers in the Village meeting house are masterpieces of wood and wire. The wood turner and the woodcarver had a hand in the making of the chandeliers, but the tinsmith's contribution was more characteristic. One tin chandelier, illustrated, is utterly simple yet subtle in line and proportion. There are many other tin chandeliers—more than one would expect in a single collection—from New York and Pennsylvania as well as New England.

Adequate light for reading was a constant problem. Much reading must have been done by the light of the fireplace, where certainly the social activities of the family also were carried on after sundown. Reminiscences of early New England life repeatedly stress the domestic importance of the fire. E. H. Arr, in *New England Bygones* (Philadelphia, 1880), wrote a typical description: "My grandfather's kitchen was a sombre room, ceiled and painted brown; with huge beams, high dressers, and yawning fireplace. It had only two small windows . . . What it lacked by day was light and sunshine. At night, brightened by a roaring backlog, it was full of cheer. Then its beams and ceilings and simple furnishings were enriched by shadows, and the pewter dishes upon its brown dressers shone like silver."

The fire had to be augmented by close light, nevertheless. Iron "hogscraper" candlesticks, ubiquitous in New England farmhouses, were equipped with hooks for hanging on a slat of a ladder-back chair. Adjustable candlestands were fashioned of wood by the village joiner, or simply contrived at home. These were perhaps more frequent in Pennsylvania than New England, but were common to both, and there are many in the collection.

Candleholders for shop work range from simple to complex. Crude little L-shape sconces of wood were used in shoemakers' shops. So was an iron hook-shape device ending in an upright point to impale the candle. An ingenious contraption, also for a cobbler's bench, is the adjustable jointed toggle arm terminating in a hole for a candle or peg lamp.

Pierced tin cylindrical lanterns with conical tops were used in New England from early times to within living memory, and square types with tin frames and glass sides were common. But, as a rule, wooden examples are far rarer in New England than in Pennsylvania. Small portable lanterns were used in New England, as elsewhere; there is a wealth of European lanterns in the collection, some closely resembling New England types. After 1825 or so the whale-oil enclosed lamp made possible the general adoption of improved lanterns with blown-glass globes. The many handsome examples of these include several designed for railroad and marine use.

Before 1800, lamps were little used in New England, particularly inland. Higginson in 1630 mentioned the abundance of fish oil available for lamps, and early probate records bear him out. These were probably iron crusie types and Dutch-style brass spout lamps, of which numerous examples are in the collection. As for the interior towns, Judd states unequivocally that oil was not used. However, grease lamps, or sluts, were known, though only for kitchen or similar use. So-called betty lamps (crusies with wick supports), when they were used in the interior at all, probably burned fat. Betty

lamps in use are shown in the Fitch house and Fenno house kitchens (see Interiors).

In the coastal towns a tin cylinder lamp with spout for the wick and drip-catcher underneath was often used. Known as a *kyal*, or "Cape Cod spout lamp," this type was used in shops, or ships, and in loom rooms all along the New England coast.

As late as 1819 John Miles' "agitable" whale-oil lamp, patented in 1787, was still being acclaimed in *Niles' Register*. "Its great security against many of the chances of fire, deservedly places it among the preservations of property; while its neatness recommends it to the patronage of a judicious public." Tinsmiths and pewterers in southern New England used their skill to imitate Miles' patent, braziers in the larger towns made handsome specimens, and by 1820 the glass manufacturers were making great quantities of these lamps. Many types are shown in the collection, from tiny "wine-glass" chamber lamps to elaborate specimens with pressed bases.

After 1830 whale-oil lamps gave way to fluid lamps, designed to burn camphene and other volatile commercial fuels. These are represented, as are the complicated lard lamps that entered with the period of invention.

Meanwhile, scientifically designed lamps based on the Argand principle were introduced in the cities. We know that both Washington and Jefferson owned Argand lamps, and hardware catalogues in the Essex Institute show that they were available to northern contemporaries. There are several rare examples of the Argand lamp, and many variations, such as astral and sinumbra lamps with their ring-shape reservoirs, and the elaborate hydrostatic and Carcel lamps. The Carcel found use in city houses in the early decades of the century, but its occurrence in country villages must have been exceptional. A unique display of Count Rumford's "portable illuminators" shows a rare lamp type which did reach inland.

This is not the place to describe the subsidiary collections of Jewish ceremonial lamps, Catholic processional lanterns, miner's lights, candle snuffers, Renaissance candlesticks, marked Pennsylvania betty lamps, Continental glass lamps, sixteenth-century Swiss soapstone lamps with wick supports, or medieval Spanish candelabra. We leave it to the visitor to survey this rich background as a means of evaluating the history of artificial lighting in New England. In its entirety, the remarkable collection of lighting devices at Old Sturbridge Village is a most significant part of one of the nation's great assemblages of rural art.

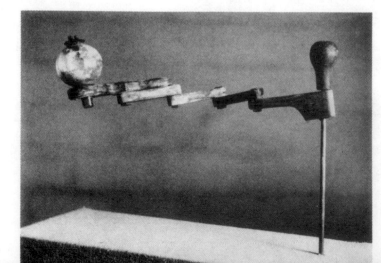

Published by permission of the Secretary of the Smithsonian Institution.

Wooden toggle arm (c. 1825), fitted with glass whale-oil peg lamp designed by a shoemaker to give light at his bench.

Chandelier with a charming rural flavor (southern New England, early 1800's). Turned wooden shaft and candle cups; wire branches to which delicate tin leaves are soldered.

Adjustable wooden candlestand from Connecticut, a characteristic New England example. The short turned arm with candle socket bored near each end moves up and down the threaded shaft, which is secured in a rough octagonal block on four splayed legs. In the Fitch house; a similar stand is shown in the Fenno house east room (see Interiors).

Tin chandelier of ageless simplicity (early 1800's). Probably designed for a tavern ballroom.

Homemade candle lantern with glass panes set in solid pine sides and conical tin top probably salvaged from a pierced tin lantern. In the Fitch house.

Left to right: *Kyal*, or "Cape Cod spout lamp," one of a pair; coastal New England, late 1700's or early 1800's. Sheet-iron betty (the wick support is missing). Tin shop lamp, consisting of a whale-oil lamp mounted in a tin pan for a reflector. Early nineteenth-century whale-oil lamp from the Hartford area made by a tinsmith with a flair for the classical. Tin whale-oil lamp (c. 1800) modeled closely after Miles' patented "agitable" lamp of 1787. The last three are developments of Miles' patent.

Left to right: Painted tin Argand lamp made in London by the firm of R. Bright, "late Argand & Co.," about 1800; a glass chimney originally fitted on the flange around the tubular burner. Engraved portrait of Ami Argand, lamp inventor. Two tin "portable illuminators," designed by Benjamin Thompson, Count Rumford, a native of Woburn, Massachusetts.

IN ITS COLLECTION of lighting devices the Henry Ford Museum takes, deservedly, special pride. Illustrating the whole history of lighting, it is one of the most comprehensive in the country, comparable only to those at the Smithsonian Institution and at Old Sturbridge Village. Its section on the electric light alone is the largest and most complete in the world. This special emphasis is due to Henry Ford's long and close friendship with Thomas A. Edison, for whom he named his whole cultural enterprise: the Edison Institute comprises the Henry Ford Museum, Greenfield Village, and the Greenfield Village Schools. An outstanding feature of the Village is the complex of buildings in which Edison's laboratory and workshops from Menlo Park are preserved.

Illustrated at the top of this page is Edison's first practical incandescent lamp, 1879, from the museum's collection. Other lighting devices are shown with *Furniture; English and Irish glass; English silver;* and *Other metals.*

CANDLEMAKER'S SHOP. Here candles of beeswax and bayberry are made by the old hand methods. Molds of many sizes, in tin, pewter, and pottery, are at hand and, in the foreground, a wax-pouring device with multiple orifices for filling a whole row of molds at once. Note the rare circular molds suspended from the ceiling. The dipping rack in the background works on the principle of a balance: as the dipped candles grow heavier, iron weights can be added to the balance pans in compensation.

Lights of simple basic types used in America from earliest colonial days until the mid-1800's. *Left to right:* Rush or splint holder of wrought iron set in conical wood base; height 8¼ inches. Crusie, or so-called open betty lamp, with hanger, of wrought iron. True betty lamp with wick channel and closed reservoir, of wrought iron; pivoted lid with bird finial; wire wick pick. Grease lamp of glazed redware, with wick channel, probably Pennsylvania.

English brass chandelier, early 1700's, perhaps the most impressive of a large group of chandeliers, candelabra, and girandoles. The well-modeled baluster stem with urn and ball supports two tiers of six candle arms each, the arms finely scrolled and terminating in narrow candle cups with drip pans. Diameter 27 inches.

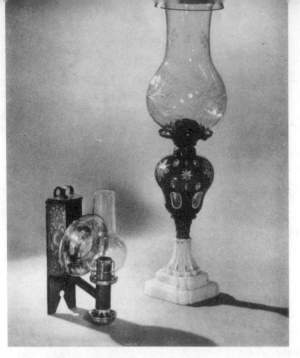

American whale-oil and kerosene lamps. Hanging wall lamp of Argand type with circular burner and blown-glass chimney, c. 1835-1840; painted and stenciled tin with brass fittings and silvered reflector. Glass kerosene lamp attributed to Sandwich, c. 1870-1880; blue and white overlay font on gilded opaque-white base; engraved blown-glass shade with rolled rim; brass fittings; height 24¼ inches.

American whale-oil and camphene lamps, c. 1830-1860. Clear blown glass with solid baluster stem and saucer base, made by the Boston and Sandwich Glass Company; reservoir fitted with tin double burner for whale oil. Glass peg lamp, rose and white overlay gilded, with brass camphene burners and pewter extinguishers; fitted in an opaque-white glass columnar candlestick; over-all height 12½ inches. Pewter swinging lamp for hanging, carrying, or setting on a table, the font suspended by copper pins; brass camphene burners with pewter caps. Cast brass lamp with saucer base and finger grip, for use with oil or camphene burner. Painted tin lamp on cast-iron base, with blown-glass reservoir and double whale-oil burner; glass bull's eye to intensify light.

Dated and marked lamps for grease or lard. Grease lamp, with swinging brass font on iron stand; stamped on font supports *1855* and *P.D.*, for Peter Derr, Berks County, Pennsylvania; height 10 inches. Lard lamp of tin on cast-iron base, gilded; stamped *SN. & H.C. Ufford,/117 Court St./ Boston/Kinnears Patent/Feb. 4, 1851.* Grease lamp of tin with iron plunger for forcing fuel from reservoir into font; stamped on plunger *I. Smith, Pat'd Aug. 8, 1854.* The collection also includes special-purpose lights, lighters, lamp fillers, snuffers, and extinguishers.

American tin lanterns. Triangular, with candle socket, pressed-glass panes; 1830-1840. Japanned folding pocket lantern; mica panes; compartments for candles and matches in hinged back; marked *Minor's Patent, Jan. 24th, 1865.* Lantern with removable tin kerosene lamp, c. 1860-1875; beveled glass panels. Cylindrical lantern with candle socket, c. 1830; the words *Jackson Forever* in the piercing confirm the nineteenth-century date; height 17¼ inches.

Chandelier for gas, American, c. 1880. Brass ceiling fixture, three scroll arms wound with tendrils; grape-leaf motif in pierced cast ball of stem, repeated in cocks; each light equipped with mantle and cylindrical glass shade. Diameter 30 inches.

The American home

Part II: Lighting devices and practices

BY ELISABETH DONAGHY GARRETT

I have now sat down to bring up my Journal from leaving Brunswick [North Carolina]; which we did last Friday, under the care of a Mr Eagle[s]. . . . We were in a Phaeton and four belonging to my brother. . . . I was charmed with the woods. . . . But by and by it begins to grow dark, and as the idea of being benighted in the wilds of America was not a pleasing circumstance to a European female, I begged the servant to drive faster, but was told it would make little difference, as we must be many hours dark, before we could get clear of the woods, nor were our fears decreased by the stories Mr Eagle[s] told us of the wolves and bears that inhabited that part of the country . . . we soon found ourselves lost in the most impenetrable darkness, from which we could neither see sky, nor distinguish a single object. . . . All I had ever heard of lions, bears, tigers and wolves now rushed on my memory . . . [but] in a few minutes we came to an opening that showed us the sky and stars, which was a happy sight in our circumstances . . . on the first turning the carriage made, we found ourselves in front of a large house from the windows of which beamed many cheerful tapers, and no sooner were we come up to the gate than a number of black servants came out with lights. Mr Eagle[s] . . . welcomed us to his house.[1]

THE "MANY CHEERFUL tapers" that beamed from the windows of Joseph Eagles' house, the Forks, were a most comforting sight to Janet Schaw as she emerged from the tenebrous depths of a North Carolina wood in March 1775. Joseph Eagles had been expecting her and the tapers and lights were synonymous with hospitality and a warm welcome. Within the intimacy of the family circle adequate lighting was a cherished comfort and indicated a well-regulated and, thus, happy household. Light suggested an inner warmth and a feeling of security and solace. Ulysses Prentiss Hedrick alluded to the emotional impact of light when he wrote of northern Michigan in the 1870's,

Many a time the sight of a light from a lamp or lantern brought cheer to my heart. . . . When I was coming home late on a dark night, especially in a gale in winter, [the lantern's] tiny wick all aglow warmed me all the way

Pl. I. *Mrs. Isaac Smith* (1726–1786), by John Singleton Copley (1738–1815), 1769. Oil on canvas, 50⅛ by 40⅛ inches. A wealthy patron's high esteem for sparkling, polished surroundings is evident in the pearls in Mrs. Smith's hair, around her neck, and at her elbows; the blue-green changeable silk lining of her plum-color silk gown; and the sheen of the tightly stretched gold damask on her polished mahogany armchair, emphatically outlined with brass tacks. *Yale University Art Gallery, New Haven, Connecticut; photograph by Joseph Szaszfai.*

Fig. 1. *Snuffing the Candle for Grandpa,* detail of the cover of *Harper's Weekly* for Saturday, March 17, 1866. Colored engraving, 15⅜ by 11 inches over all. It is not possible to determine if the glazed doors of the desk-and-bookcase in the background have been lined, but this was a frequent practice, often with bright green silk, making these bookcases a significant feature in a candlelit room. ". . . when our grandmother proposed stories, and she had a marvellous treasury of that kind to draw from, how eagerly we sought our places in the sitting room around the low-cushioned chair, which was placed in the warmest corner, the room all aglow with the bright, blazing fire. 'There is no need to light the candles,' she would say; and we were very glad to avoid the interruption occasioned by snuffing them, especially when so unfortunate as to snuff them out" (Emily R. Barnes, *Narratives, Traditions and Personal Reminiscences* [Boston, 1888], pp. 61–62). *Private collection; photograph by Helga Photo Studio.*

154

Pl. II. *Making Believe*, by Seymour Joseph Guy (1824–1910), 1870. Oil on canvas, 15 by 12 inches. The vigorous crest rail and stiles of the Chippendale side chair cast an exaggerated shadow on the wall. In *Snow-Bound* John Greenleaf Whittier recalled his boyhood evenings before the fire and captured the exaggeration of cast shadows in the couplet: "The cat's dark silhouette on the wall/A couchant tiger's seemed to fall" (quoted in Wallace Brockway and Bart K. Winer, eds., *Homespun America* [New York, 1958], p. 166). *Collection of Jo Ann and Julian Ganz Jr.*

through. There was nothing comparable to lamps and lanterns in our isolated home to raise the morale of its inhabitants, whether they were outside or inside the house.[2]

In nineteenth-century books on household management good lighting is often equated with a good marriage. Underscoring the implications of a well-lit home, Eliza Leslie forewarned the bride in 1840, "A neat and well-conducted house, with fires and lights always as they should be . . . are comforts that are not lightly prized by any married man."[3]

With the innumerable tasks to be performed before sunrise and completed after dusk, light was indeed a preface to comfort in and about the house. "It was amazing how many lanterns were used on our farm," Hedrick wrote. "For eight months in the year every male on the place had to have a lantern to do early morning chores and to finish up in the evening."[4] Maria Brown recalled her years on an Iowa farm in the mid-nineteenth century: "Our work had to go on after dark by light that was none too good. We had only candles on that farm at first. I had an iron candlestick with a hook on it that hung on the back of my chair, so I could get light on my

work. The wicks of those candles were as thick as your little finger."[5]

Candles were the primary source of artificial light throughout the seventeenth, eighteenth, and first half of the nineteenth century. In Elizabeth Buffum Chace's home town of Smithfield, Rhode Island, in the early nineteenth century, "Brass candlesticks held the only lighting apparatus."[6] Even after the introduction of gas Thomas Webster and Frances Byerly Parkes counseled in 1856, "Candles, from their portability and other qualities, supply, upon the whole, the most convenient and the most general mode of obtaining artificial light for domestic purposes."[7] Before 1850 candles were made of tallow, bayberry, myrtleberry, beeswax, spermaceti, or stearine.[8] Candlemaking was a time-consuming and messy chore that was performed in the cold months. The Reverend Edward Holyoke, president of Harvard College, recorded in his diary on March 22, 1743, "Made 112 Baybery Candles," and the following day, "Made 62 lbs. tallow Candles."[9] A plaintive Mary Cooper detailed this drawn-out process at her Long Island farmhouse in 1772. She stayed up most of Saturday night, December 19, "trying tallow" and on Monday was "Up all this night trying fat," so that by Wednesday evening, exhausted, she wrote, "I am up all this night makeing candels."[10] On Maria Brown's Iowa farm, "once we dipped four hundred candles in four hours."[11]

By the opening years of the nineteenth century candles and oil lamps[12] were often used simultaneously. Both required constant maintenance. "The Saturday cleansing and polishing of the steel candlesticks and snuffers was the abhorred task usually allotted to the younger girls in the family," Frances Breckenridge wrote of her Meriden, Connecticut, childhood.[13] Charles Haswell itemized some of the inconveniences of lighting:

previous to about 1832 . . . the instruments of illumination were oil lamps and spermaceti or tallow candles. The lamps required attention to the trimming of their wicks and to guard them from smoking, and the candles required repeated snuffing and would occasionally run or drip, as it was termed, frequently involving damage thereby, as in ballrooms, dancing parties in dwellings, etc.; as such places were illuminated by chandeliers with a great number of candles therein, some one or more of which would drip, and fortunate were the parties who did not receive drops of spermaceti upon their dresses.[14]

Tallow candles in particular required frequent snuffing to remove the snuff, or charred end of the wick, which caused the candle to gutter and smoke.[15] This operation required considerable dexterity or the flame would be extinguished (see Fig. 1). Oil lamps required daily maintenance or they too smoked. Robert Roberts observed in 1827:

Lamps are now so much in use for drawings-rooms, dining rooms, and entries, that it is a very important part of a servant's work to keep them in perfect order, so as to show a good light. I have been in some houses where the rooms were almost filled with smoke and the stench of the oil, and the glasses of the lamps clouded with dust and smoke.[16]

Kerosene was introduced on a large scale about 1869, but, for all its advantages, it did not put an end to this daily cleaning. "Asked to name her most arduous work," Ulysses Hedrick wrote, "... my sister would have said 'cleaning lamp chimneys and lanterns,' a daily task as long as she was in her father's house. We burned kerosene oil and lots of it. Lamps and lanterns had to be filled and their globes cleaned, lamps one day, lanterns the next."[17]

It is understandable, then, that lighting devices were used sparingly. Having spent so many hours making candles, Mary Cooper must have been thankful to be able to note on Sunday evening, July 26, 1772, "I come home alone and went to bed with out liteing a candel."[18] "As may be supposed," wrote Frances Breckenridge, "the candles were used with severe economy."[19] George Channing had a similar recollection of his childhood in Newport, Rhode Island: "Candles were a great luxury (little children were obliged to find their way to bed in the dark)."[20] Characteristically, a room would be lit by one candle, one or two small oil lamps, or one larger lamp. "How well I remember the room, in which the family spent their evenings around the square centre table, lighted perhaps by two brass lamps, or by what was called an astral lamp," wrote William Davis[21] (see Fig. 3). Candles and small lamps would be stored in the kitchen, where they were cleaned.[22] After being lit at the kitchen fire, kitchen taper, or tinder box they would be carried to where they were needed and placed on a table or stand.[23] The table might then be drawn into the room or up to the fire for additional light and for warmth, and chairs would be brought up to it.[24] Throughout the eighteenth century standing candlesticks that remained in place; the occasional candlestick left on the mantel; chandeliers, which were found primarily in the homes of the wealthy; and candle branches or sconces, which were frequently used in fashionable middle-class homes, would probably have been without candles except when in use, as one sees in the English conversation pieces of the time.[25] By the second and third decades of the nineteenth century a couple of fluid lamps or a pair of Argand lamps might be left permanently on the mantel (see Fig. 2).[26] In Meriden, Connecticut, during the nineteenth century, "... the glass lamps were often the most conspicuous mantel ornaments in what were then supposed to be the best rooms."[27] I believe that the mantel lamps were for decoration and provided supplemental lighting only when there were visitors or a special occasion. An astral or a solar lamp might dominate the center table or the table in the window pier, and it would be around this lamp that the family would gather in the evening (see Fig. 3). The use of a single lamp is implied in Eliza Leslie's instructions for cleaning an astral lamp: "A lamp that is nightly in use should be trimmed and replenished regularly every morning, otherwise there will be no certainty in it burning, and it will go out unexpectedly at any time in the evening, leaving the room in darkness."[28] Ulysses Hedrick is explicit about having only one lamp in each room in his youth: "There were three large double-burner lamps: one in the living room, another on the dining-room table, and a third in the kitchen. There was a single-burner for each bedroom."[29]

This scarcity of light had tremendous implications for the early family. Light was a cement which held

Fig. 2. Portrait of two children, attributed to Robert Peckham (1785–1877), c. 1844. Oil on canvas, 53½ by 41 inches. The painting is believed to depict Charles Lynde Eaton (b. 1841) and his sister Emily Lynde Eaton (b. 1838) of Malden, Massachusetts. It has been attributed to Peckham by Dale T. Johnson ("Deacon Robert Peckham: 'Delineator of the Human Face Divine'," *American Art Journal*, January 1979, pp. 33, 34). The globes of the pair of Argand lamps on the mantel in this Massachusetts interior face toward the center. Paintings and prints frequently show them facing the ends of the mantel, but in all cases the globes are in directional accord. The wreath of artificial flowers around the base of the handsome astral lamp was typical of the period. *Fruitlands Museums, Harvard, Massachusetts.*

the family together, imposing a temporal regularity on its members, who were forced to gather to benefit from the single light source and to retire when it was extinguished. The difficulty of seeing in such dim surroundings meant that the privacy the extended family lost because it was so numerous was compensated for by the secrecy of darkness, and court records and literature are full of references to people who were unperceived by others in the room. Also, things simply look different by candlelight. When Elizabeth Barrett Browning wrote, "Colours seen by candle light/Will not seem the same by day,"[30] she summed up Benjamin Franklin's apology to his wife, Deborah, on February 15, 1758, concerning "7 Yards of printed Cotton, blue Ground, to make you a Gown; I bought it by Candlelight, and lik'd it then, but not so well afterwards."[31]

Pl. III. *Mrs. Ezekiel Gold-thwait* (1713–1794), by Copley, 1771. Oil on canvas, 50 by 39¾ inches. Before bringing his bride to Mount Vernon for the first time George Washington sent ahead instructions to "get out the Chairs and Tables, and have them very well rubd and Cleand; . . . the Stair case ought also to be polished in order to make it look well" (John C. Fitzpatrick, ed., *The Writings of George Washington* [Washington, D. C., 1931], vol. 2, p. 318). And in 1829 Frances Byerly Parkes advised that "mahogany . . . is capable of receiving, by mere friction, the highest polish" (*Domestic Duties; or, Instructions to Young Married Ladies* [New York, 1829], p. 166). *Museum of Fine Arts, Boston, bequest of John T. Bowen in memory of Eliza M. Bowen.*

The dim light of candles or lamps could be dramatically supplemented by firelight. On the frontier and in the deep country heart pine or other resinous wood was gathered for candlewood. Among the "regular labours" of Daniel Drake while a boy in Kentucky was picking up "chips in the corn basket for kindlings in the morning, and for light, through the long winter evenings when 'taller' was too scarce to afford sufficient candles, and 'fat' so necessary for cooking, that the boat-lamp, stuck into one of the logs of the cabin over the hearth, could not always be supplied. . . ."[32] For William Fletcher King, who lived in a two-story log house near Zanesville, Ohio, "One of my daily duties was to prepare a good stock of 'light wood' of pine or other wood affording a good blaze, to furnish better light in the evening than the feeble candle, or to supplement it. I have spent hundreds of evenings reading and studying in front of such a fire."[33]

The crepuscular interior would have resembled a dramatic chiaroscuro sketch as the flickering light of candle, lamp, or fire jumped across polished surfaces and cast exaggerated, pulsating shadows on the wall (see Pl. II). Ellen Rollins described such a "fire-changed" scene in her grandfather's kitchen:

At night, brightened by a roaring backlog, it was full of cheer. Then its beams and ceilings and simple furnishings were enriched by shadows, and the pewter dishes upon its brown dressers shone in dancing firelight like silver. The two shelves, full of leather-covered books; the weatherwise almanac, hanging from a peg; the cross-legged table and prim chairs; the long crane, with its hissing teakettle; the brush; the bellows; the settle in the corner, and whatever else was there, all became fire-changed, and were mellowed into the bright scene.[34]

Fig. 3. *Bass Otis and His Family*, by Bass Otis (1784–1861). Oil on canvas, 40½ by 51 inches. Frederika Bremer recalled with pleasure the lamplit evenings she spent with Andrew Jackson Downing and his wife: "My happiest hours here are those . . . passed in the evening with my host and hostess, sitting in the little darkened parlor with bookcases and busts around us, and the fire quietly glimmering in the large fireplace. There, by the evening lamp, Mr. Downing and his wife read to me by turns passages from their most esteemed American poets" (Adolph Benson, ed., *America of the Fifties: Letters of Frederika Bremer* [New York, 1924], p. 11). *Private collection; Helga photograph.*

It was with considerably less sentimentality that William Fletcher King reminisced:

In this day of bright illumination the thought of a candle-lit room seems gloomy. Besides giving a feeble light, the tallow dip had to be frequently trimmed with snuffers. While the candle in a small room and for a few people might have looked cozy and done fairly well, it did poor service in a larger space. I have seen at spelling schools and at religious meetings weird effects on faces and walls, where the room was dimly lit by a few candles in tin reflectors on the walls.[35]

These tin reflectors were one of the many ways in which eighteenth- and nineteenth-century homemakers maximized what little light there was. Wall branches or sconces frequently had metal reflectors or mirrors behind them—"Sconce Looking Glasses."[36] Pendant prisms might further refract light, as in the 1762 "four-armed cut glass candlesticks, ornamented with stars and drops, properly called girandoles."[37] To augment the light, candles, chandeliers, and lamps were positioned in front of looking glasses, as is evident in Henry Sargent's paintings *The Tea Party* and *The Dinner Party*[38] (see also Fig. 4). Josiah Quincy's Massachusetts desk-and-bookcase was one of many with candle slides placed in front of the mirrored doors of the bookcase.[39] By the early nineteenth century the circular convex girandole mirror with candle arms was considered the most fashionable combination of light and reflection. In 1808 George Smith extolled the virtues of the girandole mirror: "In apartments where an extensive view offers itself, these Glasses become an elegant and useful ornament, reflecting objects in beautiful perspective on their convex surfaces; the frames, at the same time they form an elegant decoration on the walls, are calculated to support lights."[40] Thirteen years later Eliza Susan Morton Quincy described the dining and drawing rooms of Ebenezer Storer's Sudbury Street mansion in Boston, where, from the center of the large summer beam that traversed each room "depended a glass globe, which reflected, as in a convex mirror, all surrounding objects. . . . Oval mirrors and girandoles" lent further brilliance to the drawing room, while in the dining room, "Between the windows hung a long mirror in a mahogany frame"[41] in which the suspended globe was undoubtedly reflected.

Despite their cost, looking glasses were a common feature in the homes of the wealthy and the middle class because they both enlivened a room and made it more fashionable. The more elegant the apartment, the larger and more numerous the looking glasses. In May 1813 Evelina du Pont penned a picture of Mrs. Ralph Izard's Charleston home, Lansdowne: "The House is elegant, built in white marble. . . . There are two immense parlors, one of which is almost covered up with large Looking Glasses."[42] The many assets of the looking glass were clearly appreciated by Otho Holland Williams of Baltimore in a letter written in the late eighteenth century regretting that the two pier glasses he had ordered from abroad would not arrive in time for a splendid dinner party he was planning. "If these same glasses were upon my drawing room [wall], the site of our treat would be splendid—splendid for Baltimore my dear fellow."[43] In that social age, looking glasses were strategically placed for maximum drama. At the new mansion he was just completing in Providence in 1788 John Brown

gave a smart ball at his home on the hill. Indeed, it will be a most elegant place. We had four rooms lighted up on the second story. . . . Two of the largest and most elegant mirrors I ever saw ornamented the rooms. Standing in the door which is in the middle of the partition you are just in line with them, so that at the head of the dance you can look down through a variegated crowd of sprightly dancers, . . .[44]

A splendid alliance of looking glasses and candles lent a luminous brilliance to the extravagant Mischianza Ball at Walnut Grove in Philadelphia on May 18, 1778, as described by Major John André:

Fig. 4. Detail of a silhouette of the Lockwood family by Auguste Edouart (1788–1861), 1842. Inscribed at the bottom, *Aug*[n.] *Edouart fecit 1842/411 Broadway.* Sepia wash and black paper cutouts on paper, 19⅜ by 28⅜ inches over all. The silhouette was cut at the Lockwoods' New York City house at 411 Broadway. The fringe and tassel of the drapery and the solar lamp have been placed so as to be reflected in the pier glass. *Henry Francis du Pont Winterthur Museum, Winterthur, Delaware.*

As soon as tea and coffee were over most of the company went upstairs into a large and elegantly painted entry. Between the many mirrors were three spermacetti candles in sconces adorned with gauze and silk. In the supper room the floor was covered with painted canvas, roof and sides hung with paintings and ornamented with fifty large mirrors. From the roof hung 12 lustres, with 20 spermacetti candles in each.[45]

The reflection of a candle or lamp flame may at least partially account for the premium placed on highly polished surfaces. Among the headings in Robert Roberts' *House Servant's Directory* of 1827, for example, are "Italian varnish, most superb for furniture," "Italian polish to give furniture a brilliant lustre," "To polish the bars of a polished steel grate," "To give Britannia metal a brilliant polish," "To give silver a beautiful polish," "A wash to give a brilliant lustre to plate," and even "A wash to give lustre to the face."[46] "Pewter must rival silver in its brilliance, the wooden-ware . . . must be like the driven snow."[47] Roberts recommended that furniture should be rubbed and polished to "a good gloss" and "a most brilliant polish"[48] (see Pl. III). In 1793 Enos Hitchcock thus described Mrs. Charles Worthy's best room: "Under the window stood a large maple table, which for its bright polish resembled the looking glass which hung over it."[49] A century later Thomas Nelson Page recalled the old plantation house, where "The furniture was old-timey and plain—mahogany and rosewood bedsteads and dressers black with age, and polished till they shone like mirrors, hung with draperies white as snow; straight-backed chairs generations old interspersed with common new ones; long sofas with claw feet; old shining tables with slender brass-tipped legs."[50] Letitia Burwell concurred on the high polish of Virginia interiors before the Civil War: "This rubbing business was carried quite to excess. Every inch of mahogany was waxed and rubbed to the highest state of polish, as were also the floors, the brass fenders, irons, and candlesticks."[51] Yet it was a process, as Frances Breckenridge recalled, "that brought out the richness of the grain of the wood as nothing else ever did or ever will."[52]

These interiors must have been spectacular by candlelight, with the lively grain of varnished and waxed mahogany spiraling up the front of a high chest or swirling across the shiny top of a pier table. Carved and polished flame finials, pinwheels, and shells would be set to revolving by the wavering flame of lamp or candle, which would highlight gilded looking glasses and picture frames, brass curtain pins, gilded or brass drawer pulls, ormolu mounts, and polished fireplace equipment. There might be "gilt bordering" around the walls,[53] which, together with the brass tacks swagged across a line of chair seats against the walls, would provide a glittering outline of the room. Henry Sargent's *Tea Party* and also his *Dinner Party* are good examples.[54]

Even interior woodwork was usually given a glossy finish. In the *American* for February 27, 1800, "Sattin Painting"[55] vied for favor with shiny satin paper.[56] Francis DeL'Orme advertised on November 18, 1790, that he could put up fashionable papers and "gives them a coat of Varnish, which adds much to their brilliance."[57] Lustrings and satins were fabrics favored for both upholstery and dresses by ladies who admired these polished apartments (see Pls. I, III, V). Upholstery fabrics were boldly patterned, waved, watered, and glazed, and then stretched tightly over the frames of chairs and sofas (see Pls. I, III). Rainbow papers[58] enlivened candlelit drawing rooms as watered silks enlivened costume (see Pls. I, IV). In Boston in 1790 one could purchase frosted, spangled, and velvet papers with frosted and spangled borders.[59] Sequined or spangled needlework or mica-flecked shellwork might further enliven such vivacious evening pageants.

Because lighting was the hallmark of hospitality, much additional lighting was provided for entertainment. "When any of the housewives ventured to have a party," William Davis recalled of evenings in Plymouth, Massachusetts, "candles with their candlesticks and snuffers were brought out and scattered about the parlors on mantels and tables."[60] Advising on the care of such supplementary lighting, Eliza Leslie wrote, "When all your lamps (mantel, etc.) have been in use for company, they should next morning be emptied completely of oil and wick. . . . Unless a lamp is used nightly, no oil or wick should be left in it."[61]

During Mr. Christian's dance assembly at Nomini Hall in December 1773 Philip Fithian thought the supper "room looked luminous and splendid; four very large candles burning on the table where we supp'd, three others in different parts of the Room;

a gay, sociable Assembly."[62] Mrs. George Fry described the luminous and triumphant party at her home in Mobile, Alabama, in 1848:

Our house was as light as day, having thirty solar lamps and sixty candles throughout the house.... I hear that everyone who was at the party said it was the nicest one of the season.... Mr. Barney said it was the handsomest and most elegant one, altogether, that he had attended in Mobile, because the company was so well selected and the rooms so splendidly lighted.[63]

A great deal of premeditation about the effect and placement of lighting preceded such a successful party. Eliza Leslie advocated that "The articles may be so disposed on the side-board as to make a very handsome appearance, particularly when it has a marble top, and is lighted up for a dinner party."[64] She further instructed,

If the dinner is in the evening, see that the lamps, candles, etc. are all in good order before you place them on the table. The table should be very well lighted, particularly at a dinner party. If the dinner is to commence in daylight, and it is so late in the afternoon that there is any possibility of its being protracted till after sunset, it is best to close the windows, and light the candles at once; as it is extremely uncomfortable to have the company overtaken by the gloom of twilight, and obliged to wait almost in darkness while the lights are preparing.[65]

One can surmise that such calculations for the best lighting effects preceded the afternoon dinner party painted by Henry Sargent, where the windows have been partially closed with shutters and blinds to limit the amount of natural light shining on the candlelit table.[66] On Tuesday, April 24, 1821, Anna Quincy Thaxter Parsons glanced admiringly once more over the Newburyport parlor she had helped prepare for Elizabeth Carter's imminent marriage to William Reynolds: "The astral lamp stood on the card table, 4 candles were displayed on the mantelpiece & 4 on the side-board.... Our parlour was now complete, with the closing of the blind, daylight throwing too great a glare upon our arrangements."[67]

"A ball-room should be brilliantly lighted," instructed Frances Byerly Parkes, "and this is done in the best style by a chandelier or lamp suspended from the centre of the ceiling, which diffuses an equal light, while it adds to the elegant appearance of the room. Lustres placed on the mantel-piece, and branches on tripods in the corners of the room, are also extremely ornamental."[68] Mrs. Basil Hall admired a festive occasion in Philadelphia in 1827, where the rooms were "lighted entirely with candles and very well done. They were not in lustres, but in the middle of each room there was a circular frame in which were placed three or four dozen candles and at the sides of the rooms were semi-circular frames fitted with candles in the same way. Each of the frames was entirely concealed by a wreath of artificial flowers."[69] This union of lighting with flowers and leaves was considered fashionable by the late eighteenth century and was much in vogue in the nineteenth.[70] Elijah Hunt Mills wrote from Washington in March 1819, "Last evening a very brilliant ball.... The room was hung with festoons and semicircles of flowers and variegated lights."[71] Indeed, the adjective brilliant was the most coveted

Pl. IV. *Mrs. Elijah Boardman (1767–1848) and Her Son William Whiting Boardman (1794–1871),* by Ralph Earl (1751–1801), c. 1798. Oil on canvas, 85¼ by 56¼ inches. The gold highlights of the fringes on the curtain and table cover, chair frame, and carpet and Mrs. Boardman's shimmering apricot-gray dress would have provided this interior with abundant glitter by candlelight. *Virginia Steele Scott Foundation, Pasadena, California; Helga photograph.*

compliment for an evening party.[72] Eliza Susan Quincy penned a sparkling picture of a party her family gave on Wednesday, April 21, 1819:

... sent to the Botanic garden for flowers, with which we decorated our drawing rooms,—placing them in vases on the mantelpieces, and in glass vases over the folding doors which were surmounted by a fan light. By ½ past 7 o'clock our rooms were brilliantly lighted, from the centre and around the walls, and we were ready to receive our guests. ... The ladies were all in full dress, gold and silver muslins, lace & jewels of all descriptions gave brilliance to the party.[73]

With what evident pride she was able to proclaim, "Our rooms were universally admired & it was pronounced the most brilliant and successful party of the winter."[74]

Pl. V. *Mrs. Benjamin Tevis*, by Thomas Sully (1783–1872), 1827. Oil on canvas, 30 by 25 inches. Mrs. Tevis' glittering jewelry and glossy dress would have added sparkle to an evening party. At a party given by Eliza Susan Quincy's family in Boston on Wednesday, April 21, 1819, "Miss Henderson wore a silk lace French dress richly trimmed over white satin. Pearl ornaments and pearls in her hair surmounted by 6 white ostrich plumes which waved far above the heads of her admirers "(M. A. DeWolfe Howe, ed., *The Articulate Sisters* [Cambridge, Massachusetts, 1946], p. 34). For such an occasion one might want to use Robert Roberts' recipe for "A wash to give lustre to the face. Infuse half a pound of wheat bran in one quart of best white wine vinegar, for the space of four hours; add to it the yolks of five eggs well beaten, and two grains of ambergris, distil the whole, and bottle it for use; cork it very close, let it stand for fourteen days before use; this must be applied at night and in the morning, mixed in soft water" (*The House Servant's Directory* [Boston, 1827], p. 115). *Winterthur Museum*.

[1] Evangeline Walker Andrews, ed., *Journal of a Lady of Quality; Being the Narrative of a Journey from Scotland to the West Indies, North Carolina, and Portugal, in the years 1774 and 1776* (New Haven, Connecticut, 1921), pp. 146–147.

[2] *The Land of the Crooked Tree* (New York, 1948), p. 189.

[3] *The House Book or, A Manual of Domestic Economy* (Philadelphia, 1840), p. 4.

[4] *The Land of the Crooked Tree*, p. 189.

[5] Harriet Connor Brown, *Grandmother Brown's Hundred Years 1827–1927* (Boston, 1929), p. 124.

[6] Malcolm Read Lovell, ed., *Two Quaker Sisters, From the Original Diaries of Elizabeth Buffum Chace and Lucy Buffum Lovell* (New York, 1937), p. 7.

[7] *The American Family Encyclopedia* (New York, 1856), p. 165.

[8] The myrtleberry was favored in Britian for making green candles but was not much used in the Carolinas, to which it was native. Janet Schaw

of Edinburgh wrote during her residence in North Carolina, "The Myrtle thro' all this swamp is the candle-berry-myrtle, which makes the green candle you have seen at home. They give a very pleasant light, and when placed in a silver candle-stick, look extremely pretty. And here for a moment let me lead you to admire what Nature has done for the inhabitants of this country. This is an Article which every house-wife grudges the expence of—here they have it for nothing, if they would only accept it. The cotton is in plenty growing every where for the wick, if they would take the trouble to spin it. The berries hang to the hand, and seem to beg you to gather them, but they generally beg in vain, not one out of fifty will take the trouble to make them into candles. The poorer sort burn pieces of lightwood, which they find without trouble, and the people of fashion use only Spermaceti, and if any green wax, it is only for kitchen use" (*Journal of a Lady of Quality*, p. 203). John Fowler and John Cornforth have written that the "Duke of Chandos . . . imported myrtlewax and green wax, from America. . . . Myrtlewax from Carolina cost 7d. a lb. . . . The myrtle candles gave off a delicate smell" (*English Decoration in the 18th Century* [Princeton, 1974], p. 222). Tallow candles were the most inexpensive and least efficient. "Tallow candles and bayberry candles were used by many less well to do people," wrote William T. Davis in *Plymouth Memories of an Octogenarian* [Plymouth, Massachusetts, 1906], p. 481).

[9] George Francis Dow, ed., *The Holyoke Diaries 1709–1856* (Salem, Massachusetts, 1911), p. 7.

[10] Field Horne, ed., *The Diary of Mary Cooper, Life on a Long Island Farm 1768–1773* (Oyster Bay, New York, 1981), p. 46.

[11] Brown, *Grandmother Brown's Hundred Years*, p. 124.

[12] By 1859 Thomas C. Grattan was able to write, "One extremely gratifying circumstance of domestic economy in the United States, arises from the cheapness of lamp oil. Tallow candles (the curse of middle life and moderate incomes in Europe) are never seen. Astral, solar, moderator, and other fanciful kinds of lamps, [l]ustres lighted with glass, and wax or spermaceti lights, are to be found everywhere" (quoted in Allen Nevins, *American Social History as Recorded by British Travellers* [New York, 1923], p. 255).

[13] *Recollections of a New England Town* (Meriden, Connecticut, 1899), p. 142.

[14] *Reminiscences of an Octogenarian of the City of New York* (New York, 1896), p. 333. William O'Dea, in his *Social History of Lighting* (London, 1958), pointed out that in addition to dripping wax, candles add heat and consume oxygen. "A hundred or more guests in a room lit and heated by a hundred candles would not take long to overheat and vitriate [sic] the atmosphere" (p. 44).

[15] O'Dea wrote in his *Social History of Lighting*, "With those [tallow candles] that I tested the [snuffing] operation had to be done every twenty minutes and in some cases was necessary after five. . . . 'Snuffing,' by which is meant the removal of an end of charred wick before it could fall into the molten tallow and cause 'guttering,' was a process requiring dexterity and judgement. . . . It is no wonder that 'snuffing' has come to mean extinguishing. The scissors with box-like contrivances in which the cutoff ends of charred wick are held, are snuffers. . . . It was only in conjunction with the newly discovered fatty acids (stearine) that the plaited wick proved self-consuming" (pp. 3, 5, 6).

[16] *The House Servant's Directory* (Boston, 1827), p. 21.

[17] *The Land of the Crooked Tree*, p. 188.

[18] Horne, *Diary of Mary Cooper*, p. 36.

[19] *Recollections of a New England Town*, p. 142.

[20] *Early Recollections of Newport, R. I., from the Year 1793 to 1811* (Newport, 1868), pp. 267–268.

[21] *Plymouth Memories of an Octogenarian*, p. 481.

[22] In Benjamin Prat's estate in Boston in 1763 were listed "Six brass Candlesticks & a Tin One," kept in the kitchen probably near the fireplace, as they are listed next to the fireplace utensils (see Abbott Lowell Cummings, ed., *Rural Household Inventories* [Boston, 1964], p. 201).

[23] "Ellen's mother, called her, in a few minutes, to go and show Lucy and her mother the way to the bedroom. 'Shall I light a candle, mother?' said Ellen. 'Yes,' said her mother. Lucy then observed that Ellen went to a sort of open cupboard, by the side of the room [kitchen], where there were a great many dishes and tins in rows, all nice and bright; and she took down an iron candlestick, with a short candle in it, and came and lighted it by the fire. Then she conducted Lucy's mother, and Lucy herself, out through a door in the back side of the room" (Jacob Abbott, *Cousin Lucy among the Mountains* [Auburn, New York, 1850], pp. 78–79).

[24] "It was a custom in our family, that if a child was ill at night, she should be brought into the parents' bedroom and put into a trundle bed, which in the daytime was pushed under the larger bed. Now once upon a time, when I was about four years old, I had a feverish cold, and after having been dosed with squills and balsam drops, much to my delight I was promoted to the trundle bed, which being rolled out with a sleepy rumble, I was tucked in by loving hands, the lamp was taken away and I fell fast asleep. But soon, either my cold or some unexpected noise waked

me, and peeping out from my many coverings, I saw a bright little picture of fireside comfort. A wood-fire was burning in the Franklin stove—'The light stand' (as we always called a pretty old-fashioned three legged round table . . . with two brass lamps upon it,) was drawn up cosily in front of the fire, while on one side sat my mother with her workbasket, and on the other my father, wrapped in a long Russian dressing gown, a real coat of many colors, reading *A Midsummer Night's Dream* aloud to her" (Caroline King, *When I Lived in Salem* [Brattleboro, Vermont, 1837], p. 169).

[25] See, for instance, Mario Praz, *Conversation Pieces* (Rome, 1971), p. 69, Fig. 29; p. 235, Fig. 218; p. 99, Fig. 60. See also ANTIQUES for January 1983, p. 217, Pl. III.

[26] See ANTIQUES for January 1983, p. 220, Fig. 5.

[27] Breckenridge, *Recollections of a New England Town*, p. 142.

[28] *The House Book*, p. 158.

[29] *The Land of the Crooked Tree*, p. 188.

[30] Quoted in O'Dea, *The Social History of Lighting*, p. 9.

[31] Leonard W. Labaree, ed., *The Papers of Benjamin Franklin*, vol. 7 (New Haven, 1963), p. 382.

[32] Emmet Field Horine, ed., *Daniel Drake, Pioneer Life in Kentucky, 1785–1800* (New York, 1948), p. 95.

[33] *Reminiscences* (New York, 1915), p. 46.

[34] *New England Bygones* (Philadelphia, 1883), p. 63.

[35] *Reminiscences*, p. 46.

[36] Quoted in Alfred Coxe Prime, ed., *The Arts and Crafts in Philadelphia, Maryland and South Carolina, 1786–1800*, ser. 2 (Walpole Society, 1932), p. 212.

[37] Quoted in Nina Fletcher Little, "Lighting in Colonial Records," *Old-Time New England*, vol. 42, no. 4 (1952), p. 100.

[38] Illustrated in ANTIQUES for May 1982, p. 1178, Pl. VIII; p. 1180, Pl. X; and p. 1175, Pl. IV.

[39] The desk-and-bookcase is illustrated in Joseph Downs, *American Furniture: Queen Anne and Chippendale Periods* (New York, 1952), Fig. 226.

[40] *A Collection of Designs for Household Furniture and Interior Decoration* (1808; New York 1970), p. 25.

[41] Eliza Susan Quincy, *Memoir of the Life of Eliza Susan Morton Quincy* (Boston, 1861), p. 89.

[42] Quoted in Betty-Bright P. Low, "The Youth of 1812 More Excerpts from the Letters of Josephine du Pont and Margaret Manigault," in Ian M.G. Quimby, ed., *Winterthur Portfolio 11* (Charlottesville, Virginia, 1976), p. 195, n. 104.

[43] Quoted in Rodris Roth, "Interior Decoration of City Houses in Baltimore: The Federal Period," in Richard K. Doud, ed., *Winterthur Portfolio 5* (Charlottesville, Virginia, 1969), p. 86.

[44] Quoted in Wendy A. Cooper, *In Praise of America* (New York, 1980), p. 258.

[45] Little, "Lighting in Colonial Records," p. 101.

[46] Pp. vi, viii.

[47] Jane de Forest Shelton, *The Salt-Box House* (New York, 1900), p. 112. While at her aunt and uncle's house in Walpole, New Hampshire, Emily Barnes was happy that the "supper was soon ready, and I ate my corn cake, with maple syrup, on a bright pewter plate. There were two rows of these plates on the shelves, turned up against the wall, bright as polished silver (*Narratives, Traditions and Personal Reminiscences* [Boston, 1888], p. 160).

[48] Roberts, *The House Servant's Directory*, p. 30. See also ANTIQUES for January 1983, p. 221, Pl. VII.

[49] *The Farmer's Friend, or the History of Mr. Charles Worthy* (Boston, 1793), p. 100.

[50] *The Old South; Essays Social and Political* (New York, 1892), p. 7.

[51] *A Girl's Life in Virginia Before the War* (New York, 1895), p. 43.

[52] *Recollections of a New England Town*, p. 141.

[53] Minshull's Looking Glass Store advertised "gilt bordering for rooms by the yard" in New York City in 1775 (see Rita Susswein Gottesman, ed., *The Arts and Crafts in New York 1726–1776* [New York, 1938], p. 132).

[54] See ANTIQUES for May 1982, pp. 1172–1183.

[55] See Roth, "Interior Decoration of City Houses in Baltimore," p. 68.

[56] See Catherine Lynn, *Wallpaper in America* (New York, 1980), pp. 260–261.

[57] Prime, *The Arts and Crafts in Philadelphia*, p. 219. In Baltimore in 1810 Nicholas Hacke advertised "French and English glazed Paper" which he was "determined to sell very cheap" (Roth, "Interior Decoration of City Houses in Baltimore," p. 70).

[58] Lynn, *Wallpaper in America*, pp. 274–275.

[59] "Early Paper-Hangings in Boston," *Old-Time New England*, vol. 12, no. 3 (January 1922), p. 117.

[60] *Plymouth Memories of an Octogenarian*, p. 330.

[61] *The House Book*, p. 160.

[62] Hunter Dickinson Farish, ed., *The Journal and Letters of Philip Vickers Fithian* (Williamsburg, Virginia, 1965), p. 34.

[63] Quoted in ANTIQUES for September 1977, p. 522.

[64] *The House Book*, p. 259.

[65] *Ibid.*, p. 261.

[66] Illustrated in ANTIQUES for May 1982, p. 1173.

[67] "A Newburyport Wedding One Hundred and Thirty Years Ago the Bride, Elizabeth Margaret Carter," *Essex Institute Historical Collections* (Salem, 1951), vol. 87, p. 322.

[68] Mrs. William Parkes, *Domestic Duties; or Instructions to Young Married Ladies* (New York, 1831), p. 82.

[69] Una Pope-Hennessy, ed., *The Aristocratic Journey* (New York, 1931), p. 137.

[70] At seven o'clock on the evening of Thursday, February 8, 1827, Mary Wilder Foote "went to Mrs. Barstow's ball, where we saw a great show of splendor. Everybody looked very handsome. The rooms were beautifully lighted and dressed with wreaths" (Mary Wilder Tileston, ed., *Caleb and Mary Wilder Foote* [Cambridge, Massachusetts, 1918], p. 26). At Powhatan Seat in Virginia, Letitia Burwell recalled the occasions when "the house was illuminated by wax lights issuing from bouquets of magnolia leaves placed around the walls near the ceiling, and looking prettier than any glass chandelier" (*A Girl's Life in Virginia Before the War*, pp. 143–144).

[71] Quoted in *Proceedings of the Massachusetts Historical Society* (Boston, 1882), vol. 19 (1881–1882), p. 26.

[72] Antithetically, the word dull had denigrating connotations and was used to describe an old and devalued object or a listless, tired, or depressed person. On May 14, 1769, for example, Mary Cooper felt "senceles dul and sleepe" (Horne, *Diary of Mary Cooper*, p. 12).

[73] M. A. DeWolfe Howe, ed., *The Articulate Sisters* (Cambridge, Massachusetts, 1946), pp. 33–34.

[74] *Ibid.*

Fig. 5. Evening scene, artist unknown, 1800–1850. Watercolor on paper, 10⅝ by 14³⁄₁₆ inches. The extended family has gathered around the common candle for the nine-o'clock Bible reading. The vivacity of the bold, polished veneers and the restlessness of the shadows on the walls have been suggested by the artist of this candlelit scene. *Present whereabouts unknown; photograph by courtesy of the Decorative Arts Photographic Collection, Winterthur Museum.*

The lamps and candlesticks
of the Meriden Britannia Company

BY RICHARD L. BOWEN JR.

OVER THE YEARS I collected unmarked "pewter" lard, or grease, lamps, all of which had the same wide, slotted wick holders, on the assumption that one day I would find a marked example that would identify the whole group (Fig. 1). Although it now appears likely that none of these lamps was ever marked, I unexpectedly identified the manufacturer when I found lamps identical to mine illustrated in the 1855 catalogue of the Meriden Britannia Company of West Meriden, Connecticut (Fig. 2).[1]

The Meriden Britannia Company was organized in December 1852 by seven partners, all of whom had been

involved in the manufacture of britannia.[2] In January 1853 it published its first price list (unillustrated). It issued illustrated catalogues in 1855, 1861, 1867, and 1872. All included britannia candlesticks and lamps.[3] Once one becomes convinced that the illustrations are accurate it is evident that some of the finest "pewter" lamps and candlesticks in various collections are in fact britannia ware manufactured by the Meriden Britannia Company.

The lamps shown second and third from the left in Figure 1 are depicted in Meriden's 1855 and 1861 catalogues as numbers 410 and 405 (Fig. 2). The other three lamps shown

Fig. 1. Britannia lard, or grease, lamps. Height of the tallest, 8 inches; height of the smallest, 3½ inches. In all cases the copper wick holder (illustrated in ANTIQUES for January 1928, p. 45, Fig. 15) is 1¾ inches wide, and extends two inches down into the fuel reservoir to heat the lard. *Private collection.*

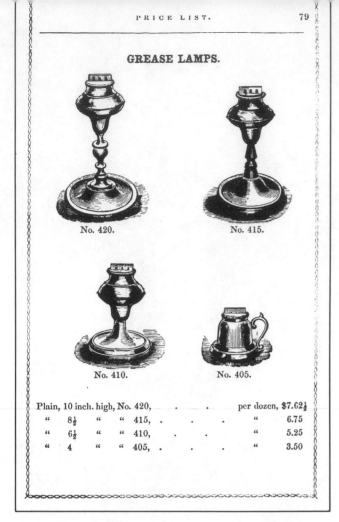

GREASE LAMPS.

No. 420.

No. 415.

No. 410.

No. 405.

Plain,	10 inch. high,	No. 420,	. . .	per dozen,	$7.62½
"	8½ "	" 415,	. . .	"	6.75
"	6½ "	" 410,	. .	"	5.25
"	4 "	" 405,	. . .	"	3.50

Fig. 2. Britannia lard, or grease, lamps from the 1855 catalogue of the Meriden Britannia Company, Meriden, Connecticut. The same lamps are shown in the 1861 catalogue.

Fig. 3. Britannia grease lamp similar to Meriden Britannia's style number 415 as shown in Fig. 2. The photograph is reproduced from the R. A. Bourne auction catalogue of January 9, 1971, lot number 252. Other examples of this lamp are shown in A. H. Haywood, *Colonial Lighting* (New York, 1962), Pl. 37; and in ANTIQUES for March 1933, p. 97, Fig. 4. Still another is in the collection of the Rhode Island Historical Society.

Fig. 4. Britannia fluid lamp similar to Meriden Britannia's style number 114 as shown in Fig. 5. The illustration is from the R. A. Bourne auction catalogue of November 27, 1971, lot number 53.

in Figure 1 do not appear in the catalogue, but since their fonts were cast from the same molds as those of the other two lamps and since the burners are identical there is reason to believe that these three were also made by Meriden— after 1861 but before 1867, since no grease lamps were shown in the 1867 or 1872 catalogues. The lamp shown in Figure 3 is similar to lamp number 415 in Figure 2, while the fluid lamp shown in Figure 4 is nearly identical to lamp number 114 of Figure 5. Note that stem and base of the lamps shown in Figures 3 and 4 appear to have been cast in the same mold.

The lamp shown in Figure 6 is similar to Meriden's number 115 (Fig. 7). The knurled bands that appear in three places on the body of this lamp are found on only a few Meriden Britannia lamps. The handle of this and certain other surviving lamps differs from the handle shown on the lamp in the catalogue illustration, but not from other handles illustrated in Meriden Britannia catalogues. There appear to have been five types of handle used by the company on lamps: a ring (for saucer bases), and four scroll shapes. To judge by the catalogues, at least, the most frequently used handle was the type shown on lamp number 117 in Figure 7.

While the 1867 catalogue offered forty-five fluid and oil lamps, only three were shown in the 1872 catalogue, presumably reflecting the growing popularity of kerosene lamps.

The search for unmarked Meriden Britannia lamps turned up an interesting group: the cigar lamps. One had previously been identified as a whale-oil lamp by Kerfoot (Fig. 8),[4] another as a "patent" lamp by Laughlin (Fig. 9),[5] and a third as a "spill holder" or "cigar counter" lamp.[6] The two lamps illustrated here appear to be nearly identical to numbers 20 and 35 in the 1855 Meriden catalogue (Fig. 10). Earlier writers were apparently not aware that each of the outside columns was filled with oil and held a removable metal rod tipped with a wick. The wicks were lit at the central burner and were used to light cigars.[7]

The most important of the few candlesticks I have been able to identify as Meriden Britannia products is the remarkably well-preserved pair shown in the foreground of Figure 11. These are very similar to number 91 with extinguisher in the 1855 catalogue (Fig. 12). They are the finest saucer-based American britannia candlesticks known.

The saucer-based candlestick shown in Figure 13 is marked LEWIS & COWLES, indicating that it was made by one of the founders of Meriden Britannia, Isaac C. Lewis, when he was in partnership with George Cowles between 1834 and 1835. What appears to have been the model for this candlestick is shown in Figure 14, which is reproduced from the 1855 Meriden catalogue. A candlestick with the same style number is listed in the 1853 price list and is the style illustrated in the 1867 and 1872 catalogues. This means that the molds for the base, stem, and trimmings were in continual use for about forty years, first at Lewis and Cowles and then at Meriden Britannia. A few unmarked examples of this candlestick have been attributed to Lewis and Cowles on the basis of the marked example,[8] but it seems more likely that they were made by Meriden Britannia.

A pair of candlesticks of medium height (Fig. 11, far right and far left) are similar to the number 2 style in the 1855 Meriden Britannia catalogue (Fig. 12). An example each of the number 5[9] and 45[10] styles is also known, and I have also seen candlesticks which correspond to style numbers 3 and 4.

No. 114.   No. 446.

Fig. 5. Britannia fluid lamps from the 1855 catalogue of the Meriden Britannia Company. Both lamps were 8½ inches high. A lamp similar to number 446 is shown in J. B. Kerfoot, *American Pewter* (Boston, 1924), Fig. 355.

For the most part, the styles of the britannia candlesticks manufactured by Meriden Britannia during the first twenty years of operation remained unchanged.[11] However, because the height of the "Fancy Fluted" candlesticks shown in Figure 12 changed slightly over the years, the following table may be used for dating them.

Style number	Catalogue year		
	1853	1855, 1861, 1867	1872
No. 6	11″	deleted	—
No. 5	10½″	11″	11″
No. 4	10¼″	10″	10″
No. 3	9½″	9½″	9½″
No. 2	9½″	9¼″	9½″

By far the most common surviving candlestick in this group is number 2, which is found both nine and one-quarter and nine and one-half inches tall. Because the 1853 catalogue was not illustrated, we can only speculate that the shape of number 6 specified in it was probably similar to those shown in Figure 12 and had either a vase or a baluster stem. The candlestick shown at the center of Figure 11 may indeed be an example of a number 6. It is not depicted in any of the Meriden Britannia catalogues, yet it is in the general style of the fancy fluted candlesticks and was obviously made by Meriden Britannia.

Heretofore all britannia lamps and candlesticks with the type of gadrooning on, for example, the lamp shown in Figure 6 and the candlesticks shown in Figure 11 have been attributed by pewter collectors to Sellew and Company of Cincinnati.[12] It is clear that the Meriden Britannia catalogues must be consulted before future attributions are made.

None of the Meriden Britannia lamps or candlesticks illustrated in this article is marked, and indeed no marked unplated britannia lamps or candlesticks made by the company after 1867 (and probably much earlier) are likely ever to be found. This inference is based on a statement in the 1867 catalogue to the effect that hollow ware of triple-plated nickel silver would be stamped as indicated in Figure

Fig. 6. Britannia fluid lamp similar to Meriden Britannia's style number 115 as shown in Fig. 7. Height without burner, 6; height over all, 7½ inches. *Private collection.*

Fig. 7. Britannia fluid lamps from the 1855 Meriden Britannia catalogue. Number 115 was 6 inches high and number 117, 6½ inches high.

No. 115.   No. 117.

15, top, while all articles of triple-plated superior white metal (britannia) were to be stamped with the mark shown in Figure 15, bottom. The catalogue went on to say that the company would also make some articles single plated on a pure white metal which would not bear any marks. This suggests that the company would not have marked unplated britannia ware either.

One would expect Meriden Britannia to follow the tradition of its predecessors, who marked at least some of their britannia. However, britannia ware marked by the company is almost nonexistent. The only example I know of is a britannia baptismal bowl marked MERIDEN BRITA COMPANY around the circumference of a circle three-quarters of an inch in diameter. At the center of the circle appears the number 1390.[13] Since no marked lamps or candlesticks have turned up, we may assume that Meriden's policy of not marking britannia was started early.

Collectors should be on guard when they find britannia wares bearing the trade marks of the Meriden Britannia Company. If the mark is either of the two shown in Figure 15 or some other Meriden Britannia mark, it undoubtedly indicates that the article was originally plated and has been stripped. Plated britannia was originally two to three times as expensive as unplated ware, while by a strange reversal a britannia item today is worth ten to thirty times as much as the same article plated. Neither britannia lamps nor candlesticks could be marked with a maker's name after they were manufactured. The mark was invariably stamped on the bottom of the base and once the base was soldered to the column it was impossible to insert an anvil against which to strike the die stamp. By contrast, it was a simple matter to mark hollow ware after manufacture.

The Meriden Britannia Company was founded by the following seven men: I. C. Lewis, H. C. Wilcox, D. C. Wilcox, James A. Frary, Lemuel J. Curtiss, and W. W. Lyman, all of Meriden, and John Munson of Wallingford.

Isaac C. Lewis (b. 1812) was apprenticed at age fifteen to Hiram Yale of Wallingford. In 1834 Lewis opened a shop with George Cowles, and in 1836 he was associated with Lemuel J. Curtiss under the name of Lewis and Curtiss. In 1839 Lewis organized I. C. Lewis and Company with a former apprentice, Daniel B. Wells. This partnership remained in business until the Meriden Britannia Company was organized.[14] Lewis became its first president, a position he held for about twelve years.

James A. Frary was one of Ashbil Griswold's many apprentices; by 1833 he was supervising Griswold's shop with Ira Couch.[15] Frary worked with Luther Boardman for a year under the name Frary and Boardman after the latter ceased working in South Reading, Massachusetts, in 1837.[16] By 1845 Frary had eight employees and was running his own fairly large shop. By 1849 he was in partnership as Frary and Benham, with ten employees.[17] When the Meriden Britannia Company was formed his firm was called James A. Frary and Company.

Lemuel J. Curtiss (b. 1814) was Isaac Lewis' partner from 1836 to 1838. He worked with his brother Edwin until 1840, then ran his own shop until 1846, when he joined W. W. Lyman for a short time.[18] When Meriden Britannia was organized he was presumably running a shop of his own.

William W. Lyman (b. 1821) was born in Vermont and moved to Connecticut at an early age. He served a five-year apprenticeship in the shop of Griswold and Couch in Meriden, beginning at age fifteen. By 1844 he was in

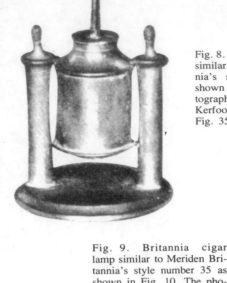

Fig. 8. Britannia cigar lamp similar to Meriden Britannia's style number 20 as shown in Fig. 10. The photograph is reproduced from Kerfoot, *American Pewter*, Fig. 356.

Fig. 9. Britannia cigar lamp similar to Meriden Britannia's style number 35 as shown in Fig. 10. The photograph is reproduced from Ledlie I. Laughlin, *Pewter in America* (Barre, Massachusetts, 1969), vol. 2, Fig. 655.

Fig. 10. Britannia cigar lamps from the 1855 catalogue of the Meriden Britannia Company. The same cigar lamps appear in the catalogues up to 1872.

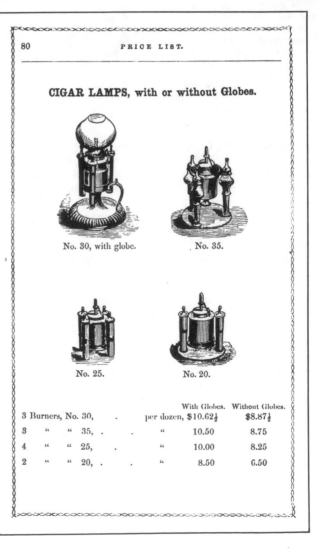

80   PRICE LIST.

CIGAR LAMPS, with or without Globes.

No. 30, with globe.   No. 35.

No. 25.   No. 20.

			With Globes.	Without Globes.
3 Burners, No. 30,	.	per dozen,	$10.62½	$8.87½
3 " " 35,	.	"	10.50	8.75
4 " " 25,	.	"	10.00	8.25
2 " " 20,	.	"	8.50	6.50

167

Fig. 11. Britannia candlesticks. Height of the pair at extreme left and right, 9½ inches; height of the center one, 11 inches; height of the saucer-base pair, 4⅜ inches. The pair in the foreground is similar to Meriden Britannia's style number 91 with extinguisher as shown in Fig. 12, while the pair at the extreme right and left is similar to style number 2 as shown in Fig. 12. All the candlesticks shown have removable *bobèches*, which are interchangeable on the two pairs. *Private collection.*

business with Ira Couch making spoons. In 1845 the firm is listed as Bull, Lyman and Couch. He was later briefly associated with Lemuel J. Curtiss, before moving into James A. Frary's shop until Meriden Britannia was organized.[19]

John Munson of Wallingford was the only founder not from Meriden. In 1846 he purchased the plant and equipment at Yalesville of Samuel Simpson who had, in turn, purchased it from Hiram Yale and Company in 1837.[20]

Horace C. (b. 1824) and Dennis C. Wilcox (b. 1829[21]) formed H. C. Wilcox and Company about 1848. Horace is said to have been a peddler for James A. Frary, and indeed both brothers were basically traveling peddlers of merchandise from various manufacturers. They apparently marketed the britannia products of the other concerns which later organized Meriden Britannia as well as a variety of other goods. Presumably they also manufactured britannia wares, since britannia teapots marked H. C. WILCOX & Co. have survived. Horace Wilcox was elected secretary and treasurer of Meriden Britannia when it was formed, but he was replaced as treasurer in 1853 by George R. Curtis, who had banking experience.[22]

Fig. 12. Britannia candlesticks from the 1855 Meriden Britannia catalogue. The same candlesticks appear in the catalogues up to 1872.

CANDLESTICKS.

No. 5.   No. 4.   No. 3.   No. 2.

No. 45.   No. 91.   No. 91. with exting'r.

Fancy Fluted,	Inches high.	No.	Per dozen.	
	11	5,	$8.75	
"	10	4,	8.25	
"	9½	3,	7.62½	
"	9¼	2,	7.00	
"	7½	45,	5.87½	
"	4½	91,	5.87½ with extinguisher, $6.75	
	11			

168

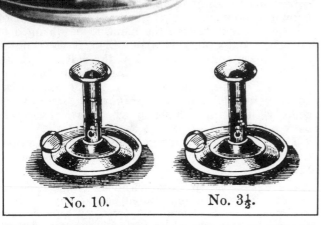

Fig. 13. Britannia saucer-based candlestick marked on the base LEWIS & COWLES. It is similar to Meriden Britannia's styles 10 and 3½ as shown in Fig. 14. The photograph is reproduced from Laughlin, *Pewter in America*, vol. 2, Fig. 634.

All Goods bearing our Trade Marks are Triple Plate.

Fig. 15. Trade marks stamped on Meriden Britannia's triple-plated ware. Diameter of each mark, ⅜ inch. The marks were not registered until 1887, when it was stated that they had been adopted in 1866. They were first shown in the 1867 catalogue, from which they are reproduced here. The catalogue states that the top mark would be used on hollow ware of triple-plated nickel silver and the bottom mark would be used on articles of triple-plated superior white metal (britannia).

No. 10.   No. 3½.

Fig. 14. Britannia saucer-based candlesticks from the 1855 Meriden Britannia catalogue. Both are 4½ inches high.

[1] D. T. and H I. Rainwater, *American Silverplate* (Nashville, 1968), p. 408. Copies of the 1853, 1855, 1861, 1867, and 1872 catalogues of the Meriden Britannia Company are in the possession of the International Silver Company in Meriden. My thanks are due to Edward P. Hogan of the library at, International Silver for making them available to me. The 1861 catalogue at International Silver does not include a section on britannia ware, but a large section on the subject is included in a copy of the 1861 catalogue at the Connecticut Historical Society.

[2] The original capitalization was $50,000. In 1957 this was increased to $100,000, in 1860 to $200,000, in 1866 to $550,000, and in 1879 to $1,100,000 (C. B. Gillespie and G. M. Curtis, *A Century of Meriden*, Meriden, 1906, part 3, p. 44). It has been estimated that the sales of the merging companies in 1852 totalled only $50,000, while in 1853 the total sales of the Meriden Britannia Company amounted to $250,000 (E. C. May, *A Century of Silver*, New York, 1947, pp. 68, 71). In 1860 the company employed 320 and had sales of $112,000 worth of britannia wares and $460,000 worth of electroplated wares. Of the latter, 30 per cent was plated on German silver and 70 per cent on britannia (1860 Connecticut Census, "Meriden: Products of Industry," n.p.; ms. in the Connecticut State Library). By 1866 the company's sales totalled well over $1,000,000 and in 1878 they had reached $2,500,000 (May, *A Century of Silver*, p. 109).

[3] The 1853 price list gives the style numbers for fifty-five lamps and twenty candlesticks. The 1855 catalogue illustrates fifty-eight britannia lamps and twenty-three britannia candlesticks. The 1861 catalogue contains fifty-eight pages of silver-plated ware followed by twenty-two pages of britannia ware. In the britannia section there are twenty-six candlesticks and sixty-two lamps (three kerosene lamps and one cigar lamp were added to the 1855 catalogue). The 1867 catalogue contains more than 150 pages of silver-plated ware followed by forty pages of britannia ware comprising forty-five lamps and twenty-three candlesticks. In 1872 a special sixty-four page catalogue of "Britannia and Planished Ware" was issued. It contained five cigar lamps, three fluid lamps, and the same twenty-three candlesticks that had been illustrated in 1867. With the exception of a single cigar lamp, no lamps were ever shown among the silver-plated ware. On the other hand, the candlesticks shown in Fig. 11, and certain other styles of candlesticks, were always offered in silver plate. No britannia was catalogued by Meriden Britannia after 1872, so that the end of the britannia era for this company can be dated to about 1875.

[4] J. B. Kerfoot, *American Pewter* (Boston, 1924), Fig. 356.

[5] Ledlie I. Laughlin, *Pewter in America* (Barre, Massachusetts, 1969), vol. 2, Fig. 655.

[6] W. A. Macfarlane, "Shedding Light on Pewter Lamps," *Pewter Collector's Club of America Bulletin*, no. 49 (1963), p. 182. The lamp in question is identical to the one shown in Fig. 8 but is missing its lighters.

[7] The 1853 price list contains three cigar lamps. Style number 35 (see Fig. 10) was added in the 1855 catalogue. A style number 45 first appeared in the 1861 catalogue, where it was offered both in britannia and silver plate. The 1867 and 1872 catalogues show all five cigar lamps. Miraculously, a cigar lamp with gadrooned base and globe resembling style number 30 (see Fig. 10) has been preserved (J. C. Thomas, *Connecticut Pewter and Pewterers*, Hartford, 1976, p. 45).

[8] Carl Jacobs, *Guide to American Pewter* (New York, 1957), p. 128, and K. Ebert, *Collecting American Pewter* (New York, 1973), p. 81.

[9] N. Hudson Moore, *Old Pewter, Brass, Copper, and Sheffield Plate* (New York, 1905), Fig. 31.

[10] R. F. French, "Some Thoughts on Lamps and Candlesticks," *Pewter Collector's Club of America Bulletin*, no. 52 (1965), p. 47.

[11] In the 1855 catalogue three of the style numbers from the 1853 price list were dropped, but five new numbers in an "Imperial" design with rope moldings were added, along with two gadrooned candlesticks with saucer bases. In the 1861 catalogue two tall candlesticks were added, and in the 1867 catalogue three short candlesticks were dropped. The twenty-three candlesticks shown in the 1867 catalogue appeared without change in the 1872 catalogue.

[12] The lamp in Fig. 6 was sold as made by Sellew, as were the saucer-based candlesticks shown in Fig. 11. The outside tall candlesticks in the latter illustration were sold as Cincinnati.

[13] Illustrated in C. V. Swain, "American Baptismal Bowls," *Pewter Collector's Club of America Bulletin*, no. 61 (1969), p. 50. Undoubtedly this baptismal bowl was originally silver plated. It is shown in the 1861 Meriden Britannia catalogue as number 1390 under "plated white metal" (Thomas, *Connecticut Pewter and Pewterers*, p. 42).

[14] C. H. S. Davis, *History of Wallingford* (Meriden, 1870), p. 573.

[15] Laughlin, *Pewter in America*, vol. 3, p. 84.

[16] *Ibid.*, vol. 3, p. 176.

[17] *Ibid.*, vol. 2, p. 102.

[18] *Ibid.*, vol. 2, p. 100.

[19] Davis, *History of Wallingford*, p. 575.

[20] Laughlin, *Pewter in America*, vol. 2, p. 108.

[21] 1850 Census of Connecticut, "Meriden, ..."

[22] May, *Century of Silver*, p. 68.

Cornelius and Company of Philadelphia

BY J. KENNETH JONES, *Curator of decorative arts, Charleston Museum*

THE FIRM FOUNDED in Philadelphia by Christian Cornelius has long been known for the superb cast and gilded lighting devices it made. Examples were shown at the 1851 Crystal Palace Exhibition in London and at other major international and regional fairs in the nineteenth century and were installed in numerous American public buildings, including the United States house of representatives and senate chambers.

Christian Cornelius came to Philadelphia from Amsterdam in 1783[1] and established himself as a silversmith. He later became a manufacturer of plated wares, but by the mid-1820's his firm was making lamps and chandeliers and by 1833 silverplating was not even mentioned in the firm's entry in the Philadelphia directory.[2] Robert Cornelius joined his father in partnership in 1831 and the company was known as Cornelius and Son until the addition of another partner caused the name to be changed to Cornelius and Company about 1840. It was known by that name until the death of the elder Cornelius in 1851.[3] By 1845 it was the largest lamp manufacturer and ornamental founder in the United States,[4] and it remained important through the end of the century, its name changing as different partners were taken in.[5]

The scope of the company's endeavors is summarized in the following review of its operations in 1860:

There is great variety in the character of the labor bestowed on articles manufactured here. Every grade of workman, from the common laborer to the artist and chemist is engaged.... The various processes through which the articles pass in this department (the dipping rooms) are exceedingly curious and interesting. Here everything is done by chemical agents ... burnishing is an

Fig. 1. Candelabrum, one of a pair, made by Cornelius and Company, Philadelphia, 1840–1851. Marked on the cast-iron weight in the base, "C & Co." Bright and mat-finish gilt bronze, height 20¼ inches. *Except as noted, the objects illustrated are in the collection of the author and photographs are by Alterman Studios.*

Fig. 2. Pair of candelabra attributed to Cornelius and Company, 1840–1851. Patinated and gilt bronze, height 32¾ inches. *Photograph by courtesy of Peter Hill.*

Fig. 3. Wall sconce attributed to Cornelius and Company, 1840–1851. Gilt bronze, height 15 inches.

important process. Much of the beauty and character of the work depends upon a judicious selection of the parts to be brought out by the burnisher.... After the brass is burnished it is again cleansed by means of acids, and finally washed in hot water.... [In the lacquering room] the various pieces are taken from their paper bed and placed upon the hot iron, after being carefully brushed. When heated to a certain degree, the articles are taken ... to a table, where the lacquer is applied with flat brushes made of camel's hair.... The different parts and ornaments are now ready to be placed in the hands of the fitter, or finisher, and are therefore selected and carried to the respective places arranged for putting them together. One room is occupied entirely by a number of men who are constantly employed in fitting together such gas work as chandeliers, pendants, brackets, etc.; another to girandoles and candelabra; and a third to the numerous class of solar lamps designed for standing upon the table, or for being suspended from the ceiling or against the wall. From all these departments the goods are taken to meet once more in the packing room previous to bidding a final farewell to their birthplace. Some of the ornamental work is painted in parti-colors to please fanciful tastes; some is bronzed with different shades; while other work is covered with a coating of fine gold, or tastefully enameled.[6]

The immense scale of Cornelius' output was made possible in part by the use of interchangeable parts, which multiplied the variety of designs that could be achieved. A study of the components of labeled Cornelius candleholders makes it possible to attribute many unlabeled pieces to the firm. The candelabrum shown in Figure 1, for instance, provided a major key to identifying other products of the firm when the stamp "C & Co" was discovered on the cast-iron plate weighting the base. The arms on this candelabrum are just like those on the unmarked candelabra shown in Figure 2, and the arms and the sockets are identical to those elements of the unmarked sconce shown in Figure 3. That sconce is nearly identical to two known sets of four sconces, one en suite with a chandelier, all of which came

from Main Line Philadelphia houses, and all were undoubtedly made by the Cornelius firm, judging by their similarity to the marked candelabrum.

The company made at least three types of sockets, two of which have turned up repeatedly, while the third has been found only on the candelabra in Figure 2. It is the most elaborate of the three sockets and was probably used on the best work done by the company. The two other Cornelius sockets are shown in Figure 4. The one at the left was used on the marked candelabrum in Figure 1 as well as on six unmarked candleholders (Figs. 3, 5, 7–9, and 12).

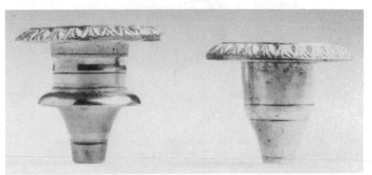

Fig. 4. The two most typical Cornelius and Company sockets. *Left*: gilt bronze, height 1⅞ inches. *Right*: gilt bronze, height 1⅝ inches.

Fig. 5. Candelabrum attributed to Cornelius and Company, 1840–1851. Gilt bronze and marble, height 18 inches.

Fig. 6. Candelabrum attributed to Cornelius and Company, 1840–1851. Gilt bronze and marble, with lead-glass prisms; height 16¼ inches.

Fig. 7. Candelabrum, one of a pair, attributed to Cornelius and Company, 1840–1851. Gilt bronze and marble, with lead-glass prisms; height 13 inches.

The plainer one at the right was used on the marked candelabrum in Figure 10 and on two other known marked three-piece girandole sets.[7] In addition, it appears on the two sets of sconces and the chandelier from Main Line houses mentioned earlier and on the unmarked candleholders in Figures 6, 11, and 13.

Other elements that Cornelius used interchangeably are upright supports, arms, and *bobêches*. The same upright is used as a socket support on all three pieces of the girandole set shown in Figure 9, as the central socket support of the sconce in Figure 3, and as the central support (behind the figure) of the candelabrum in Figure 5. The arms of the candelabra in Figures 5 and 6 are identical and those of the candelabrum in Figure 10 are the same as those on another known girandole.[8] The leafy *bobêches*, or prism rings, used on the pair of candelabra in Figure 12 are identical to those on the candelabra in Figures 5 and 10, and the floral *bobêches* on the sconce in Figure 3 match those on the candelabra in Figure 2.

In some instances Cornelius and Company's artisans used slight variations on a given design. One example is the tuliplike section of the upright supports on the candelabra in Figures 5, 6, 8, 11, and 12.

Because of the interchangeability of parts and the fact that many of Cornelius' candleholders were the same size, several combinations were possible in making up three-piece girandole sets or pairs of candlesticks. I know of one marked girandole set, for instance, in which one of the single candlesticks is a male figure in colonial costume; the other is a female figure in colonial costume; and the base of the central three-light candelabrum is a figure of Davy Crockett (see Fig. 10).[9] Another set is known that has the colonial female figure as the centerpiece and two colonial male figures as the single lights.[10] Sometimes the firm used their more elaborate figural candelabrum bases as part of their Argand and oil

Fig. 8. Candleholder, one of a pair, attributed to Cornelius and Company, 1840–1851. Bronze with a silver finish and lead-glass prisms; height 14⅝ inches. A silver finish is rare on Cornelius products.

Fig. 9. Girandole set attributed to Cornelius and Company, 1840–1851. Gilt bronze with black marble bases, and lead-glass prisms; height 18 inches. *Collection of Peter Hill; photograph by courtesy of Mr. Hill.*

Fig. 10. Candelabrum in the Davy Crockett pattern made by Cornelius and Company, 1848–1851. Marked on the back, "CORNELIUS & Co./PATENT/DECEMBER. 5/ 1848." Bronze with a silver finish on a white marble base, and lead-glass prisms; height 17½ inches. *Hill collection; Hill photograph.*

Fig. 11. Candleholder, one of a pair, attributed to Cornelius and Company, 1840–1851. Gilt bronze and marble, with lead-glass prisms; height 15 inches.

the arms are the same as those in Figures 5 and 6, the socket is identical to the one at the left in Figure 4, and a decorative gilt band between the two blocks of the marble base matches the band on the bases of the girandole set and candelabra shown in Figures 9 and 12, respectively. However, the marble used for the base appears to be slightly thinner than that usually found on Cornelius and Company's pieces and lamps. The female figure used on the candelabrum in Figure 1, for example, was also used as a support for the font of Argand and astral lamps, and an elaborate Gothic base has been found on both an astral lamp and a candelabrum.[11]

An interesting girandole has recently come to light[12] that shares many elements with the pieces discussed above. The lower half of the upright support is identical to the socket supports in Figures 3 and 9,

Fig. 12. Pair of candelabra attributed to Cornelius and Company, 1840–1851. Gilt bronze and marble, with lead-glass prisms; height 17¾ inches. *Charleston Museum, Charleston, South Carolina.*

the Gothic building used as the base is not known on any other lighting device attributable to the firm. Moreover, the building is marked "W. F. SHAW, BOSTON 1849," raising the question of whether Cornelius and Company provided elements to other lighting-device manufacturers and dealers who added their own base designs, or whether other manufacturers commissioned Cornelius to cast designs for them. Surely this question will be answered as more marked products of the Cornelius firm turn up and the extent of their design repertory is defined.

[1] Charles S. Cornelius, *History of the Cornelius Family in America* (Grand Rapids, Michigan, 1926), chap. 8, p. 2.

[2] *Lamps and Other Lighting Devices, 1850–1906* (Princeton, New Jersey, 1972), p. 21.

[3] Denys Peter Myers, *Gaslighting in America, A Guide for Historic Preservation* (Washington, D.C., 1978), p. 39.

[4] Joseph T. Butler, *American Antiques, 1800–1900* (New York, 1965), p. 131. One of the firm's outstanding cast ornaments are the gilt handles with an eagle or griffin terminal on a porcelain urn made by the Tucker company and now in the Philadelphia Museum of Art. The handles were designed by John Henry Sachse, who worked for Cornelius and Company, and were cast in the company's workshops. See *Philadelphia: Three Centuries of American Art* (Philadelphia Museum of Art, 1976), pp. 295–296.

[5] After Christian Cornelius' death, his son Robert and son-in-law Isaac F. Baker formed a partnership known as Cornelius and Baker. In 1853 William C. Baker joined the firm. In 1859 Robert Cornelius' son Robert Comeley Cornelius became a partner, followed in 1861 by another son, John C. Cornelius. By this time the firm was known as Cornelius, Baker and Company, as it remained until the partnership was dissolved in 1869. By the following year the concern was known as Cornelius and Sons. In 1886 the name was changed to Cornelius and Hetherington, and, finally, in 1888, it became Cornelius and Rowland, which it remained until it was dissolved in 1900.

[6] J. B. Chandler, *Description of the Establishment of Cornelius & Baker, Manufacturers of Lamps, Chandeliers & Gas Fixtures, Philadelphia* (Philadelphia, 1860), pp. 8–18.

[7] One pair is illustrated in *Seymour-5114*, Christie's, New York, January 23, 1982, p. 66, Lot 238. The other is shown in ANTIQUES for September 1973, p. 361.

[8] ANTIQUES, September 1973, p. 361.

[9] *Seymour-5114*, p. 66. Lot 238.

[10] ANTIQUES, September 1973, p. 361.

[11] *Ibid.*, May 1976, p. 1021, Pl. VI.

[12] *Ibid.*, March 1983, p. 520.

Fig. 13. Candle bracket, one of a pair, attributed to Cornelius and Company, 1840–1851. Gilt bronze, height 8 inches. These candle brackets were recently found attached to a Philadelphia cheval glass of 1825–1830. The arm is secured to the backplate by a pivot pin in the bottom of which is a screw of the type usually found on adjustable gas wall lights or to secure the gas valve.

Index